Exceptions
Are the Rule

New Perspectives in Sociology

Charles Tilly and Scott McNall
Series Editors

*Exceptions Are the Rule: An Inquiry into Methods
in the Social Sciences,* Joel H. Levine

FORTHCOMING IN 1993

Criminological Controversies, John Hagan, A. R. Gillis,
and David Brownfield

Freudians and Feminists, Edith Kurzweil

*Contact Westview Press for information about
additional forthcoming titles.*

Exceptions Are the Rule

An Inquiry into Methods in the Social Sciences

Joel H. Levine

Dartmouth College

Westview Press

Boulder • San Francisco • Oxford

New Perspectives in Sociology

Figure 4.3 is from Robert H. Somers, "Statistics, Descriptive: Association." Reprinted with permission of Macmillan Publishing Company, a Division of Macmillan, Inc., from INTERNATIONAL ENCYCLOPEDIA OF THE SOCIAL SCIENCES, David L. Sills, Editor, Vol. 15, p. 244. Copyright © 1968 by Crowell Collier and Macmillan, Inc. Reconstructed by Somers from William Erbe's "Social Involvement and Political Activity: A Replication and Elaboration," *American Sociological Review,* Volume 29, 1964, p. 207.

Copyright © 1993 by Joel H. Levine

Published in 1993 in the United States of America by Westview Press, Inc., 5500 Central Avenue, Boulder, Colorado 80301-2877, and in the United Kingdom by Westview Press, 36 Lonsdale Road, Summertown, Oxford OX2 7EW

A CIP catalog record for this book is available from the Library of Congress.
ISBN 0-8133-1646-4
ISBN 0-8133-1647-2 (pbk.)

Printed and bound in the United States of America

The paper used in this publication meets the requirements
of the American National Standard for Permanence of Paper
for Printed Library Materials Z39.48-1984.

10   9   8   7   6   5   4   3   2   1

We still carry the historical baggage of a Platonic heritage that seeks sharp essences and definite boundaries. . . . This Platonic heritage, with its emphasis on clear distinctions and separated immutable entities, leads us to view statistical measures of central tendency wrongly, indeed opposite to the appropriate interpretation in our actual world of variation, shadings, and continua. In short, we view means and medians as the hard "realities," and the variation that permits their calculation as a set of transient and imperfect measurements of this hidden essence. . . . But all evolutionary biologists know that variation itself is nature's only irreducible essence. Variation is the hard reality, not a set of imperfect measures for a central tendency. Means and medians are the abstractions.

— Stephen J. Gould, "The Median Isn't the Message"
Discover, June 1985

Contents

EPILOGUE

Students Should Ask

To Nicholas C. Mullins

with thanks for the contributions of Joel R. Reidenberg

First, what is a "student"? My pocket dictionary tells me a student is "one who attends school." Wrong! A student is one who actively attempts to acquire knowledge — not as a librarian acquires a book and not as one who *attends* school to acquire a degree — but for understanding. "Student" includes many of those "who attend school" as well as those who stand before them at the lectern.

That being said, there are questions I would like to whisper in the ear of students who attend statistical methods classes, particularly the good students, questions they should ask. Such mischief might enliven these classes. More important, it would alert the student to discriminate between ends and means, between what we wish to accomplish as a science and what we are able to accomplish, so far. The end is understanding, not warm sympathy that "understands" human pain, but understanding that is communicable, testable, valid, and offers real hope. The end is understanding that provides the base for affecting the human world, just as physics and biology provide the base for engineering and medicine.

That's the goal. Statistics is one means. I hesitate to criticize it because too many who criticize it reject statistics, and science and rationality as well. That's foolishness. That is unilateral disarmament in the face of the unknown, disavowing the best resources of the human mind. But all too often we fail to criticize statistical means with respect to scientific ends — what do they say? How do they help me understand? Answering that is not the statistician's job, nor is it the job of a sociological "methods" course. But both should alert you to the questions.

I would have a student ask: "Professor! When you tell me that education predicts income, what does that tell me? How does it work?" The question would give your methods professor the all-important opportunity to pass the buck, reminding the student — one who learns — that that is a question for research, for theory, and ultimately, perhaps, for other mathematical models.

The two parts of this book divide most easily into part one, summary statistics, and part two, distributions — the stuff not usually described by summary statistics. Equally well I could divide it into part one, "Everything you thought you knew is wrong," and part two, "This is where I look for answers." That is flip, inaccurately critical, and overly optimistic, but it should make the point. The point is that "modern" methodology hasn't accomplished a whole lot, not when it is measured against the unknowns of sociological research. Do we yet have one precise testable statement we would care to call a "law"? So let's relax and try to do better; there is not a whole lot to lose by releasing the death grip of one-generation-old traditional methods.

Perhaps the difficulty in relaxing, playing with new questions, is that the advances of the last generation were hard won against real opposition, forcing "methodology" into a defensive posture. Quantitative social science was "jump started" after World War II by a generation of determined social scientists, mathematicians, statisticians, foundations, and, yes, federal bureaucrats, motivated, I like to think, by a feeling of great human need for a real social science. They won the battle. Students on both sides of the lectern can now handle mathematical reasoning. They won, but now the agenda is to get on with the analyses for which the older generation created us — even when we find we must gently revise or set aside the techniques and the style of that older generation. Sometimes they proffered their command of probabilities and significance and Greek symbols as stigmata proving they had established a science. They proved no such thing, but the rituals do seem to have done their job on the opposition. They won. Now, to work . . .

Joel H. Levine

Part One
Summary Numbers

1

Introduction:
Numbers for Religion and Politics

Philosophy is written in that vast book which stands forever open before our eyes, I mean the universe; but it cannot be read until we have learnt the language and become familiar with the characters in which it is written. It is written in mathematical language, and the letters are triangles, circles and other geometrical figures, without which it is humanly impossible to comprehend a single word.

— Galileo Galilei, *Il Saggiatore*[1]

How do you put numbers on things like religion and politics? Social science cannot yet describe political position with numbers and equations. It cannot yet make a statement like "Senator X is 2.5 units to the left of Senator Y and moving left at a velocity of one unit per year." How do you put numbers on such things and describe them by the equations of simple mathematics? Such questions are a torment to the practicing social scientist. We deal with messy variables, variables like politics, religion, and race. We deal with roles like "parent" and "child," with organizations that may be "hierarchical" or "democratic"; we deal with grand things like "social order" and "revolution." The variables that social scientists must deal with and the theories we construct seem, at times, generically different from the physical continua and the measurable intervals of conventional physics.

These chapters attempt to put numbers and equations on such things and, more broadly, to introduce concepts that get the job done. To

---

1. Cited by James R. Newman in "Commentary on Galileo Galilei," *The World of Mathematics,* Volume 2, edited by James R. Newman, Simon and Schuster, New York, 1956, p. 731.

do that I have to accomplish two things: First, I have to create doubt. These days social scientists trust numbers and equations, and that's not altogether a good thing. Everyone learns the methodological canon — learns to fit lines to data, learns a little about correlation, and learns to use a few elementary statistical techniques. Beyond that, it is supposed that "methods" can be relegated to specialists while the rest of us focus our attention on the substance and content of the science. Not so.

The reasons for doubt are plain to every new student. Take something simple like the generalization "Education pays off" — literally, with dollars. That's true. On the average the well-educated are, in fact, better off economically than the rest. But when you look at the facts behind that statement, when you look at the data and the equations, they are a shock. What you expect to see is a line: Go out and interview a few thousand people. Ask them about their educations. Ask them about their incomes. Plot their data on an ordinary piece of graph paper and you expect to see a line — so many years, so many dollars. More years, more dollars. But that's not what you get. Not at all. What you see when you graph the data is a cloud, not a line. The exceptions, the deviations from the rule, are more than the occasional millionaire who dropped out of pre-school. The exceptions are large and frequent. That's the general case in social science: One of the pioneers in sociological theory, now retired, used to preface some of his more risky assertions about social systems by saying, "It would not be altogether incorrect to state . . . ," and then he would proceed with his generalization of the day. The phrase should be applied to our methods: "It would not be altogether incorrect to state . . . that more highly educated people have higher incomes, on the average." Exceptions are the rule. The genius of the methodological canon is that it is able to extract central tendencies from the midst of such variation. When you translate textbook methods from the textbooks to practice, with real data, they don't tell us very much about the data. Specialists in "methodology" already know this and are amazed at the confidence, and non-involvement, that other people show for their work. But because people trust the basics and, trusting them, set them aside, I have to begin with doubt. I have to bring out the canon, part of it, and argue in language as plain as I can muster that the old standbys don't work, not easily, not well. There is work to be done.

That's my first task, creating doubt — not about mathematics or science, but about the basic methodological canon. The second task is, of course, to provide answers, or progress — where I can. How do you describe the messy data of social science with numbers and equations? To give you a preview, imagine two variables, height and weight. Height and weight are not the kind of thing social scientists worry about, but they are the kind of thing we practice on, so bear with me: I collect data describing the heights and weights of a few thousand people and then organize the data in a table in which columns specify the height and rows specify the weight. The table shows me how many six-footers weighed 200 pounds, how many weighed 210 pounds, how many weighed 220 pounds, and so forth. Very good — I'm ready to analyze the relation between height and weight. But before I begin let me make the problem more interesting: It turns out that my research assistant (that's me) lost part of the data. In fact I lost all the labels. I still have all the counts, five people of this kind, ten people of that, but I no longer know which people were six foot five and which ones were five foot six or how much they weighed. Artificially, my well-behaved data have become messy, and here's the challenge: Can I still analyze height and weight? There is an order to these variables, but I don't know it. There is a scale to these variables, but it's lost.

Surprisingly, I can come very close to a normal analysis, even without the labels, and the trick is to use the variation. Just looking at the data I can probably spot which rows are similar to each other. The numbers of six-footers weighing 200 pounds, 210 pounds, and 220 pounds are undoubtedly similar to the numbers for people who are five foot ten. And the numbers for those who are five foot ten are surely similar to the numbers for people who are five foot eight. Just from the numbers, I can probably reconstruct the correct order by height. And again, just from the variation, I can probably reconstruct the order by weight. So even without the labels I can probably get the rows and columns of the table back in order.

That's just the beginning. I started with unknown intervals and reconstructed the order. If I take the next step and quantify "similarity" with an equation, then I can estimate that "five foot ten" is halfway between "six foot" and "five foot eight." Without knowing X and Y I could use the equation for similarity to estimate the scale and then graph the data. I could tell you whether or not the relation between X and Y was linear and I could estimate the strength of the correlation. And what of the equation that I used to quantify "similarity"? If I'm careful, then that too can be tested.

Not bad, considering that I lost the measures of height and weight. But who cares about height and weight? I don't, except as an example. Now for the payoff: Suppose I lied to you. "Really" my unlabeled table was not about height and weight at all. Instead, it was a table describing political preference and religion, messy variables. If I had told you that, in advance, then you wouldn't have tried to recover the unknown intervals. But you did: You put the categories in order and estimated their intervals, including a scale for X and Y. You verified that the pattern was linear and estimated the correlation. *A priori*, political preference and religion are not supposed to behave that way, but they did in this hypothetical example. If such a thing happened, it would be best to believe, or consider, the evidence of your eyes and doubt *a priori* ideas about what can and cannot be done with the variables of social science. And such things do, in fact, happen. The details are different. The equation changes from problem to problem. And the "fit" is always a matter of degree. But it happens.

You will have to trust me on that, for the moment. But now let me re-state my opening question: Is there something different about social science? Is it limited to classification and counting, classifying people as "Democrats" and counting their number? I think not. But there is a difference among the sciences, and it lies in practical matters, like: How do you get started? How do you get your science off the ground? In physical science the first step seems obvious, at least in hindsight. You could start with familiar things that you could see and touch. You could assign numbers to things that were accessible to the senses — to length, to mass, and, with more difficulty, to time — and then get on with the labor of genius that was eventually able to discover "elementary" physical law. In social science, by contrast, the most familiar objects are the ones we trust least. The more our culture tells us about freedom and democracy, class, wealth, and country, the less objective is our knowledge of these things. That's a real problem.

But it is not fundamental. Even in physical science the appearance of simplicity, the appearance that it is a science of things you can see and touch, is an illusion. Remember the conundrums of elementary physics: A *unit of force* accelerates a *unit of mass* up to a *unit of velocity* in a *unit of time*. And, of course, what is a unit of mass? A *unit of mass* is the mass that the *unit of force* accelerated. The verbal tangle of the riddle tells us that it's all circular — and it's supposed to be. Nothing in the physical theory exists in isolation. Neither force, nor mass, nor velocity can be measured apart from the equations that bind one to the others. This is what Carlsson called "intrinsic measurement" and what Campbell called "derived measurement":   Everything fits together and is defined together, using the physical laws that describe their relation.[2]   Modern students can think of objects as having size and mass and temperature, all of which can be weighed and measured independently. That's wrong, but in physical science you can get away with it. And that, I think, is the difference between social science and physical science. In social science you have to think right, from the beginning: The illusion of simplicity is not allowed and you have to figure out the equations while you are still trying to figure out the measure of the things that are subject to the equations. That is the special burden of the social sciences.

That's tricky, but science does it all the time. And that trick liberates social science from the tyranny of the obvious: *Intrinsically,* using measures derived from the problem at hand, no variable can be taken at its obvious value: Neither sex, nor age, nor income, nor education. We are, for example, rarely interested in "Sex" as a categorical statement about a person's physical endowments, not as social scientists. *Intrinsically,* "Sex" can only be measured by the equations that link it to other variables. *Intrinsically,* it can be entirely correct to measure the difference between the sexes in terms of intervals, observing that there is no difference between sexes with respect to behavior X, or that there is a great difference between sexes with respect to behavior Y, or that there is a changing difference between sexes with respect to behavior Z. We are interested in sex differences with respect to income, attitude, education, religion, and politics by which the variable is linked to other variables and thus, intrinsically, even a variable like "Sex" can be measured in

---

2. Gösta Carlsson, *Social Mobility and Class Structure*, Lund, Sweden, 1958, page 141, and Norman Robert Campbell, *What Is Science*, Dover Publications, Inc., 1921. Excerpts from Campbell's work are reprinted in Newman, ed., *op. cit.*, pp. 1797-1829.

terms of numerical intervals defined with respect to other variables. Scales and measures and, with them, elementary equations and laws will apply to social science just as surely as they do to physical science. They will be just as real but a whole lot harder to find.

The next three chapters, Chapters 2, 3, and 4, focus on summary measures for two-variable relations, with frequent reference to problems that lurk within the conventional methods — creating doubt. These problems follow, most often, not from the summary measures themselves but from common *a priori* assumptions that are, in varying degree, untested, untestable, or false. Chapter 2, "Lines, Damned Lines, and Statistics," tackles the measures for two-variable linear correlations, the most trusted of our methods. Chapter 3, "Calculus and Correlation," explores the basic meaning of correlation *per se*, what does it *mean* to say that two variables are correlated? And Chapter 4, "The Rule of Safety: Gamma Is Wrong," tackles the measure for ordinal correlation. Behind both types of relation, both linear correlation and ordinal correlation, there are subjective components with large effects on the numerical results. Behind the meaning of correlation, as used by social scientists, there is a still broader concept of contrast and change common to all of the quantitative sciences and mathematics.

The succeeding six chapters, Chapters 5 through 10, examine the "scatter," that part of the data which is *not* described by the summary measures — attempting to provide answers. Chapter 5, "Introduction: The Strength of Weak Data," introduces the argument that these exceptions are often well patterned. It argues that the pattern of exceptions makes it possible to infer information *about* variables *from* their correlation, reversing the usual order of research and replacing unnecessary assumptions with testable working hypotheses.

Chapter 6, "Big Folks and Small Folks," begins the examples with data for which classical summary statistics seem appropriate, with data for the relation between the height and the weight of five thousand women. The example is a textbook classic and should be an exemplar for standard technique. But, in truth, the data are used to teach students about linear analysis, not about height and weight. If the example is taken seriously, on its own merit, examining what it tells us about big people and small people, the answer is that the standard linear analysis "linear regression" tells us depressingly little. Applying scatter technology: Dropping the *a priori* assumption that pounds specify the intervals of weight, dropping the *a priori* assumption that inches specify the intervals of height, and adding an analysis of the scatter allows us to retain most of the classical analysis while adding some insight into the underlying physical process.

Chapter 7, "Democrats, Republicans, and Independents," continues with work-horse variables of sociological analysis, examining "Political Identity" in relation to "the usual," in relation to age, education, income, race, region and sex. Ordinarily, political identity is treated as an ordinal variable, ordered from "Strong Democrat," to "Democrat," to "Independent," "Republican," and "Strong Republican," with some equivocation about the insertion of "Independents" between the Democrats and the Republicans. But dropping the *a priori* decision that this variable is ordinal, and leaving the question open, produces some contrary results: The order and intervals of this variable obey at least three distinct patterns. Were the variable used as an ordinal scale, the estimated correlations would be misleading (see "Gamma Is Wrong"). Were the variable used as an interval scale, maintaining the *a priori* order, some strong correlations might still be overlooked because, often enough, the order is not as advertised.

Chapter 8, "Friends and Relations," looks at sociometric relations of the sort "A likes B," "B likes C," and "C never heard of A." *A priori*, these relations seem different from the stuff of ordinary social science and studies of sociometric relations have provided a stimulus for the mathematical imagination. For these social relations we can discuss behavior in mathematical terms as "reflexive," or "symmetric," or "transitive," sometimes using the pure mathematical definitions of these properties. For these relations we have developed methods that examine centrality of individual persons and connectivity of a group. Without doubt the theoretical stance of the network researchers who study these things is different, sometimes radically different, from the mainline sociology of twenty years ago. But we are not entirely free to construct methods according to the mathematical possibilities. Reality must be heard from. And dropping the presumption of uniqueness, while inferring the structure of these relations from the evidence, suggests that these sociometric relations are not radically different from other forms of data.

Chapter 9, "Time and Money," looks at the stock market as a wonderfully mundane example of "time series," looking at the pattern of one or more variables as they evolve and, one would hope, may be extrapolated through time. The issue in question here is nothing less than the nature of time. Usually we adopt physical time, intact, as behavioral time, assuming *a priori* that it moves forward, in one direction, at intervals paced out by the metronome of the physical universe. The assumption is not obviously correct, nor is it necessary, and as a social science variable, the structure of the variable time is open to question and subject to inference from the data.

Chapter 10, "*Real* Social Distance," analyzes occupational mobility, occupation of son as related to occupation of father. Such data are central to sociological debates and subjected to a variety of *a priori*, before-the-research assumptions. Occupation may be classified as an interval-scale variable (identified by Socio-Economic Status), it may be classified as an ordinal-scale variable (identified as High- Middle- or Low-status or, perhaps, as White Collar, Blue Collar, and Farm), or it may be classified as a categorical variable (using combinations of occupation, Clerical, Sales, Labor, . . . and industry, Retail, Wholesale, Construction, . . .). With these data people really care about the outcome, as it tends to support or deny claims about the existence of social class, as it tends to confirm or deny expectations regarding the "openness" of society. Accordingly, perhaps no other problem area of contemporary sociology has been attacked by more classes of high-tech mathematical artillery. My intention is to suggest, first, that the type of the variable "Occupation" is not entirely up to us; reality must be consulted. Second, I suggest that the appropriate descriptive methods are not drastically different from those required for supposedly simpler problems.

Finally, in Chapter 11, I take the liberty of closing my discussions of method with a chapter titled "Theory," discussing where we are going and what we are trying to accomplish in the social sciences.

Each of the five empirical "problems" discussed in Chapters 6 through 10 will be recognized by cognoscenti as an exemplar extracted from its home specialty within a sub-area of social science. How do these specialties become joined in the span of this one short discourse on method? I suppose that the irresistible answer has to be "Very carefully": I do not suggest for one moment that these problems are theoretically equivalent. If we ever develop a theory of "positive affect relations" (i.e., friendship), it will probably have little relation to any theory of occupational mobility or any model of the stock market. But descriptive tools cross the boundaries of disciplines and sub-disciplines — both sociologists and physicists have been known to use straight lines. And the scatter technology developed in these chapters is such a tool. I can argue that the tool is new and exciting by relating its development to log-linear models. I can argue that this tool is old and comfortable by relating it to the normal/Gaussian distribution — No matter. My colleagues who call themselves "structuralists" could wink and observe that the scatter methods are my secret attempt to extend their structural approach to a host of more traditional problems. They would be correct, but my non-structuralist colleagues need not take offense: At this level of generality the whole concept of "correlation" would have to be classified as structural. At this level of generality, turf boundaries are not worth defending.

The techniques of intrinsic measurement are "strong" in the sense that they are based on strong working hypotheses about equations governing the relation between weakly specified variables. But the assumptions can be tested, and their testability is a good thing because they come up with sometimes-surprising implications:

- Where there is a conflict between intrinsic measures and *a priori* "extrinsic" measures, the corrected correlations among variables are generally stronger than the correlations estimated by conventional means.

- There is evidence of surprisingly physics-like distance and distance-squared "laws" in the relations among variables.

- The concept of correlation, as used in the social sciences, is the same as the mathematical concept of the derivative, as expressed in the classical calculus.

- The commonly used measure for ordinal data, gamma, is wrong because the data are usually more than ordinal. In the usual case the standard procedure gives biased results.

- The methods indicate ways of writing a generalized linear equation even for behavior like the careers of persons moving through a multi-dimensional system of occupations.

The origin of these intrinsic techniques is difficult to nail down because what would need to be nailed down is a way of thinking, not a set of techniques. And this way of thinking seems to be "in the air" at this time, consolidating itself in various work over the last fifty years. Some of it lies in my own work beginning twenty-five years ago, work that is, to be sure, obscure and unavailable. Some of it lies in work of Leo Goodman, readily available but obscure in its own way. Some of it lies in work on "variance stabilization" by M. S. Bartlett. Some of it I absorbed from Frederick Mosteller. Some of it lies in the work on mobility models, thereby adding to the mix contributions by Harrison White, by Robert Hauser, and by John Goldthorpe. Let us hope that the whole enterprise will someday prove to have sufficient merit so that someone, other than the participants, will care about its origins. For myself I remember the heady day when I first "figured it out" for myself. It was an encounter with Truth, straight out of a C. P. Snow novel, but I soon discovered that the opening of the heavens I had witnessed had been, after all, a semi-private revelation, witnessed by few of my colleagues. Surprised, I made a pest of myself trying to get people to hear the work until, finally, I gathered my courage to explain it to one of the great living statistician-scholars. His response was different. He responded with something like, "Yes, yes, we know all that, but what are you going to do with it?" That stopped me. "We" turned out to be a small group, and little of this shared understanding was in writing, but the question was, and remains: What are you going to do with it? His terms were different from mine, but he understood and, obviously, he had figured it out before me. Then he, in turn, showed me a piece of the puzzle he had discovered, as well as the reference to another scholar who had discovered "his" work before him, as he had preceded me. The question really *is*, what are you going to do with these methods? What will they do for us? And the audience is not my friend or his small group. The audience is students and colleagues who will ask: "What are these intrinsic techniques? Why should I pay attention? How, concretely and with data, will they help us understand nature?" These chapters begin to answer the questions concretely, using data, addressing a series of problems.

2

Lines, Damned Lines,
and Statistics

Prediction Versus Explanation

I f there is one technique that we want students to know well, we want
them to know how to associate straight lines, "$y = mx + b$," the kind of
thing they learn in high school mathematics, with data: We want them
to "fit" a line to the data. If I report that for each additional year of
education you may expect to earn $2,000, and that people with zero years
of education earn about $8,000, then I am talking about a line, $y = 2,000x
+ 8,000$. The line is absolutely basic. It is also more versatile than it looks
because logarithms, square roots, and so forth, allow many non-linear
relations to be re-expressed in linear form. Even non-linear things like
radioactive decay, population growth, and long-term changes of GNP
may be treated with linear techniques.

The person interested in education and income may just want a
report: "Have the technician look at the data and let me know: Do you
get $1,000 per year of education, or $2,000 per year, or $3,000? Is it rising
or falling? Is it different for men than for women, for blacks than for
whites, in the cities than in the suburbs? Spare me the technical details."
Unfortunately, the action is in those details. Let me loose on your data
for income and education, let me choose the method of analysis, and I
could give you different answers, all of them correct but unequal, differing from each other by an easy factor of four. And I could generate these
numbers without faking the data or outright cheating — Cheating is for
amateurs. I would do it by the book, following the rules we teach. And
that, I suggest, is a serious problem: We think of statistics as objective,
the facts and just the facts, but it simply is not true. What's the problem?
A priori assumptions. The most commonly used technique for "fitting" a
line to data, called "regression analysis," is not just "math." It is a rich

and treacherous blend of facts and assumptions, all bound together in the two numbers, the slope and the intercept, the 2,000 and 8,000, or whatever, that get reported.

Right here at the heart of what positivistic social scientists think of as the objective core of our trade, *a priori* assumptions, something quite distinct from *facts*, are influencing — seriously and dramatically influencing — the reports. Let's take a look at the problem, beginning at the beginning. How do you "fit" a line to a set of data? Let's suppose I am studying a group that presents these data: There are seven people in the group, each of whom has an education and an income. Two of the seven people have completed high school, three have completed college, and two have Ph.D.'s that they completed in exactly four years (for my convenience), giving me people with 12 years, 16 years, and 20 years of formal education. Of the two people completing high school, one now earns $20,000 per year and the other $30,000, averaging $25,000. Among the three completing college, the incomes are $20,000, $30,000, and $40,000, averaging $30,000. And of the two Ph.D.s, one is earning $30,000, the other $40,000, for an average of $35,000. Plotting the seven combinations, I get the graph in Figure 2.1.

How do I fit a straight line to these data? Well, strictly speaking, I

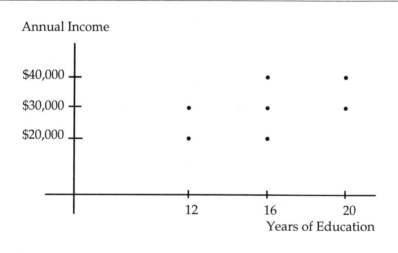

Figure 2.1
Graph of Hypothetical Data for Years of Education and Annual Income

don't. Anyone looking at these data — anyone who has not spent years battering his or her head against the wretched data we social scientists have to use — will look at these data and say, "It isn't a straight line." True enough. But then what is the "best" straight line, using the line as an approximation that summarizes the data?

What we use most frequently for the "best" line is the line of means: At 12 years of education, the mean income is $25,000. At 16 years of education the mean is $30,000, and at 20 years of education the mean is $35,000. The conventional best straight line would pass through, or near, these means. In this case the means fall on a straight line with slope $1,250: Each four years of education returns, on the average, another $5,000, which works out to $1,250 per single year of education. Extrapolating backwards to get the intercept of the straight line, 0 years of education would average $10,000. Then putting the slope and the intercept in place, the equation for the means is $y = 1,250x + 10,000$, predicting average income as a function of education. That is one "best" line, called the "regression line," describing the means of the data.

Very good, I've described the data. Or have I? Let's take another look at the same data. In Figure 2.2 I'm using the same facts, but reporting them differently. Here I have two persons with an income of $20,000, three persons with an income of $30,000, and two persons with an average of $40,000. For these three incomes the means are 14 years of education, 16 years of education, and 18 years of education, falling on a line increasing by 2 years of education for each $10,000 of income. That comes out to $5,000 per year.

The problem is obvious. From one set of data I have two different slopes, $1,250 per year and $5,000 per year: Same data, same facts, different numbers. The difference between the two does not lie in the data or in the math. That's the point. The difference lies in human intention, my own in this case. "Math" is supposed to be innocent of this kind of response to human intention and, of course, it is. But this isn't math. It's science and data analysis in which human intention, my own, has worked its way right through the equations into the results. In the first case it was my intention to predict income from education. The line I used, at $1,250 per year, went right through the means. It was correct. Given that the data were not strictly linear, lying scattered both above and below a line, it was the best answer because it correctly "predicted"

the average income. In this first case, I was using the data as an educa-
tor, trying to find out how much education is worth (in dollars).

In the second case it was my intention to predict education. I
assumed the role of a television advertiser using the data to determine
the education of people with a $30,000 income. Knowing that, I will be
able to adjust the vocabulary of my pitch in order to match the education
of my target audience. My intention in this case was to predict
education, and the line at 2 years per $10,000, or $5,000 per year, went
right through the means. It correctly predicts the average education for
each income. In fact, both lines are correct, even though they differ by a
factor of four. They are different, usually very different (with real data).

None of this is particularly surprising to the professional, but it

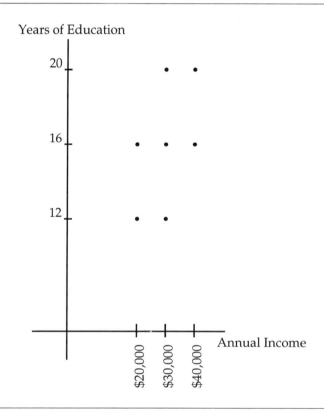

Figure 2.2
Graph of Hypothetical Data for Annual Income
and Years of Education (Transposed)

comes as a shock to the student. After all, these are "methods," real science, not that flabby intellectual stuff they teach in theory courses. Besides, we spent a lot of time in high school, and we know our algebra:

If	$y = mx + b$	(showing y as a function of x),	[2.1]
then	$y - b = mx$		[2.2]
and	$x = (1/m)\,y - b/m$	(showing x as a function of y).	[2.3]

True enough, that's algebra, but it is not necessarily statistics. Here the line through the means of income was

$$y = 1{,}250x + 10{,}000 , \qquad\qquad [2.4]$$

for income as a function of education, Figure 2.1, while the line through the means of education showed 2 years of education for each $10,000 of income, equal to .0002 years per dollar,

$$x = (.0002)y + 10 , \qquad\qquad [2.5]$$

which inverts and transposes to $5,000 per year,

$$y = 5{,}000x - 50{,}000 . \qquad\qquad [2.6]$$

So, ".0002," from Equation 2.5, ought to be the inverse of "1,250," from Equation 2.4, just as $1/m$ in Equation 2.3 is the inverse of m in Equation 2.2. But of course it isn't. It is off by a factor of four.

There you have it, two very different descriptions of one reality. Now that you know it can be done, how do you cope with it? You cope by very careful handling of a two-hundred-and-fifty-year-old debate: We send students over to the Philosophy Department where they are supposed to read David Hume, who wrote circa 1750, and learn in the discussion that a sophisticated person is supposed to snicker, knowingly, when an unsophisticated person speaks the word "cause."[1] What's

---

1. Referring to *Enquiry Concerning Human Understanding*, available in many reprints. I am using excerpts published in *Basic Problems of Philosophy*, edited by Daniel J. Bronstein, Yervant H. Krikorian and Philip P. Weiner, 2nd Edition, Prentice-Hall, Englewood Cliffs, N.J., 1955. The posthumous edition of Hume's *Enquiry* was published in 1777.

wrong or, at least, unsophisticated about using the word "cause"? What's wrong is that the word refers to an intrinsically unobservable event. This is the philosopher's version of the regression problem: Watch my hand move a pencil across the table. Did my hand move the pencil, did the pencil move my hand, or did they both just happen to be traveling together in the same direction? Whatever your answer, you did not actually *see* a cause. Personally, I'm convinced that I caused the pencil to move. But nothing that enters your eye and heads toward your brain gives you the answers about causality. How do you cope with invisibility? One solution is to excise the word "cause" from your vocabulary: If it has no empirical referent then it does not exist — so don't mess up your thinking by referring to it as a real thing. A second solution is to live with the ambiguity, arguing that, while cause itself is unobservable, causal *thinking* leads to useful results. Cause enters your thinking when you bring reason to the facts.

Getting back to the two equations: Notwithstanding a few hundred years of philosophical sophistication, sociologists appear to have found a third solution, making cause observable: Reasoning that X causes Y, you use one set of numbers. Reasoning that Y causes X, you use another, and that is the difference between the two sets of numbers for the one set of data on education and income. We appear to have created "observable" differences, different slopes and intercepts, that depend on the causal direction. How do we defend ourselves against this apparent naiveté? We do it by the route of plausible deniability, by upping the ante in the game of comparative sophistication. The problem, we claim, is not a lack of sophistication on the part of the social scientist. The problem is the failure of the lay person to understand exactly what we are doing when we use these equations: Neither of these equations was meant to be used as a description. So there is no contradiction. Both of these equations are predictions. Both are exactly what they claim to be: the parameters that make the best prediction of X from Y or, using different parameters, of Y from X. You only get into trouble if you use them the wrong way, and besides, we warned you to read the footnotes in your statistics book.

If the student protests, troubled by the difference between our two equations and the one reversible equation of high school algebra, then we wrap ourselves in the mantle of science. We observe that there is no reason why social science should conform to the demands of the lay person, who stopped with high school algebra, or to the too-broadly interpreted dicta of professional skeptics, two hundred years dead. We are scientists, not lay persons, not philosophers. For science, prediction is the test and "regression" is the best predictor of Y from X or (changing the parameters) of X from Y. That's science.

At this point the arguments and counter-arguments attacking alternative methods of analysis can get quite murky: At the next step we would have to argue the roles of prediction and of description in science. I think it fair to say that most practitioners will avoid such arguments, at least during working hours, ending the discussion with fair warning: Suffice it to say, for the moment, that there is a difference between statistics that predict and statistics that describe. And the custom in late-twentieth-century, "modern" social science, is to predict. Hand your data to the social statistician trained by a social scientist and you will get back statistics that predict. If you misuse them, or misunderstand them, or get caught in seeming contradictions, well . . . At least you were warned.

But let me return to the attack: There is a problem here. One can hardly blame the confusion entirely on the confused, denying responsibility with a wave toward the footnotes. After all we do sometimes talk about causal equations. And we do talk about "Dependent" and "Independent" variables. The words have a precise meaning: They refer to variables used to predict and variables that are predicted. But those words surely connote "cause" — even while they avoid the actual word. Most of us who teach data analysis, to not-always-sophisticated undergraduates, have been asked, "Professor, I forget, which ones are the dependent variables?" We usually warn students about the difference between correlation and causality. We warn students that "regression equations" are the best predictors, but how often do we offer them a viable alternative: Use this method if you want to predict; use that method if you want to describe or wish to make no commitment about causal order? In fact, how often do we describe two-variable data objectively, without the subjective assignment of "Dependent/Independent" variables that actually changes the numbers? Intimidating the critic, or the confused, by pointing to the footnotes is a bit of an evasion.

Let me continue the attack with a second example: I think that the "professional" will have been unmoved by my seven-person first example and will have found all this subjective stuff distasteful, so let me delve further. Let me consider a second hypothetical example, a thought experiment designed to question the "truth" that science means prediction. (It is a truth, but not a simple one, and not easily applied.) In this hypothetical example you are given data for 100 pairs of persons, data recording their physical height in feet and inches. Now, secretly, these data are from 100 pairs of brothers and, quite randomly, one brother in each pair was assigned to group I, while the other was assigned to group II. Secretly, I know there is no meaningful difference between the two groups, other than the luck of the draw. I know this. But can you, the analyst, figure it out from the data? I submit that this is an important test of the methodology: It's true that no one would bother with this experiment because we know the answer. But that's exactly why it's worth considering. When you know the answer, you can test the method. And if your methods fail to say "equal," the correct answer, then why should I trust your methods in another experiment where the answer is unknown? So let's see what would happen if you were trained to use "regression."

Figure 2.3 shows the regression line, predicting height from weight, and the line of equality: If the first person were 8' tall, what would you predict for his brother? If you had money on the bet, and wanted to be as close as possible, then you would and should predict that his brother is also far above average, but not quite so extreme as 8'. You would predict something a little less than eight feet, perhaps a mere 7' 6''. If the next person were 3' tall, you would use the same logic, but in the opposite direction: You would predict a brother far below average but not quite so extreme. That's what you should do if your objective is to have the smallest possible amount of error between the number you predict and the number you measure. That is what "regression analysis" will do for you.

But now we've got a problem. That is the right thing to do if your purpose is to make the smallest possible errors, but look where it leads you: You are predicting that a man who is 8' tall will have a somewhat shorter brother, at 7' 6". And what of the man who is 7' 6"? You are predicting that *his* brother will be a shade over 7'. There's the problem:

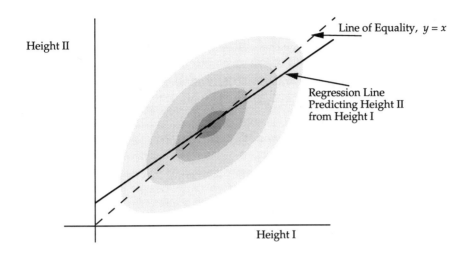

Figure 2.3
Schematic Diagram, Regression of Height II on Height I

8' predicts 7' 6", 7' 6" predicts approximately 7', not 7' 6", and 7' predicts something less. Those are the numbers you would use with a regression slope of about .94 and a complete description of

$$y = .94x + .045 .$$ [2.7]

And if your purpose were to minimize the errors in your predictions, that would be correct. But it is certainly not correct that you have "figured out" what is going on here. You have missed the key point about these two groups, which is that they are equal. Frankly, if I were doing a true comparison, testing whether "Wonder Bread" plus genes really makes people taller, then I wouldn't trust your methods. I'm not sure what they told me about the simple warm-up experiment in which, lacking any experimental intervention, the two sets were the same. So I'm loath to adopt these methods for a real experiment for which the answer is unknown. The problem is that the best *predictor*, which is what you got from the regression equation, is not usually the best clue to the underlying mechanism: The two tasks, describing what's going on and predicting the result, are different.

Perhaps, you might protest, this is an odd example, so clearly symmetrical that no one would use the asymmetrical regression method, not that we often teach students any alternative. So let me offer a third example for which I have created a hypothetical New England town and given it a simple pattern of population growth. I can eliminate one of the two competing equations immediately by freely admitting that this town's population does not cause the year. But I still submit that regression is not the best description of the underlying mechanism.

Let me tell you about this town: Unlike most towns that tend to grow in proportion to their previous size, *p*-percent per year, this little place grows by 100 people per year, *on the average*.[2] What I want to do is check: Is that what the data "tell" me when they speak to me through the language of regression? In detail, the population bounces around a bit, down 100, up 300, down 100, up 300. In 1900 my mythical town was founded with exactly 1,000 people. In 1901 it had 900, down 100 people, but by 1902 it was up to 1,200, averaging an increase of 100 per year. In 1903 it was down again to 1,100, and by 1904 it was up again to 1,400, as shown by the left-most points of Figure 2.4.

I am going to "analyze" these data for four different time periods, for the four years 1900 through 1903, the four years 1904 through 1907, the combined eight years from 1900 through 1907, and the long haul from 1900 through 1999. It's one process. But regression, showing population as a function of time, will give four answers.

For the first time period, for 1900 through 1903, I plug in the numbers and grind out the answer:

$$\text{Population} = (60 \text{ people/year}) * \text{time} + 960 \qquad [2.8]$$

(for 1900 through 1903) ,

---

2. The same problem would occur with proportional, or "exponential," growth, but the discussion would be less transparent. I would have to begin the linear analysis by transforming the numbers to their logarithms and then continue the discussion using quantities, the logarithms, which have less immediate appeal to intuition.

Population

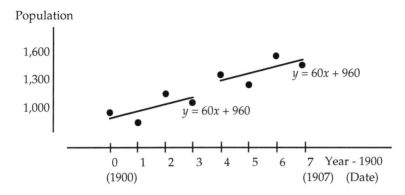

The two separate regression lines are estimated from "data" for 1900 through 1903 and from "data" for 1904 through 1907.

Figure 2.4
Population Growth for a Mythical New England Town, 1900 Through 1907

where "time" is measured in years since 1900. In 1900 regression "predicts" 960 people. In 1901 it "predicts" 1,020. Holding this equation in mind, without comment, let's repeat the computation with data for the second time period, 1904 through 1907. For these years the answer is

Population = (60 people/year) * time + 1,120   [2.9]

(for 1904 through 1907).

Now that's a little bit odd: Equation 2.8 has the same slope as Equation 2.9, but the intercept is different. If you extrapolate Equation 2.8 forward or Equation 2.9 backward, the two equations give you different numbers, the second equation being consistently "higher" than the first.

For the third time period let's combine the two data sets, using data for 1900 through 1907, inclusive. Now the correct answer is

Population = 90.48 people/year * time + 933.333   [2.10]

(for 1900 through 1907).

The plot thickens: The process remains the same, but this is a third, and different, description, differing in both slope and intercept. And finally, if I look at the long haul, using data for 1900 through 1999, the fourth result is still different:

Population = 99.94 people/year ∗ ttime + 902.97   [2.11]

(for 1900 through 1999).

Different again. What's going on? The process is constant, but the answers are not. There's nothing wrong: The regression equations are doing just what they are supposed to. But the best predictor, represented by these regression equations, is not usually the best cue to the underlying mechanism. In this example the best predictor is not even constant, although in each case it is using "data" that are absolutely well-behaved indicators of the same mechanism.

When-in-Doubt:
The Orthogonal Least Squares Line for Description

Regression techniques are exquisite techniques, but they serve a special purpose. It's hard to track down why they have become all but universal in sociology and political science, universal as compared to other ways of fitting lines to data. It is the right technique when you are predicting hospital beds, schoolrooms, traffic patterns, and making general policy-oriented predictions. But most of us, as scientists, have policy as at best a secondary consideration. Somehow, this results-oriented technique has spilled over into the more research-oriented domains of the science.

There are alternatives, but just as regression is not a universally appropriate technique, there is no universally appropriate alternative. My own when-in-doubt favorite is the line that splits the angle between the two regression lines. It goes under at least four names, corresponding to different derivations: It is the line of standard deviations,[3] it is also the orthogonal least squares line, it is the major axis of the bivariate Gaussian distribution (when the data are bivariate Gaussian), and it is the first component of a two-variable principal components analysis.[4]

Let me use two derivations, beginning with the orthogonal least squares derivation. In this derivation I want a line that is close to the data. So I go back to that student of high school algebra and ask, "Student: What is the distance between a data point and a line?" To that, the well-trained student responds by instructing me to "drop a perpendicular" from the point to the line. The length of that perpendicular is the distance from the point to the line. That high school definition of distance or, conversely, of closeness, is the definition used by the orthogonal least squares line: It is the line closest to the data points, using straightforward geometrical definitions of distance and closeness. It is the line with the *smallest average squared perpendicular* distance from the data points to the line.

The derivation of this "orthogonal least squares line," as it is called, is a little trickier than the derivation of the ordinary regression line, were I to present it. But the result is rewarding because it is easy, almost too easy, to compute: The magnitude of the slope of this line is the ratio of the two standard deviations, while the sign, plus or minus, is the sign of the correlation coefficient. As an added bonus, this line conforms nicely to the rules you would expect from the rules of high school algebra, whether you describe y as a function of x or x as a function of y, reversing the equation. Writing y as a function of x, it is the line

$$y = \pm\frac{s_y}{s_x}x + \left(\overline{y} - \left(\pm\frac{s_y}{s_x}\right)\right)\overline{x}$$

[2.12]

or, reversing the equation,

---

3. David Freedman, Robert Pisani, and Roger Purves, *Statistics*, W.W. Norton & Company, New York, 1980.

4. The computations, for both regression and for orthogonal least squares are shown in Appendix 2.1, but they can be easily inferred from standard statistical programs.

$$x = \pm\frac{s_x}{s_y}y + \left(\overline{x} - \left(\pm\frac{s_x}{s_y}\right)\right)\overline{y}$$

[2.13]

where $\overline{x}$ is the mean of x and s_x is the standard deviation of x.

That's one derivation of this alternative fit of a line to the data. Another derivation of the same line, showing different features, can be achieved by generalizing a property of the line *as it would be* if the fit were perfect: Suppose that two variables were, truly and without exception, related by the line $y = mx + b$. In that rare case two useful relations would hold true and determine the line: One is that the known point (x-mean, y-mean) must lie on the line: If a person's "x" were exactly equal to the mean of the x's then that person's "y" would have to be exactly equal to the mean of the y's. That determines one point on the line. In addition, if a person's "x" were exactly one standard deviation above the mean x, then that person's "y" would have to be exactly one standard deviation away from the mean of the y's (above or below). That determines a second point on the line. Seizing these two properties of the "perfect" line, and extending them as criteria for the usual (imperfect) case, you get the same solution as the orthogonal least squares line, again matching Equations 2.12 and 2.13.

Whatever derivation you choose, the orthogonal least squares technique does *not* build in a hidden agenda about "predicting" y from x or x from y. If I choose to think that x causes y, or y causes x, that's my business — and I do, in fact, choose to think this way, at times. But the cause is not in the data, so all I want from the line is a summary description of the data. The rest is up to me. That is why I use the orthogonal least squares line. Compared to the regression line, the line of means, it uses fewer hidden assumptions and is closer to a purely descriptive statistic: *closer* to the facts and nothing but the facts.

Perhaps the best solution, combining the good points of both the descriptive line and the predictive line, is to describe the best-fit line by three numbers, not the usual two: using two numbers for the line and one for the variation. Reporting the orthogonal least squares (descriptive) slope, plus the orthogonal least squares intercept, plus a third number called "r," which is a correlation coefficient, gives you what you need to either describe or predict — take your choice. For those who are not familiar with r, now is not the time to derive it; it is too important to be slighted at this late point in the discussion. The charm and the hazard of "r" are that it accomplishes many things, including the conversion between the slope of the descriptive line and the slope of the predictive line. Careful insertion of r accomplishes the conversion:

For orthogonal least squares,

$$y = \pm \frac{s_y}{s_x} x + \left(\bar{y} - \left(\pm \frac{s_y}{s_x} \right) \bar{x} \right) ,$$
                                                                            [2.14]

while inserting r, as marked by the arrows, yields regression, the line of means

$$\downarrow \qquad\qquad \downarrow$$
$$y = r \frac{s_y}{s_x} x + \left(\bar{y} - \left(r \frac{s_y}{s_x} \right) \bar{x} \right) .$$
                                                                            [2.15]

If I use the orthogonal least squares line as the descriptive statement and tell you the value of r (and the means of x and y), then you have everything. You can, if necessary, convert the orthogonal least squares description into the regression line for prediction. The numbers can be combined or separated at will, leaving description and prediction unentangled.

For my hypothetical data on education and income the orthogonal least squares line yields:

Income = ($2,500/year) ∗ years − $10,000   [$r = .5$] .   [2.16]

For the short, medium, and tall brothers, it yields simply:

Height = Height   [r not specified] .[5]   [2.17]

And for the four sub-sets of data from my fictitious New England town it yields one description:

_____

5. That is (Height of Brother I) = 1 ∗ (Height of Brother II) + 0.

Population = (100 people/year) * (year–1900) + 900 people   [2.18]

where $r = .6$,   for 1900 to 1903,
          $r = .6$,   for 1904 to 1907,
          $r = .905$,   for 1900 to 1907,
and $r = .999$,   for 1900 to 1999.

The comparison to ordinary regression suggests that the orthogonal least squares line is better, sometimes. When in doubt, I use it. More so than ordinary regression, the orthogonal least squares line is a summary description of the facts.

Appendix 2.1

```
!Program:      Lines - Simple lines: Regression and Orthogonal Least
!Squares
!Language:     True Basic
!By:           Joel Levine 9/91

!Note:         The printed reproduction of the Basic wraps some long lines
!              of code onto the next printed line.  These line fragments
!              should be entered in their correct positions.

!Data taken from file.  If two variables are present, 2 are plotted. If
!3 variables are present, then the third variable is plotted with
!respect to the other two.
!Data in the file should follow a format of pairs or triples:

!5                number of data points (number of pairs or triples
!3                Number of Variables (always either 2 or 3)
!12               First element of first pair
!20000            Second element of first pair
!12               First element of second pair
!30000            ...
!16
!20000
!16
!30000
!16
!40000
!20
!30000
!20
!40000

DIM X(1,1), labl$(1)        !Create arrays (size is determined later)

!Down to work:
CALL get_data(ncases,nvariables,X(,),labl$(),v_name1$,v_name2$)
CALL get_mean(ncases,X(,),1, mean1)
CALL get_mean(ncases,X(,),2, mean2)
CALL get_sd(ncases,X(,),1,mean1, sd1)
CALL get_sd(ncases,X(,),2,mean2, sd2)
CALL get_r(ncases,X(,),mean1,mean2,sd1,sd2, r12)

!Display
DO                          !Infinite loop:  End program by breaking
    CALL print_summary(mean1,mean2,sd1,sd2,r12,v_name1$,v_name2$)
    GET KEY ks              !Pause, until signalled to continue
    CLEAR
    CALL
plot_it(ncases,X(,),labl$(),v_name1$,v_name2$,mean1,mean2,sd1,sd2,r12)
    GET KEY ks              !Pause, until signalled to continue
LOOP

END
```

```
!****************************
!*   External Subroutines   *
!****************************

SUB get_data(ncases,nvariables,X(,),labl$(),v_name1$,v_name2$)
    LET yes=1
    LET no=0
    LET debug=no
    IF debug=no then
       PRINT "Enter name of data file: ";
       INPUT fname$
    ELSE
       LET fname$="Test_line"      !Used during debugging
    END IF
    OPEN #1: name fname$

    INPUT #1:ncases
    INPUT #1:nvariables
    MAT redim x(ncases,2),labl$(ncases)
    FOR i=1 to ncases
        INPUT #1:x(i,1)
        INPUT #1:x(i,2)
        IF nvariables=3 then LINE INPUT #1:labl$(i) else LET labl$(i)=""
    NEXT i
    LINE INPUT #1:v_name1$
    LINE INPUT #1:v_name2$
END SUB
SUB get_marks(left,right,   from_h,to_h,step_h)
    LET range=right-left
    LET step_h=range/3
    LET step_h=log10(step_h)
    LET step_h=int(step_h)
    LET step_h=10^(step_h)
    DO until range/step_h<=7
       LET save=step_h
       IF range/step_h>7 then LET step_h=step_h*2
       IF range/step_h>7 then LET step_h=save*5
       IF range/step_h>7 then LET step_h=save*10
    LOOP
    LET from_h=left/step_h
    LET from_h=int(from_h)
    LET from_h=from_h*step_h
    LET to_h=right/step_h
    LET to_h=int(to_h)
    LET to_h=(to_h+1)*step_h
END SUB
SUB get_mean(n,X(,),column, mean)
    LET sum=0
    FOR case=1 to n
        LET sum=sum+x(case,column)
    NEXT case
    LET mean=sum/n
END SUB
```

```
SUB get_r(n,X(,),mean1,mean2,sd1,sd2, r12)
    LET sum_product=0
    FOR case=1 to n
        LET first_factor=(x(case,1)-mean1)/sd1
        LET second_factor=(x(case,2)-mean2)/sd2
        LET sum_product=sum_product + first_factor*second_factor
    NEXT case
    LET r12=sum_product/n
END SUB
SUB get_sd(n,X(,),column,mean, standard_deviation)
    LET sum_squares=0
    FOR case=1 to n
        LET sum_squares=sum_squares+(x(case,column)-mean)^2
    NEXT case
    LET mean_sum_squares=sum_squares/n
    LET standard_deviation = sqr(mean_sum_squares)
END SUB

SUB plot_it(n,X(,),labl$(),v_name1$,v_name2$,mean1,mean2,sd1,sd2,r12)

    !Find the limits, left, right, bottom, and top of the plot
    LET left=x(1,1)
    LET right=x(1,1)
    LET bottom=x(1,2)
    LET top=x(1,2)
    FOR case=2 to n
        IF left>x(case,1) then LET left=x(case,1)
        IF right<x(case,1) then LET right=x(case,1)
        IF bottom>x(case,2) then LET bottom=x(case,2)
        IF top<x(case,2) then LET top=x(case,2)
    NEXT case

    !Now extend these boundaries a little to allow room for labels,
    ! on the graph
    LET horizontal_range=right-left
    LET window_left=left-(.1)*horizontal_range
    LET window_right=right+(.1)*horizontal_range
    LET vertical_range=top-bottom
    LET window_bottom=bottom-(.1)*vertical_range
    LET window_top=top+(.1)*vertical_range

    !Simple plot:
    SET WINDOW window_left,window_right, window_bottom,window_top
    FOR case=1 to n
        !PLOT TEXT, AT x(case,1),x(case,2):labl$(case)
        PLOT x(case,1),x(case,2)
    NEXT case
    FOR case=1 to n                !Draw a cross (in case the label was blank)
        PLOT x(case,1)-horizontal_range/80,x(case,2);
        PLOT x(case,1)+horizontal_range/80,x(case,2)
        PLOT x(case,1),x(case,2)-vertical_range/60;
        PLOT x(case,1),x(case,2)+vertical_range/60
    NEXT case
```

```
    !Plot 3 lines, for reference:
    SET COLOR 4                        !Shaded line
    !First regression:
    LET slope = r12*(sd2/sd1)
    LET Intercept = mean2-r12*(sd2/sd1)*mean1
    PLOT left,slope*left+intercept; right,slope*right+intercept

    !Second regression:
    LET slope = r12*(sd1/sd2)
    LET Intercept = mean1-r12*(sd1/sd2)*mean2
    LET transposed_slope=1/slope
    LET transposed_intercept=-intercept/slope
    PLOT left,transposed_slope*left+transposed_intercept;
    PLOT right,transposed_slope*right+transposed_intercept

    !Orthogonal least squares line:
    LET Slope = sgn(r12)*(sd2/sd1)
    LET Intercept = mean2-sgn(r12)*(sd2/sd1)*mean1
    PLOT left,slope*left+intercept; right,slope*right+intercept
    SET COLOR 1                        !reset computer to normal black lines

    !Mark some points
    !horizontal bench marks
    CALL get_marks(left,right,  from_h,to_h,step_h)
    FOR k=from_h to to_h step step_h
        PLOT k,(window_bottom+10*bottom)/11;k,(window_bottom+3*bottom)/4
        PLOT TEXT, AT k,(2*window_bottom+1*bottom)/3:str$(k)
    NEXT k

    !and some vertical bench marks
    CALL get_marks(bottom,top,  from_v,to_v,step_v)
    FOR k=from_v to to_v step step_v
        PLOT (window_left+8*left)/9,k;(window_left+3*left)/4,k
        PLOT TEXT, AT window_left,k:str$(k)
    NEXT k

    !Label the axes
    PLOT TEXT, AT window_left,top-step_v/2:v_name2$
    PLOT TEXT, AT right-step_h/2,window_bottom:v_name1$

END SUB
SUB print_summary(mean1,mean2,sd1,sd2,r12,v_name1$,v_name2$)
    PRINT v_name1$;tab(15);"Mean = ";mean1;tab(40);"Standard Deviation =
";sd1
    PRINT v_name2$;tab(15);"Mean = ";mean2;tab(40);"Standard Deviation =
";sd2
    PRINT "            Product Moment Correlation, r = ";r12
    PRINT
    PRINT "Regressing: "
    PRINT tab(5);v_name1$;" 'predicted' from ";v_name2$
    PRINT "        slope = ";r12*(sd1/sd2);
    PRINT "units of ";v_name1$;" per unit of ";v_name2$
    PRINT "    Intercept = ";mean1-r12*(sd1/sd2)*mean2;"units of
";v_name1$
    PRINT
```

```
    PRINT tab(5);v_name2$;" 'predicted' from ";v_name1$
    PRINT "          slope = ";r12*(sd2/sd1);
    PRINT "units of ";v_name2$;" per unit of ";v_name1$
    PRINT "    Intercept = ";mean2-r12*(sd2/sd1)*mean1;"units of
";v_name2$
    PRINT
    PRINT "Orthogonal Least Squares, 'Descriptive', SD-Line"
    PRINT tab(5);v_name1$;" as a function of ";v_name2$
    PRINT "          slope = ";sgn(r12)*(sd1/sd2);
    PRINT "units of ";v_name1$;" per unit of ";v_name2$
    PRINT "    Intercept = ";mean1-sgn(r12)*(sd1/sd2)*mean2;"units of
";v_name1$
    PRINT
    PRINT tab(5);v_name2$;" as a function of ";v_name1$
    PRINT "          slope = ";sgn(r12)*(sd2/sd1);
    PRINT "units of ";v_name2$;" per unit of ";v_name1$
    PRINT "    Intercept = ";mean2-sgn(r12)*(sd2/sd1)*mean1;"units of
";v_name2$
    PRINT tab(15);"[r = "&str$(r12)&"]"

END SUB
```

Test File

```
7
2
12
20000
12
30000
16
20000
16
30000
16
40000
20
30000
20
40000
Education
Income
```

3

Calculus and Correlation: A Calculus for the Social Sciences

Thirty years ago optimistic social scientists dreamed of a calculus of the social sciences. The logic of this calculus would mirror the logic of social events and it would be the natural language with which to formulate laws of behavior. With it, social science would become "science." That distant dream expressed both admiration for physical science and hope. The admiration was for the incredible fit between the calculus and basic concepts of physical science, a fit so apt that it is no longer possible to think about phenomena like "velocity" and "acceleration" apart from their mathematical expressions. And, seeing that fit, social scientists hoped for a calculus of our own, a mathematics that would confer upon us the blessings that classical calculus had bestowed upon physics. Our present generation of survey researchers would be our Tycho Brahes, documenting the basic facts of social existence. Our Newton would lie just ahead, discovering law.

Why invent a calculus of our own? Why not borrow? Presumably because social science is built from variables like class and power, from roles like "mother," from religion and politics, and because such variables defy the scientific heritage of physics. The science of these things will require a new math. That's one view. But one way that science moves forward is by looking backward to re-assemble its understanding of what it has already accomplished and I'm going to look backward to argue that the calculus, or a calculus, of the social sciences is already here — even for such variables. What's more, I suggest that the Newton and Leibniz of our calculus are none other than the original Isaac Newton and Baron von Leibniz — because it is the same calculus.

My theme is that our basic idea of correlation, in the social sciences, and their basic idea of the derivative, in the calculus, are fundamentally the same. The similarity is well disguised by convention and context, but the two are essentially the same. In one sense my task is simple: I have to show the correspondence between the two forms of the one concept. In another sense the task is difficult because I have to break through the disguises of convention and context, playing with uncomfortably basic questions like what *is* correlation and what *is* a derivative. It's tricky to deal with broad generalities while retaining useful content, but that's the task. The immediate implications are for the concept of correlation: Currently, two-variable correlation is reasonably well understood among social scientists. But partial correlation is something we know more by practice than by intellect, and three-variable, four-variable and n-variable correlation are hardly understood at all, at present. James A. Davis put it well in successive chapter headings for his book on survey analysis, referring to "Two Variables," "Three Variables," and "Too-Many Variables."[1] But we can do better than that. If we rely on the ideas of the calculus as the organizing principle, then the whole intellectual picture of correlation becomes "obvious."

The Logic of Contrasts: Change of One Variable

Let's begin on neutral turf, neither correlation nor the derivative, beginning with the basic problem of comparing two numbers. Suppose that the great oracle who prepares data for data analysts encodes a sequence of four messages about the world, shown in Figure 3.1.

My job as analyst is to read these four messages and interpret them. But, oracles being what they are, the messages are both badly labeled and ambiguous, leaving me little to work with. One fact that's clear about them is that the two numbers in each pair are different: 2 is not equal to 4; 4 is not equal to 8. So I can ask the question, "How different are they?" If I compare the two numbers by their ratio, then I think the

---

Message	Message	Reading One: Ratios	Reading Two: Differences
#1:	[2, 4]	2	2
#2:	[4, 8]	2	4
#3:	[6, 12]	2	6
#4:	[8, 16]	2	8

Figure 3.1
Four Sets of Data Read as Messages Describing the Real World

great oracle is telling me "2" in the first message, and then "2" again, and again "2." That's clear enough. Reading the messages as fractions, the sequence of four messages is constant. The data vary, but the message is constant.

Unfortunately, there is another obvious interpretation for the same data and if I compare the two numbers by their difference, instead of their ratio, then I get a conflicting result: If I compare two numbers by their difference, then I think that the great oracle is telling me "2" and then "4," "6," and "8." That's also clear. Reading the messages as differences, the sequence is a regular progression, not a constant. And, of course, having found two ways to read the data I can probably find more, and that leaves me with a choice: Which is correct? Do the messages describe a constant, or a progression, or something else? Which reading of the data connects to reality? Without labels and clarity, the question is undecidable and that's the point: The numbers do not speak for themselves. Here at the very lowest level of quantification, comparing numbers, they require human intervention and choice. Quantification is about ideas. Get the numbers right with respect to reality and you have a foundation that lets you progress to the next level of difficulty. Get them wrong here, at the beginning, and any subsequent analysis of the data, and of the reality behind the data, is in jeopardy.

But in one important sense there really is a universal answer to the question, or at least a preferred answer, for all cases: How different are

$$\lim_{x \to x_0} \frac{f(x) - f(x_0)}{x - x_0}$$

Figure 3.2
The Derivative of "f" with Respect to "x"
Expressed as the Ratio of Two Differences

two values of one variable? I'll have to justify this answer, but as a matter of form *the correct answer is always their difference*: Never their ratio, never a percentage, always the difference. Always, for any variable and any problem. And the way you make this rule work is by including a generous escape clause: If theory or intuition suggests ratios, then use logarithms before computing the differences of the logs. Whatever it takes, logarithms, inverses, whatever: Transform the variable and then compare values by computing their difference.

Such abstraction may seem distant from the work of a practical scientist — discussing universal answers and content-free rules. But there is solid practical reason for it. This is the kind of thing that mathematicians learn, but rarely teach, because the message is only implicit in the mathematics. It's implicit, for example, in the derivative — the mathematical form, content free, by which we describe velocities and accelerations of all kinds of particular cases. Take a look at a derivative, defined in Figure 3.2, and note the abstraction. The derivative uses two variables, an "x" and an "f," and each variable has two values. In the denominator, the derivative compares two values of x, using subtraction. In the numerator, the derivative compares two values of f, again using subtraction. Thus, if x_0 is the starting time of an experiment and x is the current time, then the denominator, $x - x_0$, is the time elapsed. And if $f(x_0)$ is a location at time x_0 and $f(x)$ is a location at time x, then the numerator, $f(x_0) - f(x)$, is the distance between locations. Putting the two variables together, the derivative divides one difference by the other, giving the rate of change in units of distance divided by time, in miles per hour or centimeters per second.

Part of the genius of the derivative lies in the stunning simplicity of this rate of change at the heart of the concept. A rate of change expressed as "miles per hour" is so obvious to us now, hundreds (or thousands) of years after its invention — so built in to the culture, that math students go right past it, focusing on the less familiar concept of limit, also built in to the definition. But there was a time, I'm told, when physical scientists weren't at all sure that a precise concept of velocity was important. If, for example, you hadn't observed that falling objects fall at different velocities — if you thought they all did the same thing under the influence of what we now call gravity — then you might not be well focused on the concept of velocity. It probably took some serious thinking to define "velocity" as a rate of change and serious creativity to re-use the same idea for acceleration, defining it as the rate of change *of* a rate of change.

What's so clever about the derivative and the rate of change? What's clever is the foresight to begin with subtraction. The derivative compares two values of one variable by subtraction. You would think that flexibility might be a virtue here, when it comes to comparing numbers: When social scientists compare two people's educations, or two counts, or two prices of a commodity, we are ready to use differences, or ratios, or percentages. Whatever makes sense, we'll use it. Compared to our flexibility, in the social sciences, Newton and Leibniz's derivative is the work of monomaniacs, monomaniacs with foresight.

You have to violate the rule of subtraction, temporarily, in order to demonstrate the trouble that would develop without it. For example, let me attempt the mathematical description of a population that doubles each year, and let me compare population to population by division instead of subtraction. Having specified, at the outset, that the population doubles each year, you would think that division would be the natural arithmetic for this population. But watch: If I compare population to population using division, then I have to compare change of population to change of time with an exponent. Thus, if I begin the comparison with division, I have to follow up with the unpleasant expression at the left of Figure 3.3.

This expression does the job, but one thing that Newton and Leibniz did *not* do is work with this kind of thing. It's not just "ugly." The problem is that to generalize this expression, to create a calculus that could calculate its implications would require a whole new branch of the calculus, just for this expression. And mathematicians and physicists

$$\left(\frac{f(x)}{f(x_0)}\right)^{\frac{1}{(x-x_0)}} = 2 \qquad \frac{\log f(x) - \log f(x_0)}{x - x_0} = \log 2$$

Using Division   Using Subtraction

"Population doubles each year" — expressed by division, left, and by subtraction, right, where "f" is Population and "x" is time.

Figure 3.3
Doubling of Population

$$\left(\frac{\left(\frac{f(x)}{f(x_0)}\right)}{\left(\frac{x}{x_0}\right)^{\text{Constant}}}\right) = 1 \qquad \frac{\log f(x) - \log f(x_0)}{\log x - \log x_0} = \text{Constant}$$

Using Division   Using Subtraction

"Proportional growth of the population is directly proportional to the growth of the food supply" — expressed by division, left, and by subtraction, right, where "f" is population and "x" is food supply.

Figure 3.4
Proportional Growth of Population and Food Supply

don't do that, not if they can avoid it. They keep it simple, which means, in this case, being rigidly simple-minded with respect to form, by subtracting. How do I replace division by subtraction? Using logs. That is what logarithms do for positive numbers, replacing multiplication and division of the original numbers by addition and subtraction of their logarithms. If I transform population to log population and subtract, then the whole concept reverts to standard form as a rate of change, Figure 3.3, where it is subject to well-known methods of inference and easily handled by anyone with a term of calculus.[2]

And if this example doesn't worry you, then try something more troublesome: Try expressing something like "the rate of growth of a population is directly proportional to the rate of growth of the food supply." If I compare population to population and food supply to food supply using division, then the comparison between change of population and change of food supply requires the distinctly unpleasant expression on the left of Figure 3.4, another new object requiring another new mathematical development. By comparison, changing the numbers to their logarithms and subtracting re-expresses the same concept in standard form as a rate of change. Keeping it simple, the derivative conserves the user's intellectual muscle for something more productive, further down the road.

The popular culture views math as something complicated, but the truth is that math places high value on simplicity, acknowledging the humble fact that human beings have limited cognitive capacity. And the trick to doing better is not to work yourself into a frenzy to make yourself a smarter human being. The trick is to work on the problem to make it simpler — without any change in the problem. Mathematics keeps it simple.

To be sure, there is a price to be paid for simplicity: You have to switch from population to log population, from the kind of thing you can count, one person, two people, three . . . to a different kind of unit. That

---

2. Working with the calculus, on the left, the math establishes the mutual implication between this rate of change and exponential growth. Working with the thing on the right, the same implication is there — it must be. But it is difficult to prove.

isn't easy. Everyone knows what a person is. But a log-person? Everyone knows what a dollar is. But a log-dollar? That's uncomfortable. It
takes time to get used to such things. But it pays off with simplicity:
Even if you have no direct interest in equations and take no joy from the
beauty of the math, even if your interests are immediate and practical,
change the variables. Suppose, for example, that I am watching the price
of a corporation's stock on Wall Street — that's as immediate and
practical as I can get: Suppose I buy a security priced at $100 and
observe a change of price to $110. Everyone in this culture knows about
percentages. So how could the difference of logarithms, which I recommend, be simpler than percentages as a description of this change? The
answer is that percentages are not simple, just familiar, and if you insist
on using them for practical work you quickly get into as much trouble as
you would if you insisted on using them in equations. Suppose I buy
this security at $100 and observe its changes, using percentages. And
suppose its price moves up ten percent one day, down ten percent the
next, up ten percent the next day, and down ten percent again, regularly.
That's steady and sounds stable, but if I keep that kind of steadiness
going, day after day, in percentages, I will lose about seventy percent of
my money in the course of a year: Check the numbers. Ten percent up
from $100 is $110. Ten percent down from $110 is $99. Ten percent up
from $99 is $108.90. Follow that out for a year and what's left is about
$30.[3] In fact, to stay even, expressing change in percentages, I would
have to climb ten percent while holding my loss to about nine and one-
tenth percent: 10% up and 9.1% down, just to stay even.

If that surprises you, then I've made my point that percentages are
not simple. A little thought will show you the problem — the base from
which you must compute the percentages keeps shifting. And, seeing

---

3. Assuming 250 days of trading, on the stock exchange, each year,
and using as many digits of accuracy as my computer will allow, the
sequence begins
100.0000, 110.0000, 99.0000, 108.9000, 98.0100, 107.8110, 97.0299,
106.7329, . . .
and concludes
. . . , 29.6387, 32.6025, 29.3423, 32.2765, 29.0488, 31.9537, 28.7584,
31.6342, 28.4708.

the problem, you might figure out a way to compensate for it. But now, adding some sort of built-in compensation to the discussion, you are no longer talking about a sequence that is simple, using percentages. (In fact, you are probably on your way to re-inventing logarithms.) Better to convert the price to logs and observe, plus log(1.1), minus log(1.1), plus log(1.1), minus log(1.1). Logs are simpler.

Again, I'll admit there is a price: Tell someone, "Today the logarithm of the price of a share of General Motors stock moved up by log(1.1)," and they will look at you strangely. But there is no easy way out. The same people who object to logarithms and claim to be at ease with percentages will look at you strangely when they find that a precise balance of gains and losses, 10% gained, 10% lost, can wipe out 70% of their money in the course of a year.

To follow the same point, that changing the numbers pays off, even in empirical work, consider the data for the relation between the total populations of nations and their gross national products (GNPs). There should be nothing exciting about population and gross national product: Large nations, like China, the former Soviet Union, India and the U.S. should show large populations and large gross national products. (I'm using GNP, not GNP *per capita*.) Using "people" for population and "dollars" for GNP, think about the graph of these two variables. You might expect something like a line extending from low to high, from low population and low GNP to high population and high GNP, from Tokelau (an island nation in the South Pacific) on one end to China on the other. And when you have a clear mental image of the graph you expect for these data, look at the facts graphed in Figure 3.5. In fact, the real graph of "people" (left to right) by "dollars" (bottom to top) is, in non-technical terms, a mess: More than 90% of the nations clump together in a blur at the lower left-hand corner of the graph. The lay explanation for this mess is practical. Practically, it appears that the U.S. and a few large nations are too big, so big that these super-states are different in kind from other nations and don't belong on the same graph. You don't mix "apples" and "oranges" and you don't mix Tokelau with China, for which differences of degree have become differences in kind, as one is almost one *million* times larger than the other.

So, following this explanation, you solve the problem by removing the U.S. and other very large nations from the graph and drawing it again, without them. Sounds good, but it doesn't work: If I oblige by removing the special cases, I get the revised graph in Figure 3.6, which is basically a re-run of the same phenomenon, minus a few of the original data points. And if you fix it again, simply by removing more cases, then you will be disappointed, again and again. Holding on to the familiar units of dollars and people, these data will not behave. And each time you compensate for your difficulties, keeping track of what has not been placed on the graph, as well as trying to make sense of what has, the analysis gets more complicated.

The real problem here is the mathematics: You may not be inter-

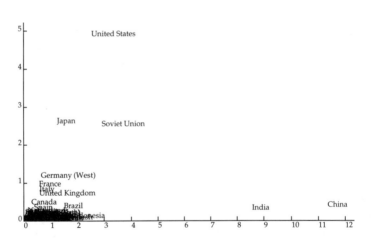

1988 population in hundreds of millions, left to right, by 1990 gross national product in trillions of dollars, bottom to top. For example, the United States is plotted at 251 million people and 4.86 trillion dollars. Data from 1991 *Britannica Book of the Year*, Encyclopaedia Britannica, Inc., Chicago, 1991.

Figure 3.5
Gross National Product Versus Population

ested in it — your interests may be practical and data oriented, but you can't escape it. The practical problem with these data is directly comparable to the mathematical problem in the equations of Figure 3.4. And, fortunately, the solution is also the same: Fix up the comparison between one population and another, and the comparison between one GNP and another, by converting to logs. Then, comparing differences of population to differences of GNP, you will be rewarded with the graph in Figure 3.7. In "theory" the two graphs, Figures 3.5 and 3.7, display exactly the same information. In practice there is a big difference. Even Tokelau, with its two thousand people, and China, with its one billion, line up. Mathematics keeps it simple.

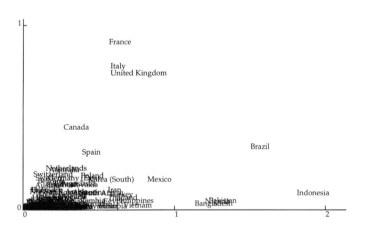

1988 population in hundreds of millions, left to right, by 1990 Gross National Product in trillions of dollars, bottom to top. For example, France is plotted at 57 million people and 898 billion dollars. Data match Figure 3.5.

Figure 3.6
Gross National Product Versus Population — Truncated

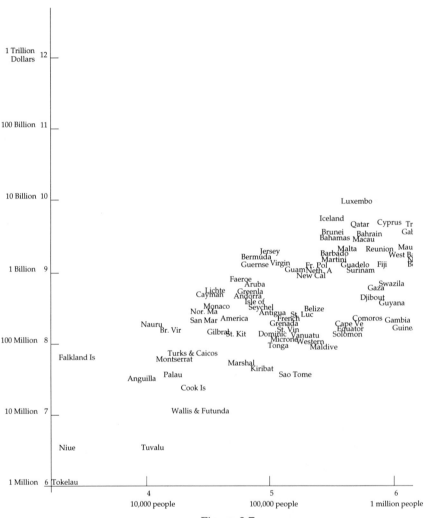

Figure 3.7
Gross National Product Versus Population in
Logarithms, Base 10

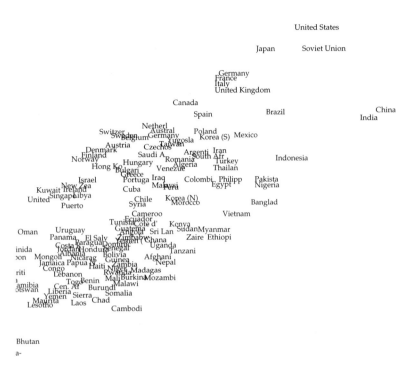

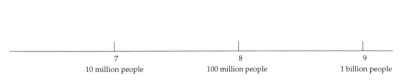

	7	8	9
	10 million people	100 million people	1 billion people

1988 Population, left to right, by 1990 gross national product, bottom to top, plotted logarithmically, using logarithms base 10. For example, the U.S. population of 251 million is plotted at 8.4, between the 100 million mark at 8 and the one billion mark at 9. The U.S. GNP of 4.8 trillion dollars is plotted at 12.7, between the 1 trillion dollar mark, at 12, and the 10 trillion dollar mark, at 13. Data match those in Figure 3.5

The Logic of Correlation

In summary, regardless of context and meaning, when you compare two values of one variable, subtract. Change the numbers, if necessary, but subtract. And that simple lesson in the virtue of good form is half of what I need to connect correlation to the derivative. The other half is a good look at correlation, looking at what correlation *is* in the abstract. To anticipate the argument: In the abstract, correlation expresses a particular kind of comparison, involving two or more variables. By custom, however, correlation and its implied comparison, are not generally expressed by subtraction. And that is where the two halves of the argument get joined: When correlation is re-expressed, using subtraction, the form of the comparison shows that both concepts, both correlation and the derivative, are expressing with the same idea.

Let's look at correlation. To illustrate, let me capture the first two messages from my oracle and give them labels. Shown in Figure 3.8, the first message is now a message about "Democrats": Four of them voted for Bush, two for Dukakis. And the second message is a message about "Republicans": Eight of them voted for Bush, four for Dukakis. In these hypothetical data, is there a correlation between party and vote? How do you answer the question? Paraphrasing the answer by G. Udny Yule, circa 1903, the answer begins by asking the meaning of a single number:[4] Look at the "2" at the upper left of Figure 3.8, two Democrats voted for Dukakis. Does this single number, "2," say anything about the correlation between Vote and Party? No, "2" is neither large nor small, except in comparison to some other number.

All right then, reading the first message, Yule would have compared 2 to 4, using the odds: These Democrats voted for Bush, two to one. Now, does this comparison, using odds, say anything about the correlation between party and vote? Still, the answer is no. The 4 to 2 odds, favoring Bush, are neither large nor small except by comparison to

---

4. Over the years, Yule's *Q*, which I am about to derive, has been derived by alternative methods and has been related to other measures, but it is the original logic of Yule's derivation that I am after.

Data as Numbers

	Votes for Dukakis	Votes for Bush
Democratic Party	2	4
Republican Party	4	8

Data as Symbols

	Votes for Dukakis	Votes for Bush
Democratic Party	$n_{\text{Dem,Dukakis}}$	$n_{\text{Dem,Bush}}$
Republican Party	$n_{\text{Rep,Dukakis}}$	$n_{\text{Rep,Bush}}$

Figure 3.8
Data for Two Two-Valued Variables

the odds among Republicans. The fact that these Democrats favored Bush tells us nothing about the correlation between the two parties and the vote. For that we need to compare the Democrats to the Republicans. So Yule would have read the second message, again using odds, and then compared message to message by the ratio of their odds, which he named κ, the "odds ratio." In this example the odds ratio is 1, and now, with this ratio of two ratios, this comparison of comparisons, we know about the correlation between party and vote: In this example, there is no correlation. The logic of this correlation is summarized in Figure 3.9.

Evidence:

Among Democrats:	Odds favoring Bush = 4/2
Among Republicans:	Odds favoring Bush = 8/4
Contrasting odds among Republicans to odds among Democrats:	Odds ratio, κ = (8/4) / (4/2) = 1

Conclusion:

"Vote," represented by the odds favoring Bush, is not correlated with Party: Comparing Republicans to Democrats, the odds do not change.

Figure 3.9
Logic of Contrasts for Two-Valued Variables

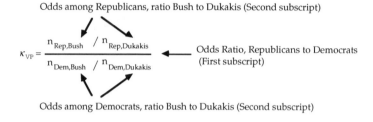

Figure 3.10
Yule's odds ratio, κ

Yule used ratios, not differences, but his logic is clear enough. Correlation lies in the double contrast measured by the ratio of odds. Visually, his logic is crystallized by the notation for κ, shown in Figure 3.10. In both the numerator and denominator the second subscript changes — expressing the comparison between Bush and Dukakis. Then, between the numerator and the denominator, the first subscript changes, expressing the comparison with respect to party.

The Conventions of Correlation: Yule's Q

Unfortunately, Yule too had a public that liked some kind of numbers and disliked others. The issue, in this case, was not a matter of subtraction, or division, or percentages. Rather, the issue was custom and custom in Yule's day, and our own, demanded that a measure of correlation satisfy three conventions. Logic aside, custom demanded:

1. That the value of a correlation coefficient would lie between +1 and –1 (or between +1 and 0 where "negative" correlation is undefined)

2. That the value of a correlation would be 0 for uncorrelated variables and

3.   That the values of a correlation coefficient might change sign, but not magnitude, if the order of the rows or the columns were reversed.

Yule's odds ratio, κ, violated custom on all three counts: Violating the first convention, as a ratio, Yule's odds ratio lies between 0 and infinity, not plus-one and minus-one.   Violating the second convention, Yule's odds ratio is one for uncorrelated variables, not zero.   And violating the third convention, the ratio changes from κ to $1/\kappa$, not $-\kappa$, if the order of the rows or columns is reversed.   Yule responded by transforming his κ to a new expression he named Q, bending and stretching κ to the demands of custom, using Equation 3.1. Yule's Q, named for Adolphe Quetelet, satisfied convention, but the logic was buried.

$$Q_{XY} = \frac{\kappa_{XY} - 1}{\kappa_{XY} + 1},$$

[3.1]

And, after ninety years of historical drift, the form of Yule's Q has itself been altered with the result that the presence of the odds ratios and the logic of Yule's contrasts are entirely hidden, using the form in Equation 3.2. In theory, the original odds ratio and this modern expression of Q embody the same information. In practice there is a difference.

$$Q_{PV} = \frac{n_{RB}\, n_{DD} - n_{RD}\, n_{DB}}{n_{RB}\, n_{DD} + n_{RD}\, n_{DB}}.$$

[3.2]

The Logic of Contrasts:
Correlation and the Derivative

This transformation from κ to Q was, in a sense, a change of language — expressing the concept in the argot of statistics. But differences in language matter, the classical example being the difference between

Roman numerals and Arabic positional numerals as two different expressions of numbers. Just try subtracting "C" from "XL" and then try subtracting "100" from "40." One language works for science; the other is reserved for tombstones. In science language is active. It can block access to the logic of the science or simplify that access and accelerate it. And in this technical sense the conventional language of correlation, in Yule's day and in our own, is barbaric. Like Roman numerals, it labels the objects, but it inhibits their use by disguising the logic. It satisfies convention while obscuring the link between the principle of correlation and ideas of broad currency in the wider community of science.

Now, I'm ready to link correlation to the derivative. On the one side, correlation encodes a double contrast. On the other side, in the calculus there is a comparable double contrast: the rate of change with respect to x of the rate of change with respect to y (or, in the limit, the derivative with respect to x of the derivative with respect to y). If I link the two halves of the argument by using differences to express correlation — changing the language of correlation — then it becomes clear that these ideas are the same.

Using the difference, among Democrats, the contrast with respect to vote is the difference, Δ:

$$\overset{\leftarrow \textit{Difference of log n with respect to Vote} \rightarrow}{\Delta_{\text{Vote}}(\text{among Democrats}) \;=\; [\,\log n_{\text{Dem,Bush}} \;-\; \log n_{\text{Dem,Dukakis}}\,]}$$
$$= [\,\log 4 - \log 2\,]. \qquad\qquad [3.3]$$

Using the difference, among Republicans the contrast with respect to votes is the difference:

$$\overset{\leftarrow \textit{Difference of log n with respect to Vote} \rightarrow}{\Delta_{\text{Vote}}(\text{among Republicans}) \;=\; [\,\log n_{\text{Rep,Bush}} \;-\; \log n_{\text{Rep,Dukakis}}\,]}$$
$$= [\,\log 8 - \log 4\,] \qquad\qquad [3.4]$$

And then, using difference for the contrast with respect to party of these contrasts with respect to vote, Δ^2:

Difference with respect to Party
of Differences of log n
←with respect to Vote →

Difference of log n   *Difference of log n*
←with respect to Vote →   *←with respect to Vote →*

$$\Delta^2_{\text{Party,Vote}} = [\log n_{R,B} - \log n_{R,D}] - [\log n_{D,B} - \log n_{D,D}] \qquad [3.5]$$

There it is, "correlation" as the difference of two differences, the difference with respect to party of the differences with respect to vote. And to see why I find this exciting, let me juxtapose it with the derivative of the derivative — the mixed partial derivative. For well-behaved functions, the derivative of the derivative can be written in the form of Equation 3.6, which is itself the difference of two differences.

Difference with respect to x
←of Differences with respect to y→

Difference   *Difference*
←with respect to y→   *←with respect to y→*

$$\frac{\partial^2}{\partial y \partial x} g(x,y) = \lim_{y \to y_o} \lim_{x \to x_o} \frac{[g(x,y) - g(x,y_o)] - [g(x_o,y) - g(x_o,y_o)]}{(y - y_o)(x - x_o)}$$

$$[3.6]$$

In Equation 3.5 you have correlation as a double contrast; in Equation 3.6 you have the mixed partial derivative as a double contrast and I submit that these two are the same. The terms within the square brackets of each expression are change with respect to one variable. And the difference between the terms in brackets is the change with respect to the other. Now I grant that describing these two equations as "the same" is sloppy: In the calculus, the expression "$x - x_0$" has numerical value where, in the table, there is only a difference between categories, like Bush and Dukakis. In fact, I'm willing to go all the way when I declare that these are the same — including the introduction of numerical values for all sorts of social science objects that have been presumed to be non-numerical, including Bush and Dukakis — but not in this chapter. For the moment I want to continue the single point that correlation is a disguised form of the basic concept of the derivative.

Gaussian, or "Normal," Correlation

So far I've attached my argument to a single measure of correlation, Yule's expression of correlation as k or Q. I'll admit that I'm using Yule: The test of the concept lies in its utility. And had Yule's example of correlation not illustrated my point, I would have chosen another example. But it was not necessary. Nor is it necessary in the case of another correlation, in the case of Gaussian, or "normal," correlation, ρ. If Yule's two-valued variables are the crudest variables that social science has to contend with, then Gaussian variables may be the most sophisticated, so sophisticated that they are not even real: In one dimension, Gaussian variables are the prime example of the bell-shaped curve, with values symmetrically distributed around their average value. In two-dimensions, Gaussian variables are the prime statistical model of a linear relation, with values of both variables symmetrically distributed around the line that describes their averaged relation. Gaussian variables are a statistical ideal, a mathematical norm to which the real world may or may not comply. For these idealized things there is an idealized correlation coefficient, ρ. And for ρ, as for Q, there is a direct link between correlation, Gaussian correlation, and the mixed partial derivative.

To show the correspondence, I am going to be intentionally abrupt: Never mind first principles of correlation that appear in any textbook on correlation. Never mind careful discussion of why the correspondence is reasonable. Instead, I am going to use the principle we have already developed, outlined in Figure 3.11, simply running the argument for ρ in parallel to the argument for Q: Thus, first transform the numbers. For the Gaussian this means using the logarithm of the Gaussian formula. Second, measure the change with respect to one of the two variables. For the Gaussian, this is the derivative. Third, measure the change with respect to the second variable of these changes with respect to the first. For the Gaussian, this is the mixed partial derivative. And that's the end of the argument because what's left shows ρ-correlation in a one-to-one correspondence with the mixed partial derivative. For ρ, as for Q, in each case the correlation coefficient carries the same information as the appropriate measure of change, stretched and shrunk to the limits of plus-one and minus-one, by the equations of Figure 3.12.[5]

---

5. My apologies for word difficulties beyond my control: I am avoiding the conventional term "mixed partial derivative" and substituting "two-variable derivative." This is to avoid the word "partial" because partial has a different meaning in the context of correlation.

Contrasts with Respect to Two-Valued and with Respect to Gaussian Variables

Step 1

Table

Original Table for Two Variables

	Column D, Dukakis	Column B, Bush
Row D, Dem	n_{DD}	n_{DB}
Row R, Rep	n_{RD}	n_{RB}

Function

Original Gaussian Function of Two Variables, x and y.

$$f(x,y) = \frac{1}{2\pi\sqrt{1-\rho^2}}\, e^{-\dfrac{x^2 - 2\rho x y + y^2}{2(1-\rho^2)}}$$

Step 2
Preparing for Subtraction

Transformed Table, using logarithms

$g(D,D) = \log n_{DD}$	$g(D,B) = \log n_{DR}$
$g(R,D) = \log n_{RD}$	$g(R,B) = \log n_{RB}$

Transformed Function, g, Defined as the Logarithm of f

$$g(x,y) = \log f(x,y)$$

Step 3
Contrast with Respect to One Variable

Derivative with respect to Y

For X = x:

$$g_y(x,y) = \lim_{y' \to y} \frac{g(x,y') - g(x,y)}{y' - y}$$

For X = x':

$$g_y(x',y) = \lim_{y' \to y} \frac{g(x',y') - g(x',y)}{y' - y}$$

For both cases:

$$g_y(x,y) = \frac{1}{(1-\rho^2)}(y - \rho x)$$

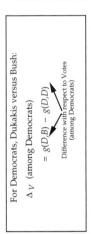

For Democrats, Dukakis versus Bush:

Δ_V (among Democrats)

$= g(D,B) - g(D,D)$

Difference with respect to Votes (among Democrats)

For Republicans, Dukakis versus Bush:

Δ_V (among Republicans)

$= g(D,B) - g(D,D)$

Difference with respect to Votes (among Democrats)

Step 4
Contrast with Respect to the Second Variable
(Between Contrasts with Respect to the First)

$$g_{xy}(x,y) = \lim_{x \to x} \frac{g(x',y) - g(x,y)}{y' - y}$$

$$= \frac{\rho}{(1-\rho^2)}$$

$\Delta_{PV} = \Delta_V$ (among Republicans)
$\quad - \Delta_V$ (among Democrats)

$= \log \kappa_{PV}$

(the logarithm of Yule's κ)

Figure 3.11
Procedural Correspondence Between Δ Correlation and the Derivative

Q – Correlation Versus the Two-Variable Difference	ρ – Correlation Versus the Two-Variable Derivative

Correlation to Contrast

$$Q_{XY} = \frac{e^{\Delta_{XY}^2} - 1}{e^{\Delta_{XY}^2} + 1} \qquad\qquad \rho = \frac{-1 + (1 + 4\,g_{xy})^{\frac{1}{2}}}{2\,g_{xy}}$$

Contrast to Correlation

$$\Delta_{xy}^2 = \frac{1 + Q_{XY}}{1 - Q_{XY}} \qquad\qquad Q_{XY} = \frac{e^{\Delta_{XY}^2} - 1}{e^{\Delta_{XY}^2} + 1}$$

where $\Delta_{xy}^2 = \log \kappa$, the log odds ratio, and where $g(x,y) = \dfrac{\partial^2}{\partial y\, \partial x} g$

Graphically

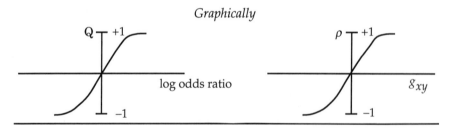

Figure 3.12
Transformations: Correlation to Change and Change to Correlation,
Shown Algebraically and Graphically, for Both Q and ρ.

More-Variable Correlation

And there, in two instances, is Newton and Leibniz's concept disguised, but functioning, as correlation. You discover the underlying rhythm, uniting our concept with theirs, by translation. And that's what I have to say about two-variable correlation, for the moment. Personally, I take pleasure in a concept that unifies ideas, ordering them and simplifying them. And the pleasure is all the greater when the unifying concept is already a classic, extending its reach. But we scientists are supposed to be practical too, and for that it is necessary to extend the concept beyond two variables to three variables and more.[6] Three-variable correlation is not in the vocabulary of statistics. There is three-variable linear regression, which is something else. And there is three-variable partial correlation, which is a special form of two-variable correlation, extracted from the complicating presence of other variables.

---

6. The subject is surely broader than I've indicated here and the parallels seem to continue for partial correlation. For partial correlation between Gaussian variables, the correct difference coefficient appears to be the average with respect to z of the derivative with respect to x and y. This average derivative corresponds to the usual "partial correlation" coefficient by exactly the same formula that translates the simple two-variable derivative into ρ.

For partial correlation between Yule's two-valued variables, you get something different in form from the partial Q suggested by Goodman and Kruskal but very similar in its numerical values when both are applied to real data. Goodman and Kruskal reasoned their way to a partial Q by working with the form of Q shown in Equation 3.2. Working, instead, with the difference form of Equation 3.5, and then translating from differences to kappa to Q leads to a partial Q that corresponds to the average odds ratio:

$$Q_{XY \cdot Z} = \frac{\bar{\kappa}_{XY \cdot Z} - 1}{\bar{\kappa}_{XY \cdot Z} + 1}$$

where $\bar{\kappa}$ is the geometrical mean of the odds ratio, or the anti-log of the arithmetic mean of the difference of differences. In conventional form,

$$Q_{XY \cdot Z} = \frac{n_{x'yz}n_{xyz}n_{x'y'z'}n_{xyz'} - n_{xy'z'}n_{x'yz'}n_{xy'z'}n_{x'yz}}{n_{x'y'z'}n_{xyz}n_{x'y'z'}n_{xyz'} + n_{xy'z'}n_{x'yz'}n_{xy'z'}n_{x'yz}} \quad .$$

Both of these are interesting, but there are lots of things you can do with three variables. The narrower question is what do you get if you extend the logic of differences or derivatives to three variables and then use the result as correlation? The question is almost irresistible to anyone with the nasty turn of mind to push: to push for the next step, to push for more generality, to push to an extreme in which the argument will either fail or add insight. If this two-variable derivative corresponds to two-variable correlation, then what does the three-variable derivative or the three-variable difference correspond to? You have to ask what happens if you push the argument to more variables.

Precisely because we are using a calculus, the formulas for three-variable correlation are automatic. For the Gaussian it's very simple: There is none. Or, to be more precise, the three-way correlation is theoretically zero for Gaussian variables. By mathematical assumption the Gaussian has no three-variable "*xyz*" term that we would call three-way interaction, were it present. For real-world data such things may exist, but not for the Gaussian.[7]

For Yule's variables, however, Δ^3 is clear and not trivial. Logically, it must be the *difference* of the *differences* of the *differences*:

$$\Delta^3_{XYZ} = \Delta^2_{XY}(z') - \Delta^2_{XY}(z).$$

[3.7]

And now, simply invoking the equation that translates from Δ to κ and Q, Figure 3.12, you get the same concept expressed as a ratio, κ^3, and the same concept expressed as a Q, Q^3. What is it? As a ratio, κ^3 is the ratio of two odds ratios: It is the factor by which the odds ratio changes, as a function of a third variable, Z. As a Q it is a coefficient that juxtaposes opposite diagonals from the two different two-variable tables, multiplying the diagonal numbers, $n_{x'y'z}n_{xyz'}$, from one table by the diagonal numbers, $n_{xy'z}n_{x'yz}$, from the other.

---

7. Specifically, no matter how many variables are included in the full *n*-variable Gaussian, it has no product terms with more than two variables.

Two Diagonal Elements from One XY-Table	Two Diagonal Elements from the Other XY-Table	Two Off-Diagonal Elements from One XY-Table	Two Off-Diagonal Elements from the Other XY-Table

$$Q_{XYZ} = \frac{\overbrace{n_{x'y'z'}\,n_{xyz}}\;\overbrace{n_{xy'z'}\,n_{x'yz}} - \overbrace{n_{xy'z'}\,n_{x'yz}}\;\overbrace{n_{x'y'z'}\,n_{xyz}}}{n_{x'y'z'}\,n_{xyz}\,n_{xy'z'}\,n_{x'yz} + n_{xy'z'}\,n_{x'yz}\,n_{x'y'z'}\,n_{xyz}} \qquad [3.8]$$

This concept of three-variable correlation fits right in when you think in terms of differences — just add one more level of contrast. This "thing," implied by the logic, is what some social scientists call three-variable interaction, while others call it specification. Here it is shown as "simply" the three-variable generalization of correlation. It's certainly a known concept, but usually a negative one: When specification is present, ordinary two-variable methods fail, so we tend to watch for it and hope it isn't present. When specification is present we tend to separate the separate cases verbally, rather than quantitatively, and then discuss the separate two-variable cases.

I suspect that the limited use of the concept is caused, in part, by the lack of a number, the lack of a well-understood measure that would detect, express, and facilitate comparisons among three-way correlations — the way we use correlation to detect and compare different two-variable correlations.[8] Therefore, let me close this discussion by

---

8. In both the analysis of variance and log-linear modeling there are tests for the presence of these effects. But just as we always caution users to separate the probabilistic "significance" of a two-variable correlation from the descriptive strength of the correlation, there is a difference between detecting the probabilistic significance of three-variable correlation and measuring its strength. Similarly, in both the analysis of variance and log-linear modeling we can measure the cell-by-cell consequences of correlation, but these effects are not the correlation coefficients. (The difference between the *effects* and the *correlation* is easily seen in a two-row, two-column table: The table has four interaction *effects* and one *correlation*.)

	Low GNP/Capita	High GNP/Capita
Low Literacy	51	15
High Literacy	14	50

$$\Delta^2 = 2.50, \quad \kappa = 12.14, \quad Q = .84$$

Figure 3.13
Relation Between Literacy and Per Capita Gross National Product

	Low Military Expenditures/GNP '78		High Military Expenditures/GNP '78	
	Low GNP/Capita '75	High GNP/Capita '75	Low GNP/Capita '75	High GNP/Capita '75
Low Literacy '75	29	5	22	10
High Literacy '75	7	29	7	21

$$\Delta^2 = 3.18, \quad \kappa = 24.03, \quad Q = .92 \qquad \Delta^2 = 1.89, \quad \kappa = 6.60, \quad Q = .74$$

$$\Delta^3 = 1.29, \quad \kappa^3 = 3.6406926, \quad Q^3 = .57$$

Figure 3.14
Combined Data for Literacy and GNP Per Capita Separated According to High
or Low Military Expenditures as a Fraction of GNP

applying the three-variable measure, derived from the model of the derivative, to data. For data, I've used various indicators for 155 nations, splitting each variable into two values, High and Low, accordingly as values were greater than the median for all values or less than or equal to the median.[9] Through all of these three-variable examples I've used two variables whose two-variable correlation is "obvious": Using literacy rates and per capita gross national products, the two-variable correlation is strong. Shown in Figure 3.13, nations with high literacy were twelve times more likely to show high GNP per capita. The odds were 50 to 14 for the more literate nations, compared to 15 to 51 for the less literate.

That's the way it's supposed to be — education leads to money and money leads to education, at least for a nation as a whole (nothing guarantees that the literate individuals in the country are the ones with the money). But, that's not the whole story. If military expenditures (military expenditures as a fraction of gross national product) are introduced as a third variable, then the *two*-variable correlations change: Where military expenditures are high, the correlation between literacy and wealth is relatively low. Where military expenditures are low, the correlation between literacy and wealth is relatively high.

Figure 3.14 shows the data. The correlations are positive in both sets of countries, but different. In fact, the presence or absence of high military expenditures effects a three- to four-fold change in the correlation between literacy and wealth. (The odds ratios change by a factor of 3.6.)

Habits with three variables are hard to break, so let's be clear what the data do *not* say about literacy, wealth, and military expenditures. The data do *not* say that high literacy and low military expenditures combine, or "add-up," to increase the wealth of the country. No, that would correspond to data in which the worst case for GNP would be low literacy and high military expenditures, while the best case would be the opposite, high literacy and low military expenditures. Lining up the

---

9. Using data reported in the *World Handbook of Political and Social Indicators*, Taylor and Jodice, 1983, available from the Interuniversity Consortium for Political and Social Research, Ann Arbor, Michigan.

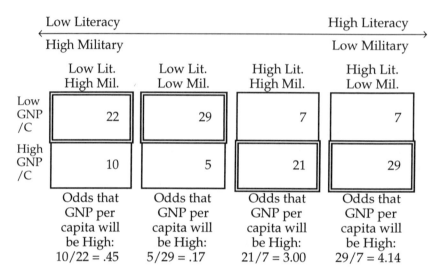

	Low Lit. High Mil.	Low Lit. Low Mil.	High Lit. High Mil.	High Lit. Low Mil.
Low GNP /C	22	29	7	7
High GNP /C	10	5	21	29
	Odds that GNP per capita will be High: 10/22 = .45	Odds that GNP per capita will be High: 5/29 = .17	Odds that GNP per capita will be High: 21/7 = 3.00	Odds that GNP per capita will be High: 29/7 = 4.14

Columns are ordered according to an additive model, with the order of the two middle categories being indeterminate. Counts indicate the number of countries displaying each combination. And the odds indicate the observed odds favoring High GNP per Capita

Figure 3.15
Comparing an "Additive Model" of the Odds Favoring High
GNP per Capita (Left to Right) to the Actual Odds Favoring
High GNP per Capita.

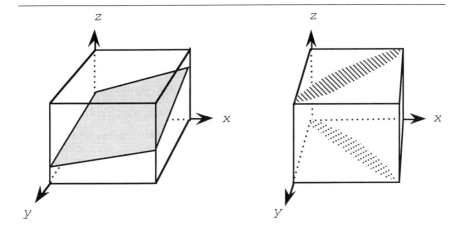

On the left the data lie in a plane; here the two-variable relations are
constant, or uniform, throughout the data. On the right the data indicate a
three-variable correlation; here, the two-variable relations change.

Figure 3.16
Two Forms of Three-Variable Relation

data in that order, in Figure 3.15, that is *not* what the data show. On the
contrary, both the best case for high GNP and the worst case involve low
military spending.

That's what is *not* in the data: In fact, the three-variable correlation
is not a statement about wealth at all. It is a statement about the correlation between literacy and wealth: The correlation changes.

The difference between the usual use of three variables and the
pattern detected by the three-variable correlation is shown graphically in
Figure 3.16. On the left, the three-variable relation is, or is presumed to
resemble, a plane: Within the plane the relation between x and y,
between x and z, or between y and z is both linear and "constant," the
same throughout the data. On the right, the correlation changes. I've
drawn it as a change in the xy correlation: It goes in one direction for
low values of z; it goes in the opposite direction for high values of z. The
two patterns, the one on the left and the one on the right, are quite

incompatible: Real data can be matched by (at most) one of these patterns.[10]

The data for these nations can be set out in two more table formats, Figures 3.17 and 3.18, both of which show the same effect, although they are conducive to different interpretations of the data: As far as the numbers are concerned, it is equally correct to observe that literacy affects the correlation between wealth and military expenditures, Figure 3.17. Where literacy is high, there is a positive correlation between wealth and per capita military spending. Where literacy is low, there is a negative correlation. Comparing the less literate nations to the more literate nations the odds favoring military expenditures shift by a factor of 3.6, necessarily the same factor as for the first presentation of the data.

And finally, the data allow a third presentation, Figure 3.18, displaying the data in their full ambiguity. Separating the nations by GNP per capita, where wealth is low, there is a slight positive correlation between literacy and military spending. Where wealth is high, there is a negative correlation.

While all three of these arrangements are the same data, they look different, illustrating the positive effects of good form, the

---

10. The diagram is, of course, an exaggeration: The correlation must change, but it need not change sign. And while the figure on the right is drawn to show the change in the xy correlation, it is also true that three-variable correlation, or specification, changes the xz correlation and the yz correlation as well as the xy correlation.

One "obvious" candidate for a measure of three-variable correlation is a generalization of the two-variable correlation coefficient r. If you define r^3 as the mean product of three standardized variables (standardized to mean 0 and standard deviation 1), then the result seems responsive to the presence of these three-variable correlations. But this r^3 is not satisfactory without modification because it is also responsive to data distributions that are not indicative of three-variable correlation: It achieves its maximum values for variables that are co-linear, and highly skewed, which is not what I'm after. (It is not bounded by plus- and minus-one, but that's a minor problem.)

	Low Literacy '75		High Literacy '75	
	Low Military Expenditures /GNP '78	High Military Expenditures/GNP '78	Low Military Expenditures/GNP '78	High Military Expenditures/GNP '78
Low GNP/ Capita '75	29	22	7	7
High GNP/ Capita '75	5	10	29	21

$$\Delta^2 = .97, \ \kappa = 2.64, \ Q = .45 \qquad \Delta^2 = -.32, \ \kappa = .72, \ Q = -.16$$
$$\Delta^3 = 1.29, \ \kappa^3 = 3.64, \ Q^3 = .57$$

Figure 3.17
Combined Data for GNP Per Capita and Military Expenditures as a Fraction of GNP, Separated according to High or Low Literacy

	Low GNP/Capita '75		High GNP/Capita '75	
	Low Military Expenditures /GNP '78	High Military Expenditures/GNP '78	Low Military Expenditures/GNP '78	High Military Expenditures/GNP '78
Low Literacy '75	29	22	5	10
High Literacy '75	7	7	29	21

$$\Delta^2 = .28, \ \kappa = 1.32, \ Q = .14 \qquad \Delta^2 = -1.02, \ \kappa = .36, \ Q = -.47$$
$$\Delta^3 = 1.29, \ \kappa^3 = 3.64, \ Q^3 = .57$$

Figure 3.18
Combined Data for Literacy and Military Expenditures as a Fraction of GNP, Separated according to High or Low GNP per Capita

negative effects when it's absent: Using Δ's to measure correlation it is clear that the differences of correlation are the same, 1.29 in each case. Even using κ's, it is almost clear that the change of odds ratios, from 24 to 6.6, from 2.6 to .7, and from 1.3 to .4, is the same in each case. Using Qs, satisfying convention, the information is present but obscure, .92 versus .74, .45 versus –.16, and .14 versus –.47. "Everyone" knows it's hard to compare two Qs, but it's also hard to resist. In the first presentation, the two Qs look "large." They look approximately equal. In the second and third presentations the two Qs differ in sign and magnitude. They look different. It would be easy to miss the specification in one case or focus on it in the other, using Q. Reverting to good form, using differences, these are all the same.

Scanning the social and political indicators for other instances of three-variable correlation yields a group of "third" variables suggesting, jointly, that the correlation between literacy and wealth (between literacy rates and per capita gross national products) is specified by the size of the country: In small countries, the correlation is relatively large, or more positive. In large countries the correlation between literacy and wealth is relative small, or less positive. The specifying variables include three measures of population, one measure of physical area, and one more measure of expenditure.

Specified by

Total Adult Population:	$\Delta^3 = 0.86,$	$\kappa^3 = 2.36,$	$Q^3 = .40$
Total Military Manpower:	$\Delta^3 = 0.90,$	$\kappa^3 = 2.47,$	$Q^3 = .42$
Total Population:	$\Delta^3 = 0.98,$	$\kappa^3 = 2.67,$	$Q^3 = .46$
Total Agricultural Area:	$\Delta^3 = 1.10,$	$\kappa^3 = 3.00,$	$Q^3 = .50$
Total Working Age Population:	$\Delta^3 = 1.22,$	$\kappa^3 = 3.40,$	$Q^3 = .55$
Total Defense Expenditures:	$\Delta^3 = 1.24,$	$\kappa^3 = 3.46,$	$Q^3 = .55$

Pushing Newton and Leibniz's concept to three variables, these six correlations indicate differences in the correlation between literacy and wealth. These correlation coefficients are Newton and Leibniz's concept at work, disguised as correlation.

Appendix 3.1

1988 Population in thousands and 1990 Gross National Product in millions of dollars. For example, the United States data indicate 251 million people and 4.86 trillion dollars. Data from 1991 *Britannica Book of the Year*, Encyclopaedia Britannica, Inc., Chicago, 1991.

	Population in Thousands	GNP in Millions of Dollars		Population in Thousands	GNP in Millions of Dollars
United States	251,394	4,863,674	Argentina	32,880	83,040
Japan	123,530	2,576,541	Romania	23,265	79,813
Soviet Union	290,122	2,500,000	South Africa	37,418	77,720
Germany (West)	62,649	1,131,265	Indonesia	180,763	75,960
France	56,647	898,671	Turkey	56,941	68,600
Italy	57,512	765,282	Hungary	10,437	64,527
United Kingdom	57,384	730,038	Venezuela	19,735	59,390
Canada	26,620	437,471	Algeria	25,337	58,250
China	1,133,683	356,490	Hong Kong	5,841	54,567
Brazil	150,368	328,860	Thailand	56,217	54,550
Spain	38,959	301,829	Bulgaria	8,997	50,837
India	853,373	271,440	Greece	10,038	48,040
Netherlands	14,934	214,458	Iraq	17,754	40,700
Australia	17,073	204,446	Israel	4,666	38,440
Switzerland	6,756	178,442	Philippines	61,480	37,710
Poland	38,217	172,774	Portugal	10,388	37,260
Sweden	8,529	160,029	Colombia	32,978	37,210
Germany (East)	16,433	159,370	Pakistan	122,666	37,153
Mexico	81,883	151,870	Egypt	53,170	33,250
Korea (South)	42,793	150,270	New Zealand	3,389	32,109
Belgium	9,958	143,560	Nigeria	119,812	31,770
Yugoslavia	23,800	129,514	Malaysia	17,886	31,620
Taiwan	20,221	125,408	Peru	22,332	29,185
Czechoslovakia	15,664	123,113	Cuba	10,603	26,920
Austria	7,623	117,644	Ireland	3,509	26,750
Denmark	5,139	94,792	Kuwait	2,143	26,250
Iran	56,293	93,500	Singapore	2,718	24,010
Finland	4,978	92,015	United Arab Emir	1,903	23,580
Saudi Arabia	14,131	86,527	Libya	4,206	23,000
Norway	4,246	84,165	Korea (North)	22,937	20,000

	Population in Thousands	GNP in Millions of Dollars		Population in Thousands	GNP in Millions of Dollars
Syria	12,116	19,540	Bolivia	7,322	3,930
Chile	13,173	19,220	Tanzania	24,403	3,780
Puerto Rico	3,336	18,520	Mongolia	2,116	3,620
Bangladesh	113,005	18,310	Gabon	1,171	3,200
Morocco	25,113	17,830	Afghanistan	15,592	3,100
Vietnam	66,128	12,600	Brunei	259	3,100
Cameroon	11,900	11,270	Bahrain	503	3,027
Ecuador	10,782	10,920	Papua New Guinea	3,671	2,920
Tunisia	8,182	9,610	Nicaragua	3,871	2,911
Cote d'Ivoire	12,657	8,590	Nepal	18,910	2,843
Luxembourg	378	8,372	Bahamas	253	2,611
Kenya	24,872	8,310	Macau	461	2,611
Sudan	28,311	8,070	Jamaica	2,391	2,610
Guatemala	9,197	7,620	Guinea	6,876	2,300
Myanmar	41,675	7,450	Haiti	5,862	2,240
Uruguay	3,033	7,430	Niger	7,779	2,190
Oman	1,468	7,110	Zambia	8,456	2,160
Sri Lanka	17,103	7,020	Madagascar	11,980	2,080
Angola	10,002	6,930	Rwanda	7,232	2,064
Zimbabwe	9,369	6,070	Burkina Faso	9,012	1,960
Ethiopia	50,341	5,760	Congo	2,326	1,950
Zaire	34,138	5,740	Mauritius	1,080	1,890
Yemen (San'a')	9,060	5,700	Reunion	600	1,830
Ghana	15,020	5,610	Lebanon	2,965	1,800
Panama	2,418	5,091	Mali	8,152	1,800
Iceland	256	5,019	Malta	353	1,740
El Salvador	5,221	4,780	Jersey	83	1,647
Paraguay	4,279	4,780	Mozambique	15,696	1,550
Costa Rica	3,015	4,690	Barbados	257	1,530
Dominican Rep	7,170	4,690	Benin	4,741	1,530
Senegal	7,317	4,520	West Bank	908	1,500
Uganda	16,928	4,480	Namibia	1,302	1,477
Jordan	3,169	4,420	Bermuda	59	1,406
Cyprus	739	4,320	Martinique	261	1,400
Trinidad&Tobago	1,233	4,160	Fr. Polynesia	197	1,370
Honduras	4,674	4,110	Malawi	8,831	1,320
Qatar	444	4,060	Togo	3,764	1,240
Albania	3,262	4,030	Burundi	5,451	1,200

	Population in Thousands	GNP in Millions of Dollars		Population in Thousands	GNP in Millions of Dollars
Botswana	1,295	1,191	Bhutan	1,442	202
Guadeloupe	380	1,170	Comoros	463	200
Fiji	740	1,130	American Samoa	40	190
Guernsey	60	1,122	San Marino	23	188
Cen. African Rep	2,875	1,080	Gambia	860	180
Virgin Islands	105	1,070	French Guiana	117	176
Liberia	2,595	1,051	Cape Verde	339	170
Suriname	411	1,050	Nauru	9	160
Guam	132	1,000	Guinea-Bissau	973	145
Yemen (Aden)	2,486	1,000	Equator. Guinea	350	140
Somalia	7,555	970	Grenada	101	139
Sierra Leone	4,151	930	Br. Virgin Is.	13	133
Mauritania	1,999	910	Dominica	82	130
Neth. Antilles	196	860	Gilbraltar	31	130
New Caledonia	168	856	Solomon Islands	319	130
Chad	5,678	850	St. Vincent	115	130
Laos	4,024	710	St. Kitts-Nevis	44	120
Lesotho	1,760	690	Vanuatu	147	120
Faeroe Islands	48	686	Micronesia	108	107
Aruba	63	619	Western Samoa	165	100
Cambodia	8,592	600	Maldives	214	80
Swaziland	770	580	Tonga	96	80
Gaza	608	560	Turks & Caicos	15	63
Greenland	56	465	Falkland Islands	2	56
Cayman Islands	26	461	Montserrat	12	54
Liechtenstein	29	450	Marshall Islands	46	46
Andorra	51	360	Kiribati	71	40
Isle of Man	64	340	Palau	14	32
Djibouti	530	330	SaoTome&Principe	121	32
Guyana	756	327	Anguilla	7	28
Monaco	29	280	Cook Islands	19	21
Belize	189	264	Wallis & Futuna	16	10
Seychelles	69	260	Niue	2	3
Nor. Mariana Is	23	256	Tuvalu	9	3
Antigua	81	230	Tokelau	2	1
St. Lucia	151	220			

Appendix 3.2

Three-variable data, indicating the names as well as the counts of the
nations showing each combination. These are the combined data for
Literacy, for GNP Per Capita, and for Military Expenditures as a Fraction
of GNP, comparable to Figure 3.14.

	Low Military Expenditures/GNP '78		High Military Expenditures/GNP '78	
	Low GNP/Capita '75	High GNP/Capita '75	Low GNP/Capita '75	High GNP/Capita '75
Low Literacy '75	29 — Haiti, Guatemala, Honduras, Gambia, Senegal, Benin, Niger, Ivory Coast, Guinea, Liberia, Sierra Leone, Ghana, Togo, Cameroon, Central African Republic, Zaire, Kenya, Burundi, Rwanda, Ethiopia, Mozambique, Malawi, Lesotho, Swaziland, Madagascar, Afghanistan, Bangladesh, Nepal, Papua New Guinea	5 — Nicaragua, Gabon, Algeria, Tunisia, Libya	22 — Cape Verde, Guinea Bissau, Mali, Mauritania, Upper Volta, Nigeria, Chad, Congo, Uganda, Somalia, Zambia, Zimbabwe, Botswana, Morocco, Sudan, Egypt, Jordan, Yemen Sana, Yemen Aden, India, Pakistan, Laos	10 — South Africa, Iran, Turkey, Iraq, Syria, Saudi Arabia, Kuwait, Bahrain, United Arab Emirates, Malaysia
High Literacy '75	7 — El Salvador, Colombia, Ecuador, Bolivia, Paraguay, Sri Lanka, Philippines	29 — Canada, Dominican Republic, Jamaica, Trinidad Tobago, Barbados, Mexico, Costa Rica, Panama, Venezuela, Surinam, Brazil, Chile, Argentina, Uruguay, Ireland, Luxembourg, Switzerland, Spain, Austria, Italy, Malta, Cyprus, Finland, Denmark, Iceland, Mauritius, Japan, Australia, New Zealand	7 — Guyana, Tanzania, China, Korea South, Burma, Thailand, Indonesia	21 — United States, Cuba, Peru, United Kingdom, Netherlands, Belgium, France, Portugal, Federal Republic Germany, German Democratic Republic, Poland, Hungary, Yugoslavia, Greece, Bulgaria, Romania, USSR, Sweden, Norway, Israel, Singapore

$$\Delta^3 = 1.29, \quad \kappa^3 = 3.6406926, \quad Q^3 = .57$$

4

The Rule of Safety:
Gamma Is Wrong

The social science textbooks teach that variables come in great variety. There are nominal variables, like religion, whose categories have names, but no more. There are ordinal variables, like rank (Private, Corporal, Sergeant, . . .), whose categories have order. There are interval variables, like years of education, for which we can attempt to measure the relative sizes of the intervals between categories. And there are more. There are partial orders and semi orders. There are variables with true zeroes and variables with a true unit of "one." The diversity of these variables, and their peculiarity as compared to the "x's" and "y's" of high school algebra, create difficulty for the scientist. With nominal variables about the best you can do, mathematically, is to list the categories, Catholic, Hindu, Jew, Moslem, Protestant. . . .   With ordinal variables you can do a little inference such as "*If* Corporal greater than Sergeant and *if* Sergeant greater than Private, *then* Corporal greater than Private." And with interval variables it is possible to compute averages and to plot lines.[1]

This proliferation places a heavy burden on the user: You've got to be very careful. You can't ask for the average of a nominal variable, it makes no sense. You can't draw a graph of the correlation between two

---

1. Strictly speaking, by *a priori* reasoning some of the obvious examples of interval-scale variables are more than interval scales, depending on whether or not the variable has a natural zero or a natural unit. Income may have a natural zero, zero income. Years of education completed may have both a natural zero and a natural unit if it is defined as the number of years for which someone will certify your performance.

ordinal variables because graph paper has intervals, whereas the ordinal variables do not. Even restricting the list of types to these three kinds of variables, nominal, ordinal, and interval variables, the attentive user looking for correlations must be prepared to understand six combinations of variables, nominal-nominal, nominal-ordinal, nominal-interval, interval-interval, etc., and come up with six appropriate ways of measuring correlation.

So, if you aspire to be the "compleat" methodologist, with the right measure for every occasion, you have your work cut out for you. And even that is not sufficient because, often enough, we're not really sure about the type of a variable. Take education for example. Is it valid to say that years of education form an interval scale in which the interval between "10" and "11" is equal to the interval between "11" and "12"? Arguably, it isn't. In the U.S., 10 years of education brands you as a dropout. So does 11. But 12 years of education completed implies a high school diploma. Arguably, the intervals between years of education are unequal, with large intervals lying between 7 years and 8, between 11 years and 12, and between 15 years and 16, with each diploma that you can show to an employer.

So, even if the aspiring methodologist has a logically complete tool kit, ready for anything, it may not suffice because, in practice, it may not be clear how to proceed. Fortunately, there is a way out, or at least there is supposed to be. The way out is to realize that every interval-scale variable is also ordinal: I may not know the interval between 11 years of education completed and 12, but I am sure that "12" is greater than "11." I am sure about the order. So, if you can prove your results by assuming nothing more than order, then your results will be correct even if the variable could have been treated as an interval scale. That is what I call the "Rule of Safety." By the rule it's safe to treat an interval variable as if it were only ordinal and it's safe to treat an ordinal variable as if it were only nominal. It's safe to be wrong, as long as the error is conservative, as long as you have assumed less than you were entitled to assume, not more. Assume too much and you're in trouble because you have assumed something contrary to fact. Assume too little and you're safe. So, worse come to worst, if you can handle nominal variables you can handle anything, conservatively.

Sounds good, but it's wrong. Whether you err on the side of conservativism (assuming less than is true) or on the side of non-conservativism (assuming more than is true), wrong is wrong. The reason that the rule of safety sounds reasonable, and is accepted in practice, is that we often confuse mathematical arguments with scientific ones and, more generally, we confuse mathematics with science. Social scientists so routinely prostrate themselves before the awe of mathematics that it might help clear the air for social scientists to think of themselves as "natives" who have been colonized by a foreign culture of mathematics. Generations back, mathematicians came to our sciences bearing technology that jolted social science out of its ancestral ways and into the culture of the 20th century. For that I thank the mathematicians, and we will not abandon what they have taught us. But they've stayed too long. They have tried to impose their values upon us, what is good and what is bad, and many of our native scientists have learned to mimic the mathematician's style and the mathematician's view of the world. That's a mistake.

You can see the mathematician's style at work when someone uses a phrase like "Let X be an ordinal variable." Those are words of power and intimidation in the methods books and the books on mathematical modeling. But they're out of place in science. A sociologist, playing by the rules of science, is not free to use a phrase like "Let Social Class be an ordinal variable" and then go forward. After all, the assertion can be wrong. Class may be an interval-scale variable and not ordinal. That would certainly be consistent with decades of research that have labored to measure "socio-economic status" on an interval scale. Or, Social Class may be multi-dimensional. Or, Social Class may be none-of-the-above. That would certainly be the argument of people who claim that "class" is an ideological myth without valid meaning in American society. Given that the variable "social class" is not well defined, and *can not* be well defined *a priori*, all these points about class can be argued and the rules of science do not allow us to dismiss them by an *a priori* wave of the hand.

The rule of safety is a logical statement that has no relevance for most of science, where few of us have reason to prove mathematical theorems. Proof for us is usually an empirical exercise, comparing reality to theory. In mathematics, by their rules, it is true that any theorem you can prove for ordinal variables will be true for interval variables (provided that the intervals are embedded in one dimension). By contrast, in observational science, by our rules, it is not true that any correlation I estimate for ordinal variables will be correct, necessarily, when the same variables are treated as interval variables. In mathematics there is no world outside of the mathematician's assumptions, nothing to trip you up from outside the logic of the system. In sociology assumptions can be wrong.

I will save discussion of the *a priori* leap, "Let X be . . . ," for later: The entire second half of this book is, in a sense, a discourse on data analysis versus declaration. My contention in those chapters is that to skip the analysis and simply *declare* the type of a variable, their rules, is to walk right past one of the great repositories of information about our phenomena.

My target for this chapter is the rule of safety: It's wrong. To make the discussion concrete, I want to take on one of the workhorses of methodology: Goodman's gamma, a measure of association for ordinal variables. But I'm not really after gamma *per se*. As a piece of mathematics and a logical exercise I have little quarrel with it. If the mathematical assumptions apply, if "X" and "Y" are in fact ordinal variables, then use gamma to measure their correlation. What I'm after is the comfortable assurance that, somehow, methodological thinking can be set apart from theoretical thinking, that pure logic is somehow superior to reality. Our science is riddled with artifacts implanted by our colonial masters. For example, the widely practiced rules of "significance testing" repeatedly apply the rule of safety: If you assert that a correlation exists when that correlation is not statistically significant, that is a damnable error. But if you do not assert that a correlation exists when, with better research, you would have found one, that's OK. You're wrong but you've been prudent. Invoking the rule of safey, that's not "error," that's caution.

Such thinking has its place. But it is not an eternal verity: If you tell me that education leads to economic wealth, when it doesn't, then you've encouraged me in the direction of an image of our society that you can not support. That would be wrong. If you tell me that education does not lead to economic wealth, when it does then, again, you will have encouraged me to build a theoretical model of our society that is wrong. That's my target, the rule of safety. Casting doubt on the plausible logic and the widely used practice of measuring ordinal correlation — that's my weapon.

In fact, to focus attention, I will commit the intellectual equivalent of pinning a large target on the left side of my chest and shouting "Ready, Aim, Fire!" I will assert that I can not find a single case where the logic and practice of measuring ordinal correlation is correct. There must be one, and more, somewhere, but as a commonly used measure of association gamma is almost always the wrong measure because the methods do not fit the facts. When the ordinal measure is used anyway, invoking the rule of safety, it generally masks the true strength of correlations that are really present in our data but hidden by our methods.

Gamma: The Abstraction

To get down to it, let me present the logic of gamma for ordinal correlation. I will use what are, almost literally, "textbook examples" for gamma, beginning with Socio-Economic Status and Alienation, from Somers' illustration of gamma in the *Encyclopedia of the Social Sciences*,[2] and continuing with the defining example with which Goodman and Kruskal brought gamma into the literature.

Recall, from the discussion of calculus and correlation, that Yule's Q was originally defined in terms of an expression of contrasts, kappa, which was re-expressed, algebraically, to bring it within the conventional confines of a measure of correlation (forcing it into the range of ±1).

$$Q = \frac{\kappa - 1}{\kappa + 1} = \frac{\dfrac{n_{22}/n_{21}}{n_{12}/n_{11}} - 1}{\dfrac{n_{22}/n_{21}}{n_{12}/n_{11}} + 1} \ . \tag{4.1}$$

---

2. Robert H. Somers, "Statistics, Descriptive: Association," in the *International Encyclopedia of the Social Sciences*, edited by David Sills, MacMillan & Free Press, Volume 15, 1968, p. 244.

The logic of gamma is based on an alternative interpretation of Yule's Q, related to an alternative algebraic form of the concept: The alternative form is realized by first simplifying the double quotients

$$Q = \frac{\dfrac{n_{22}/n_{21}}{n_{12}/n_{11}} - 1}{\dfrac{n_{22}/n_{21}}{n_{12}/n_{11}} + 1} = \frac{\dfrac{n_{11}n_{22}}{n_{12}n_{21}} - 1}{\dfrac{n_{11}n_{22}}{n_{12}n_{21}} + 1} \qquad [4.2]$$

and then multiplying both the numerator and the denominator by $(n_{12}n_{21})$

$$= \frac{(n_{12}n_{21})\dfrac{n_{11}n_{22}}{n_{12}n_{21}} - 1}{(n_{12}n_{21})\dfrac{n_{11}n_{22}}{n_{12}n_{21}} + 1}. \qquad [4.3]$$

This yields the alternative form:

$$Q = \frac{n_{11}n_{22} - n_{12}n_{21}}{n_{11}n_{22} + n_{12}n_{21}}. \qquad [4.4]$$

In this guise, the product $n_{11}n_{22}$, at the left, is considered a report of "positive" information: It counts the number of *pairs* of people for which one of the two people is "higher" than the other on both variables, Figure 4.1. For these $n_{11}n_{22}$ *pairs* of people, one person from each end of the arrow, the person who is "highest" on one variable is also highest on the other, suggesting "positive" correlation.

Similarly, the product $n_{12}n_{21}$, on the right, is a report of "negative" information: For these $n_{12}n_{21}$ pairs, the person who is "higher" on one variable is "lower" on the other, suggesting "negative" correlation. By this logic, Q is simply a balance: The numerator is the surplus, if any, of "positive" over "negative," while the denominator divides by the total number of *pairs* of persons that has been used in the calculation, bringing the whole thing into the range ±1. That balance is your measure of correlation.

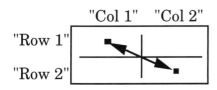

Positive Pairs: One person from Row 1 Column 1, one person from Row 2 Column 2. One person is "higher" on both variables, suggesting positive correlation. The number of pairs of people for which this comparison holds is $n_{11}n_{22}$.

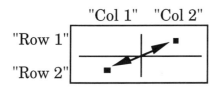

Negative Pairs: One person from Row 1 Column 2, one person from Row 2 Column 1. One person is "higher" on variable 1 and is "lower" on variable 2, suggesting negative correlation between variables. The number of pairs of people for whom this comparison holds is $n_{12}n_{21}$.

Combinations of persons evincing positive and negative correlation. In the upper table a pair of persons, one from each of the two indicated cells, is said to exhibit the pattern of positive correlation. The complementary pair indicates negative correlation.

Figure 4.1

Positive and Negative Pairs

This alternative explanation for Q uses only the order of the categories and it leads to a logical solution for tables with many rows and many columns, in order. For these tables the whole multi-row multi-column table is analyzed into many little two-row and two-column sub-tables, Figure 4.2. Then, logically, if the correlation is positive, the same surplus of positive over negative information should be observed in each of these little sub-tables. Accordingly, the overall correlation is detected by adding up the positive information and the negative information from the tables: In each case (in each of the sub-tables) the positive diagonal indicates "positive" correlation and the negative diagonal indicates "negative" correlation.

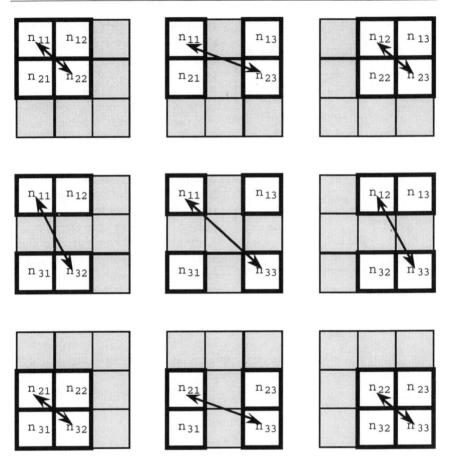

For each sub-table the double-ended arrow marks the pairs for "positive correlation."

Figure 4.2
Two-Row Two-Column Sub-Tables of a
Three-Row Three-Column Table

Now, not only does the logic make sense in every sub-table consistent with the original order but also, mathematically, under the assumption of order (and no more), the information from each of these sub-tables is equally important: There is no reason that a 1-to-3 sub-table should be "more ordered" than a 1-to-2 sub-table. Mathematicians are very strict about this kind of thing: Making the 1-3 distance greater than

1-2 assumes more than order.[3] In this context "1," "2," and "3" mark the order, and no more. So, using order and only order, consistent from table to sub-table, gamma gives the same treatment to each pair of rows and each pair of columns: It sums the positive information and the negative information, computes the balance, and supplies a denominator that brings gamma into the range ±1.

With a little bookkeeping, so that nothing gets lost, this leads to gamma measuring ordinal correlation in the entire table. For the three-row three-column case, using all nine sub-tables, the computation is

Number of Positive Pairs (following the nine double arrows) =

$$n_{11}n_{22} + n_{11}n_{23} + n_{12}n_{23} + n_{11}n_{32} + n_{11}n_{33} + n_{12}n_{33} + n_{21}n_{32} + n_{21}n_{33} + n_{22}n_{33}$$

[4.5]

Number of Negative Pairs (following the opposite diagonals) =

$$n_{12}n_{21} + n_{13}n_{21} + n_{13}n_{22} + n_{12}n_{31} + n_{13}n_{31} + n_{13}n_{32} + n_{22}n_{31} + n_{23}n_{31} + n_{23}n_{32}$$

[4.6]

Computing the balance and using the sum as a denominator yields:

$$\gamma = \frac{\text{Number of Positive Pairs} - \text{Number of Negative Pairs}}{\text{Number of Positive Pairs} + \text{Number of Negative Pairs}} \quad [4.7]$$

---

3. Strictly speaking, which is what mathematics is about, an order relation is irreflexive and transitive, that's all. Irreflexively, if A is greater than B, in order, then B is not greater than A, you can't have both orders. Transitively, if A is greater than B and B is greater than C, in order, then A is greater than C, in order. There is a temptation to say more, to say that if A is greater than B and B is greater than C, then A is *much* greater than C — but that's not in the math. There's even a symbol that appears occasionally, ">>," to express this "much greater than" concept, as in the formal looking "If A>B and B>C, then A>>C." But that is something beyond order, some sort of second-order order, beyond irreflexiveness and beyond transitivity. And if the argument is that "math" may not recognize the concept, but scientists of the real world should recognize it, then that is my point: Data commonly described as ordered are typically more than ordered and, in that case, methods assuming order, and no more, misrepresent the reality. See Kenneth Bogart's *Introductory Combinatorics,* 2nd Edition, HBJ-Saunders, 1990, Chapter 7.

Gamma: With Data

Gamma — Status and Alienation

That's gamma. So, what's the trouble with gamma? Its "math" is certainly different from Yule's logic of contrasts — I would prefer something closer to that logic — but that's not the big problem. The problem with gamma is that it is very difficult to come up with a live example, a single case using data, for which it is the appropriate measure. "Order" makes sense as a mathematical concept, but in the real world it usually means that the intervals are unknown and that's quite a different matter from asserting that they don't exist. I can not, and need not, assert that there is no appropriate example, but I can say that the "exemplars," the one with which Goodman and Kruskal brought gamma forth into the world, and the examples in current textbooks are *not* examples of ordinal scales.

		SOCIO-ECONOMIC STATUS			
		High	Medium	Low	*Total*
	High	23	62	107	*192*
ALIENATION	Medium	61	65	61	*187*
	Low	112	60	23	*195*
	Total	*196*	*187*	*191*	*574*

$$\gamma = -.57 \quad r = -.47$$

From Somers, *op. cit.*, reconstructed by Somers from William Erbe's "Social Involvement and Political Activity: A Replication and Elaboration," *American Sociological Review*, Volume 29, 1964, p. 207.

Figure 4.3
Cross-Classification of Socio-Economic Status and Alienation

	Small Interval H-M	Small Interval M-L	Large Interval H-L
Small Int. H-M	Q = –.50	Q = –.33	Q = –.63
Small Int. M-L	Q = –.33	Q = –.44	Q = –.70
Large Int. H-L	Q = –.70	Q = –.60	Q = –.92

Figure 4.4
Sub-Table Q-Correlations for Alienation and Status Data of Figure 4.3

In the *International Encyclopedia of the Social Sciences*[4] the table used to illustrate gamma is a cross-classification of 574 persons by Alienation (High, Medium, or Low) and by Socio-Economic Status (High, Medium, or Low), Figure 4.3. No numbers are attached to the category labels, they are named to suggest order. But names are not evidence and the evidence, once examined, shows the presence of intervals that trip up the logic of gamma. "Socio-Economic Status" in this example is a combination of income, education, and occupational prestige and "Alienation" is a combination of subjects' responses to a variety of statements like "We are just so many cogs in the machinery of life." At a minimum it's reasonable to suspect that High Status is closer to Middle Status than High Status is to Low Status. That would be more than order. That would invalidate the equal treatment of tables that is built in to gamma. And that is what the evidence of the sub-tables suggests.

Figure 4.4 organizes the nine sub-tables in terms of "suspected" small intervals and large ones. Sure enough, where we suspect long intervals we get a large sub-table correlation, large in absolute value ($Q = –.92$). Where we suspect short intervals we get small correlations, small in absolute value (ranging from –.33 to –.5).[5]

Known or unknown, the intervals impose themselves on the sub-tables. But gamma treats all these numbers, ranging from –.3 to –.9, as if

---

4. Somers, *op. cit.*

5. BASIC programs in Appendix 4.2 automate the computations for tables and sub-tables.

they were estimates of a single uniform quantity, "averaging" them together. That's what an average is supposed to do — give a single number to summarize a reasonably similar batch of equivalent objects. And that's where the ordinal logic gets into trouble: It uses one number for dissimilar objects. Not only do we have different kinds of sub-tables but there are almost always more of one kind than the other — four out of nine short ones, in this case, versus one long one (with four more cases in the middle). So gamma, pooling them all together, weights the average in the direction of the smaller correlations: Here it gets a number slightly larger (in magnitude) than the smaller correlations, gamma equal to –.57. That's wrong or, to be more precise, misleading — like adding my income to one of the Rockefellers' incomes and reporting the average.

Gamma — The "Defining Example"

Gamma was introduced to the literature in Goodman and Kruskal's 1954 article for the American Statistical Association.[6] To illustrate their statistic they used "Education (of Wife)" and "Fertility-Planning Status (of Couple)," using data for married Protestants living in Indianapolis. Reproduced from Goodman and Kruskal the data are displayed in Figure 4.5.

The table is more complex than the *Encyclopedia* example, in part because it has four columns rather than three. But the set-up is basically the same: For both variables "I suspect" more than order. I suspect, for example, that "1 yr. College+" is closer to "3-4 years H.School" than it is to "< 3 yrs. H.School," but that statement is not allowed under the mathematical definition of order. So we may expect their exemplar to exhibit similar anomalies. It does.

Simplifying to three columns and nine sub-tables by combining the middle columns produces a grouping of magnitudes consistent with the suspected intervals.

---

6. Leo A. Goodman and William H. Kruskal, "Measures of Association for Cross Classifications," *Journal of the American Statistical Association*, Volume 49, 1954, p. 752.

PLANNING STATUS WITH RESPECT TO CHILDREN

	All Planned (Includes 0 children)	Most-Recent Child Planned	Most-Recent Un-planned but Wanted	1 or More Un-planned and Un-wanted	*Total*
EDUCATION of WIFE					
1yr. College+	102	35	68	34	*239*
3-4yrs. H.School	191	80	215	122	*608*
< 3yrs. H.School	110	90	168	223	*591*
Total	*403*	*205*	*451*	*379*	*1438*

$$\gamma = .30 \qquad r = .25$$

Data are from both Goodman and Kruskal, *op. cit.*, re-labeled, and from the original source. The original Goodman and Kruskal column labels, left to right, were A: Most effective planning of number and spacing of children and D: Least effective planning of children. Middle columns were labeled only "B" and "C." Frequencies are reproduced as printed by Goodman and Kruskal. Labels were re-constructed from C. V. Kiser and P. K. Whelpton, "Fertility Planning and Fertility Rates by Socio-Economic Status," in Whelpton and Kiser (editors), *Social and Psychological Factors Affecting Fertility*, Volume 2, *The Household Survey in Indianapolis*, Milbank Memorial Fund, 1954, p. 402, the original source.

Figure 4.5
Cross-Classification of Wife's Education by Planning of Children

	Small Column Interval "All –Middle"	Small Column Interval "Middle –Unwanted"	Large Column Interval "All –Unwanted"
Small Row Int. Coll.–.H.S.	Q = .21	Q = .11	Q = .31
Small Row Int. H.S.–<H.S.	Q = .21	Q = .35	Q = .52
Large Row Int. Coll.–<H.S.	Q = .40	Q = .45	Q = .72

Figure 4.6
Sub-Table Q-Correlations for Education and Planning Data of
Figure 4.5 (Planning Simplified to Three Columns)

As before, known or unknown, the intervals make these nine sub-tables dissimilar. But gamma treats these dissimilar things as estimates of a single uniform quantity, yielding $\gamma = .349$.

Using the full four-column table and eighteen sub-tables, without simplification, the full set of sub-tables is organized in Figure 4.7. Column pairs are organized, left to right, by the increasing median values of the relevant sub-table correlations, and each of the eighteen tables is graphed, vertically, according to the magnitude of the sub-table Q.   Where we might expect long intervals (Rows 1 and 3 versus Columns 1 and 4), we get a large sub-table correlation.

Where we might expect short intervals, there are some surprises: At the left, the data for Columns 2 and 3 provide correlations that are not only small but slightly (very slightly) negative. The implication is that there is no difference between them or, if anything, that their order is reversed. In fact the reverse order, 3 then 2, is consistent with the other median correlations: Checking their mutual distance to Column 4, Columns 2 and 4 are closer (lower median correlation) than 3 and 4, suggesting the order 3, 2, 4. And, similarly, checking the mutual distances of both 3 and 2 to 1, 1 and 3 are closer (lower median

COLUMN PAIR

Q-Range	Col 2-3	Col 2-4	Col 1-3	Col 1-2	Col 3-4	Col 1-4
-.8 -1.00						
-.6 -.79						
-.4 -.59						
-.2 -.39						
-.0 -.19	Rows 2-3,Q=-.18 Rows 1-3,Q=-.02					
0 .19	Rows 1-2,Q=.16		Rows 2-3,Q=.15	Rows 1-2,Q=.10	Rows 1-2, Q=.06	
.2 .39		Rows 1-2,Q=.22 Rows 2-3,Q=.24	Rows 1-2,Q=.26 Rows 1-3,Q=.39	Rows 2-3,Q=.32 Rows 1-3,Q=.41		Rows 1-2,Q=.31
.4 .59		Rows 1-3,Q=.44			Rows 2-3, Q=.40 Rows 1-3, Q=.45	Rows 2-3,Q=.52
.6 .79						Rows 1-3,Q=.72
.8 1.00						
Median Q:	-.020	.238	.256	.323	.401	.521

Figure 4.7
Sub-Table Q-Correlations for the Education and Planning Data of Figure 4.5

correlation) than 1 and 2, suggesting the order 1, 3, 2. Taken together, the evidence suggest the order 1, 3, 2, 4.

So, in this example, we seem to have dual problems: On the one hand, the categories as a group are more-than-ordinal, 1-to-4 being a large interval. On the other hand, the middle categories may be less-than-ordinal, there being little and inconclusive evidence of a difference between them and some suggestion that the empirical order (with respect to education) is, if anything, the reverse of what was assumed. Gamma, of course, "knows" nothing of this detail. Assuming order, no more and no less, it combines all pairs, even those with 0-distances and potentially reversed order, as equals and comes up with the value $\gamma = .30$. That is "correct" and, as before, misleading.

The problem, in both cases, is neither subtle nor interesting, unless you happen to have believed the rule of safety. The calculations are simply churning out the consequences of applying ordinal thinking to an interval problem. And, curiously, the numerical consequences are not even conservative, not consistently: Generally I can force a gamma up, in magnitude, by giving it cruder data. You can work this out from the arithmetic (counting the number of short-interval tables) or try it empirically.[7]

---

7. The figure below is a six-row six-column table generated from a theoretically Gaussian distribution with $r = .25$. Intervals are chosen to approximate "bell-shaped" marginals, with Pascal-triangle proportions 1, 5, 10, 10, 5, 1. As a six by six table the distribution yields gamma equal to .248. As a three by three table (combining adjacent categories) or as a two by two table it yields gamma approximately equal to .312. Here gamma has been manipulated to report stronger results (by giving it cruder data).

		VARIABLE X (a theoretical Gaussian variable)				
		$-\infty < X <= -1.86$	$-.89 < X <= 0$		$.89 < X <= 1.86$	
			$-1.86 < X <= -.89$	$0 < X <= .89$		$1.86 < X < \infty$
VARIABLE Y						
$-\infty$	$< Y <= -1.86$	3	9	11	7	2	0
-1.86	$< Y <= -.89$	9	35	54	41	15	2
$-.89$	$< Y <= 0$	11	54	104	95	41	7
0	$< Y <= .89$	7	41	95	104	54	11
$.89$	$< Y <= 1.86$	2	15	41	54	35	9
1.86	$< Y < \infty$	0	2	7	11	9	3
Sums		32	156	312	312	156	32

The same non-conservative manipulation is available to anyone using the two real-data examples. Combining Alienation and Socio-Economic Status as two-way splits, Other versus Low, increases gamma's magnitude from –.57 to –.712. Combining them as Other versus High increases gamma's magnitude to –.718. For the Goodman and Kruskal exemplar, Education by Fertility-Planning status, using six columns (reported in the original source — reproduced here as Appendix 4.1) yields a gamma of .217. Using four columns, as reported, increases gamma to .349. And combining the columns to two columns, College versus Other, increases the gamma to .518 — that's .217 versus .349 versus .518, using six columns, four columns, or two.

Interval Estimates, Quick and Dirty

What's the problem? How do I fix it? Should I weight the various sub-tables? How many categories, two rows, three rows, or six rows, is correct for a particular problem? All of these questions are inappropriate because, as I said before, there is nothing subtle or intellectually engaging here. These are just the consequences of applying ordinal thinking to interval data *as if* it didn't matter. The solution is to treat these as interval data.

How do you estimate the intervals? Getting it "right" is a delicate matter. I'll show you one solution in later chapters (particularly in Chapter 7, "Democrats, Republicans, and Independents"). But getting it "almost right" can be handled by at least one quick procedure. It has problems of its own, but it is clear and straightforward, and gives us a rough idea of the "unknown" intervals and correlations: The quick and dirty approach I suggest is to use those intervals that realize the maximum "r" correlation, where r is the ordinary correlation for interval-scale variables. A simple BASIC program (included as Appendix 4.3) does the job by what we may call, politely, brute force: It assigns coordinates to the rows and columns, computes the implied correlation, and then changes the intervals so that r gets better. Let the program change the coordinates a few thousand times, checking for improvement, and you get an estimate of the otherwise hidden intervals embedded in the data.

This can, of course, go too far, using the information and even the randomness in these data to eke out a better r. But, in practice with these data the results are surprisingly stabile. (This is equivalent to a technique called "canonical correlation" for which there exist direct solutions.)

For the Somers' Status and Alienation variables this estimates $r = -.45$ with essentially equal intervals for both Alienation and Status (Figure 4.8). (For the more crude, 2-category simplifications, it gets a smaller correlation, $r = -.33$ in both two-by-two cases.)

For the Goodman and Kruskal exemplar it yields a surprisingly stable result. For the four columns, there are two interval estimates, one based on the three rows, as published, the other based on six rows, published in the original report. The estimates are essentially the same, Figure 4.9, getting −1.22, .18, −.21, and 1.46 for the first estimate and −1.23, .09, −.17, and 1.46 for the second. Both estimates suggest reversing or combining the middle categories. For the three educational categories, both the collapsed three-column table and the four-column table yield similar estimates for the three educational categories, −1.39, −.57, 1.15 for the one and −1.43, −.57, and 1.14 for the other. For the original six educational categories the estimates are peculiar, grouping the rows in three groups (the ones used by Goodman and Kruskal), yielding −1.39 for College, −.64 and −.53 respectively for 4 years and 3 years of high school, and 1.44, .95, and .92 for 2 years, 1 year or zero years of high school education. Looking at the correlations, using maximum r, the 3-row 3-column simplification, the 3-row 4-column table, and the original 6-row 4-column table yield approximately the same value or r: .2500, .2518, and .2549 (compared to .3492, .2987, and .2168 for gamma).

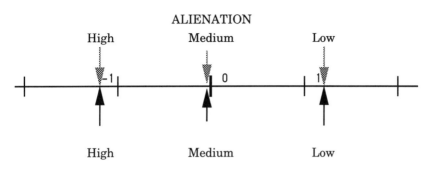

Scale values for Alienation are –1.21, –.03, and 1.22.
Estimates for Status are –1.22, .04, and 1.21.

Figure 4.8
Map of Intervals for the Alienation and Status Data

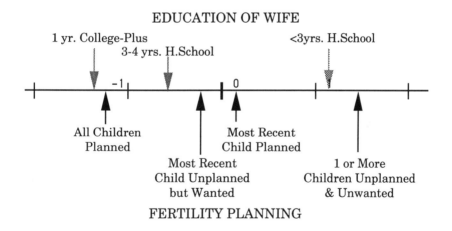

Figure 4.9
Map of Intervals for the Education and Fertility Planning Data

So? Does It Matter?

Does it matter? I think the best defense of gamma would be something like this:

> Everyone "knows" that these data are more-than-ordered, you
> don't get points for writing down what everyone knows. But
> the intervals are unknown and so we simply slip down one
> notch in the measurement scale and use the ordinal
> information. Invoking the Rule of Safety: We may lose some
> information that exists, in principle, but in practice there is no
> damage and we are sticking to information, the order, which is
> firmly established.

If that's the defense, it's wrong: There is no obvious meaning to the consolation that error does no damage. The way values of gamma can be made to increase, playing on the mismatch between intervals and order, it's not even clear that assuming less is "conservative."

In some contexts biased results are appropriate: The procedures of "hypothesis testing," or "significance testing," are the statistical equivalent of the legal rule "innocent until proven guilty." The procedures assume that no correlation exists until its existence is proven, beyond a reasonable doubt. In many contexts that standard makes sense: If you ask me to prove that some human beings, distinguished by skin color or ancestry, are intrinsically more worthy human beings, and if the consequence of my work could justify unequal access to the goodies and scutt work of society, then you can just bet that I will use "hypothesis testing" and that I will be conservative. When I venture forth from research to policy and proclaim "guilt" or argue the redistribution of resources — based on the evidence of my data — then I may well be called upon to prove my results beyond reasonable doubt.

But that is far from the usual context of data analysis. Remember the footnote in every social science "methods" class: It tells you not to confuse measures of correlation with tests of significance. Usually we are interested in correlations as "facts," helping us to know reality. Usually we work as detectives trying to figure out what makes the world tick. For that we need facts and thought, and more facts and more thought, long before we can figure it out and long before we attempt to "prove" what we claim to know.

And in this context the rule of safety is wrong. A report that the correlation between income and education is weak, when it is strong, is a false statement about reality. Whether you are a theorist or simply planning your career, it is the wrong model of the way things work. And the opposite, reporting that the correlation between income and education is strong, when it is weak, is an equal error. As a description of reality, adding up "2 plus 2" and coming up with a conservative "3" is no more accurate than an expansive "5."

In the usual case, substituting "weaker" assumptions muffles the message in the data, confuses the relation between the numbers and the underlying reality, and wastes carefully collected information. In the extreme case, if a strong correlation is lost, its loss is a misdirection, setting off new research to explain what is *already* explained, but mismeasured.

I submit that probably the greatest loss in the *a priori* game, backed up by the rule of safety, is the loss due to misdirected intellectual resources and premature closure: We direct our energies to the abstract games of the colonialist-statisticians and we ritualize the importance of summary statistics, ordinal or interval summaries, instead of analyzing data. Consider the case of Alienation by Status, above. OK, here are your summary statistics: Gamma = $-.57$ or $r = -.47$. Take your choice. And if you need to you may compute the exact level of statistical significance with which we can reject the null hypothesis that there is no correlation. Tell me, what does that contribute to your mental picture of the world? Tell someone who is not "into" the game of methodology what that means.

By contrast, look at the data. Someone, presumably Erbe, the original author, went to a lot of trouble to make the meaning comprehensible: The rows and columns correspond to the upper middle and lower thirds of the population. That keeps it simple. Now look at the numbers. Very roughly: Low-income people think they are cogs in the machine, five to one (56% versus 12%). In extreme contrast, the high-income people find life meaningful, also five to one. And that's a dramatic difference: Five to one, "life is hell," versus five to one in the opposite direction. *Now* I have a mental image of these data.

Pardon me for over-simplifying: Socio-economic status is more complicated than that, and so is alienation, but now I, at least, have a grip on what these data are telling me. If I indulge in the additional step of estimating intervals, the graph of the scores shows the message in detail, with a surprisingly simple correspondence, variable to variable: Again, low-status people are alienated, high-status people are *not* alienated, and middle-status people are right in the middle. If you like, now you may indulge in a summary statistic, $r = -.47$. That locates the strength of this whole relation vis-à-vis the strengths of other correlations in the social sciences. (It's a big one.)

Consider the case of Education and Fertility Planning, the second example. What have you learned from these data? I'll give you gamma $= .299$ or $r = .252$, but the question remains. Turning to the data, the numbers give a rough picture: Female high school dropouts have twice as many unwanted children as college women. (One out of *three* high-school dropouts have unwanted children compared to one out of *seven* for college women.) Now I have an intuitive grasp or guess about what's going on, with great reservations about causal direction: Do educated women learn to plan? Or do planners make it through high school without becoming pregnant? The intervals suggest more detail of the relation: The map suggests that the big step in education is between dropouts (two years or less of high school) and non-dropouts. For "planning" the short step between the two "intermediate" categories suggests that the key to both categories is that the most recent pregnancy was wanted, which is what they have in common. As for the summary statistic, $r = .25$: It's much weaker than the previous correlation but still, sad to say, strong for what we find in the social sciences.

"Doing science," our rules, is not the forte of the mathematicians who brought us their tools. Perhaps the greatest danger in their rule of safety is that it may deflect us from complex but real answers we would find in the data.

Appendix 4.1

PLANNING STATUS WITH RESPECT
TO CHILDREN

EDUCATION of WIFE	All Planned (Includes 0 children)	Most-Recent Child Planned	Most-Recent Un-planned but Wanted	1 or More Un-planned and Un-wanted	Total
1yr. College+	102	35	68	34	*239*
4yrs. H.School	156	53	177	103	*489*
3yrs. H.School	35	27	38	19	*119*
2yrs. H.School	35	29	73	94	*231*
1yr. H.School	26	24	43	49	*142*
Grade School	49	37	52	80	*218*
Total	*403*	*205*	*451*	*379*	*1438*

$$\gamma = .22 \quad r = .25$$

From C. V. Kiser and P. K. Whelpton, "Fertility Planning and Fertility Rates by Socio-Economic Status," p. 402, in Whelpton and Kiser (editors), *Social and Psychological Factors Affecting Fertility*, Volume 2, *The Household Survey in Indianapolis*, Milbank Memorial Fund, 1954.

Cross-Classification of Wife's Education by Planning of Children

Appendix 4.2

```
!Program:  Gamma      (Compute gamma, reading the data from a
file)
!Language:  True Basic 2.01
!Lightly updated/edited  1/21/92 by Joel H. Levine


!Set-up two arrays needed by the program

DIM d(10,10)                   !Rectangular array of data
DIM x(10)                      !Temporary array facilitating input


!Get the data file:

PRINT "Type name of data file (e.g. ed_plan)" !Name of data file
INPUT f$
OPEN #1: name f$


!Read data from file

INPUT #1:nrow                   !Number or rows
INPUT #1:ncol                   !Number of columns
MAT redim d(nrow,ncol)
PRINT "In process, reading data for row:   ";
FOR i=1 to nrow
    PRINT i;
    MAT INPUT #1:x(ncol)        !Read a row of data
    FOR j=1 to ncol
        LET d(i,j)=x(j)         !Append the row to the array
    NEXT j
NEXT i
PRINT
PRINT


!Now, compute gamma, using rows i1 and i2 with columns j1 and j2

LET positive=0
LET negative=0
FOR i1=1 to nrow-1    !First row of each two-by-two sub-table
    FOR i2=i1+1 to nrow             !Second row
        FOR j1=1 to ncol-1         !First column
            FOR j2=j1+1 to ncol  !Second column
                LET p=d(i1,j1)*d(i2,j2)
                LET positive=positive+p
                LET n=d(i1,j2)*d(i2,j1)
                LET negative=negative+n
            NEXT j2
```

```
        NEXT j1
     NEXT i2
NEXT i1
PRINT

!Output
LET gamma = (positive-negative)/(positive+negative)
PRINT "Gamma = ";gamma
MAT PRINT using "####ç:d
END
```

Sample data file name "Ed_Plan":

```
3
4
102,  35,  68,   34
191,  80, 215, 122
110,  90, 168, 223
```

```
!Program:  Gamma2 - Compute gamma  and display information
!          about subtables
!Language:  True Basic 2.01
!Lightly updated/edited 1/21/92 by Joel H. Levine
PRINT "Warning:  Gamma2 trips over zero-valued frequencies."?

!Set-up two arrays needed by the progra

DIM d(10,10), x(10)


!Read Data

PRINT "Enter name of Data File:   ";
INPUT f$
OPEN #1: name f$
INPUT #1:nrow
INPUT #1:ncol
MAT redim d(nrow,ncol)
PRINT "In process, reading data for row:   ";
FOR i=1 to nrow
    PRINT i;
    MAT INPUT #1:x(ncol)
    FOR j=1 to ncol
        LET d(i,j)=x(j)
    NEXT j
NEXT i
PRINT
PRINT


!Now, compute gamma, using rows i1,i2 and columns j1 and j2
LET positive=0
LET negative=0
LET meansubg=0
LET meanlor=0
LET count=0
FOR i1=1 to nrow-1
    FOR i2=i1+1 to nrow
        FOR j1=1 to ncol-1
            FOR j2=j1+1 to ncol
                LET p=d(i1,j1)*d(i2,j2)
                LET positive=positive+p
                LET n=d(i1,j2)*d(i2,j1)
                LET negative=negative+n
                PRINT "rows ";i1;"? ";i2;"  Cols ";j1;" & ";j2;
                PRINT "sub-gamma= ";
                PRINT using "--.###"?(p-n)/(n+p);
                LET meansubg=meansubg+(p-n)/(p+n)
                PRINT tab(55);
                PRINT "ln odds rat= ";
                PRINT using "---.###"?log(p/n)
                LET meanlor=meanlor+log(p/n)
```

```
                   LET count=count+1
               NEXT j2
               PRINT
          NEXT j1
     NEXT i2
NEXT i1
PRINT
PRINT meansubg/count;"?ean sub-table gamma"?"      "
PRINT meanlor/count;"?ean lor ~~"?
LET logk=meanlor/count
LET k=exp(logk)
LET qbar=(k-1)/(k+1)
PRINT "corresponding to q-bar apprxoximately ="?qbar

LET gamma = (positive-negative)/(positive+negative)
PRINT "Gamma = ";gamma
MAT PRINT using "####"?d
END
```

Appendix 4.3

```
!Program:  Max-r,  Brute force estimation of intervals

!Input:  Name of a cross-classification table using frequencies
!Output: Intervals and r
!Procedure:  Find intervals for which r is largest

!Language:  True Basic 2.0

!Re-constructed 9/5/88, Joel H. Levine from 3/27/88

RANDOMIZE

DIM data(10,10),scr(10)
DIM row_coord(10),col_coord(10),stzd_row(10),stzd_col(10)
!indices used to work on rows or columns in random order:
DIM rord(10),cord(10)

!Input
PRINT "Name of Data Files:  ";
INPUT name$
OPEN #1:name name$

INPUT #1:nrow
INPUT #1:ncol
FOR i=1 to nrow
    MAT INPUT #1:scr(ncol)
    FOR j=1 to ncol
        LET data(i,j)=scr(j)
    NEXT j
NEXT i

!To work:

!Initial assignment:  use order, as read, as coordinates
FOR i=1 to nrow
    LET row_coord(i)=i
NEXT i
FOR j=1 to ncol
    LET col_coord(j)=j
NEXT j
!Standardize to mean 0 and standard deviation 1
CALL
stand(row_coord(),col_coord(),data(,),nrow,ncol,stzd_row(),stzd_col())
MAT row_coord=stzd_row
MAT col_coord=stzd_col


!Now Trial and Error, checking a step "trial_change" in either
!direction from a present coordinate
```

```
LET trial_change=.2              !This gets progressively smaller
DO until trial_change<.001
   LET trial_change=trial_change/2
   !Standardize to mean 0 and standard deviation 1
   CALL
stand(row_coord(),col_coord(),data(,),nrow,ncol,stzd_row(),stzd_col())
   MAT row_coord=stzd_row
   MAT col_coord=stzd_col


   CALL evaluate(row_coord,col_coord,data,nrow,ncol, r_current)
   PRINT
   PRINT "Current r = ";r_current;
   PRINT " for adjustment size ="?
   PRINT using "---.#### ":trial_change
   CALL printcrd(nrow,ncol,row_coord,col_coord)


   LET r_better=2               !Initialized with nonsense
   DO while abs(r_better)>abs(r_current)
      PRINT " -"?               !Keep screen busy
      !Standardize to mean 0 and standard deviation 1
      CALL
stand(row_coord(),col_coord(),data(,),nrow,ncol,stzd_row(),stzd_col())
      MAT row_coord=stzd_row
      MAT col_coord=stzd_col


      CALL evaluate(row_coord,col_coord,data,nrow,ncol,
r_current)

      !Try to improve the row coordinates:
      !Work on them in random order, different each time
      CALL indexord(nrow,rord())

      FOR row=1 to nrow
         LET i=rord(row)
         !Try three values
         LET y=row_coord(i)        !Present value
         LET y_plus=y+trial_change
         LET y_minus=y-trial_change
         !Evaluate all three
         CALL evaluate(row_coord,col_coord,data,nrow,ncol, r)
         LET row_coord(i)=y_plus
         CALL
evaluate(row_coord,col_coord,data,nrow,ncol,r_plus)
         LET row_coord(i)=y_minus
         CALL
evaluate(row_coord,col_coord,data,nrow,ncol,r_minus)

            !Act on the results
            IF abs(r)>=abs(r_plus) and abs(r)>=abs(r_minus) then
               LET row_coord(i)=y
```

```
                LET r_better=r
            ELSE
                IF abs(r_plus)>abs(r_minus) then
                    LET row_coord(i)=y_plus
                    LET r_better=r_plus
                ELSE
                    LET row_coord(i)=y_minus
                    LET r_better=r_minus
                END IF
            END IF

        NEXT row

        !Try to improve column coordinate
        CALL indexord(ncol,cord())
        FOR col=1 to ncol
            LET j=cord(col)
            LET x=col_coord(j)        !Present Value
            LET x_plus=x+trial_change
            LET x_minus=x-trial_change

            !Evaluate all three
            CALL evaluate(row_coord,col_coord,data,nrow,ncol, r)
            LET col_coord(j)=x_plus
            CALL
evaluate(row_coord,col_coord,data,nrow,ncol,r_plus)
            LET col_coord(j)=x_minus
            CALL
evaluate(row_coord,col_coord,data,nrow,ncol,r_minus)

            !Act
            IF abs(r)>=(r_plus) and abs(r)>=abs(r_minus) then
                LET col_coord(j)=x
                LET r_better=r
            ELSE
                IF abs(r_plus)>=abs(r_minus) then
                    LET col_coord(j)=x_plus
                    LET r_better=r
                ELSE
                    LET col_coord(j)=x_minus
                    LET r_better=r_minus
                END IF
            END IF
        NEXT col
    LOOP                                !Continue with this step size
    PRINT
    PRINT "Maximum value realized for r = ";r_better
LOOP
!Continue with smaller step size
CALL printcrd(nrow,ncol,row_coord,col_coord)
END
```

```
SUB printcrd(nrow,ncol,row_coord(),col_coord())
PRINT "          Row          Col"?FOR i=1 to max(nrow,ncol)
PRINT using "###:   ":i;
IF i<=nrow then PRINT using "--.####    ":row_coord(i); else PRINT "
";
IF i<=ncol then PRINT using "--.####    ":col_coord(i); else PRINT "
";
PRINT
NEXT i
PRINT
END SUB


SUB evaluate(row_coord(),col_coord(),data(,),nrow,ncol, r)
    DIM stzd_row(10),stzd_col(10)
    !Prepare to compute r by computing standardized versions of both
variables
    CALL stand(row_coord,col_coord,data,nrow,ncol,
stzd_row,stzd_col)

    !Now, compute r as the mean of the products of the standardized
values of
    !the row and column coordinates
    LET r=0
    LET total=0
    FOR i=1 to nrow
        FOR j=1 to ncol
            LET r=r+stzd_row(i)*stzd_col(j)*data(i,j)
            LET total=total+data(i,j)
        NEXT j
    NEXT i
    LET r=r/total
END SUB

SUB stand(row_coord(),col_coord(),data(,),nrow,ncol,
stzd_row(),stzd_col())

    !Compute means for both variables
    LET r_sum=0
    LET c_sum=0
    LET total=0
    FOR i=1 to nrow
        FOR j=1 to ncol
            LET r_sum=r_sum+row_coord(i)*data(i,j)
            LET c_sum=c_sum+col_coord(j)*data(i,j)
            LET total=total+data(i,j)
        NEXT j
    NEXT i
    LET r_mean=r_sum/total
    LET c_mean=c_sum/total

    !Compute first-step standardized coordinates:  subtract
means
    FOR i=1 to nrow
```

```
          LET stzd_row(i)=row_coord(i)-r_mean
     NEXT i
     FOR j=1 to ncol
          LET stzd_col(j)=col_coord(j)-c_mean
     NEXT j

     !Compute standard deviations
     LET rss=0
     LET css=0
     FOR i=1 to nrow
          FOR j=1 to ncol
               LET rss=rss+(stzd_row(i)^2)*data(i,j)
               LET css=css+(stzd_col(j)^2)*data(i,j)
          NEXT j
     NEXT i
     LET rsd=sqr(rss/total)
     LET csd=sqr(css/total)

     !Complete standardization
     FOR i=1 to nrow
          LET stzd_row(i)=stzd_row(i)/rsd
     NEXT i
     FOR j=1 to ncol
          LET stzd_col(j)=stzd_col(j)/csd
     NEXT j

END SUB

SUB indexord(n,id())
     !create indices, integers 1 to n, but in random order
     DIM x(10)
     FOR i=1 to n
          LET x(i)=rnd
          LET id(i)=i
     NEXT i

     !Sort indices according to magnitudes of the random numbers
     FOR i=2 to n
          LET j=i
          DO until j<2 or x(id(j))>x(id(j-1))
               LET junk=id(j)
               LET id(j)=id(j-1)
               LET id(j-1)=junk
               LET j=j-1
          LOOP
     NEXT i
END SUB
```

Part Two
Scatter Analysis

5

Introduction:
The Strength of Weak Data

To the novice, quantitative social science offers some profound mysteries. It utters incantations that begin, "Let X be a normally distributed random variable." It lays claim to objectivity and positivism, but is laden with unobservables like "dependent" and "independent" variables and "causal" structures. "Theory" seems to be the province of word merchants with whom quantitative social scientists are in some unstated conflict, and "data" are consigned to something called "field methods." Results are cloaked in double and triple negative statements about refuting (or not refuting) a "null hypothesis." We lavish intellectual rigor on precise statements of "confidence," "significance," and "explanation," but the statements are based on assumptions that may or may not be satisfied. In the words of Oscar Hammerstein's King of Siam, " 'tis a puzzlement."

The learning of these mysteries, or some of them, is probably an appropriate price of entry. Science simply is not common sense measured to six digits, nor is it journalism formalized with tables and statistics. But, as common sense insists, there can be too much of a good thing. "Methods" can backslide into what Davis called the "ritual slaughter of data," performed to identify the performer as a practicing (and fearsome) member of the tribe.[1] The tools of quantification can become rites, ceremonial formulae that are vehicles more of awe than of content.

---

1. James A. Davis, *Social Differences in Contemporary America*, Harcourt Brace Jovanovich, 1987.

Activity

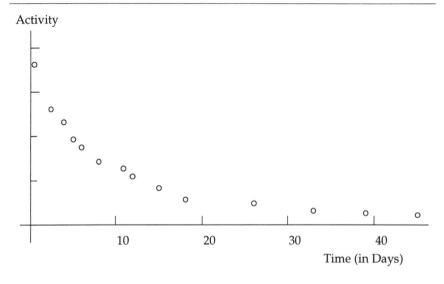

Data from *Exploratory Data Analysis* by John Tukey, Addison Wesley, 1977, p. 195, original from Meyer and Schindler, *Sitzungsberichte der Akademie der Wissenshaften zu Wien, Mathematisch-Naturwissenshaftliche Classe*, 1905, p. 1202.

Figure 5.1
The Decay of Radioactivity

What is the relation between two variables? How do you figure it out? The usual practice in the sciences is to plot the data on graph paper and then look at the pattern. For example, Figure 5.1 shows a graph of radioactivity by time.

Such data are well-behaved in the sense that the eyeball can trace an "obvious" relation — even though the follow-up, "figuring it out," may yet require the attention of genius. (In fact, Tukey used this example because of its bumps rather than its regularities.) These are the kind of *xy*-relations social scientists think about when we use the phrase "X is related to Y." And for these things, particularly when they are linear, summary parameters are entirely appropriate: When you've seen one straight line, you've seen them all. The only things that distinguish one straight line from another are the summary statistics, specifically, the slope and the intercept.

But we rarely find such relations. On the contrary, for many problems, by no means limited to the social sciences, data are different.

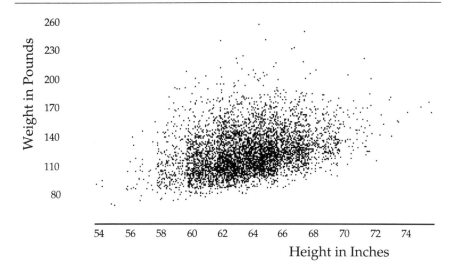

The scatter plot is based on the data used in Chapter 6, but where the original data were presented categorically, here they are spread across the width of the category interval.

Figure 5.2
Simulated Scatter Plot of Height by Weight

For example, Figure 5.2 is a plot of height by weight. We call such diffuse plots "scatter diagrams," a name that is all too suggestive of their difference as compared to the relatively clean *xy*-traces of mathematics or undergraduate physics. "Scatter diagrams," not obvious-seeming relations, are the general fare of social science.

This scatter is the root of many of the evils befalling summary measures. If there were no scatter, just the thin trace of a line, then the troubles described as "Lines, Damned Lines, . . . ," in Chapter 2, would cease: We would use the same equations and the same numbers whether predicting X from Y, or Y from X, or just describing X and Y together. If there were no scatter, just a one-to-one relation between X and Y, then the problems of unknown intervals, subtitled "Gamma Is Wrong," in Chapter 4, would disappear.

The traditional response is to make the scatter itself disappear, at least as an intellectual issue: Somewhere beneath the scatter there lies a pure form, obscure but present. The scatter is treated as an overburden

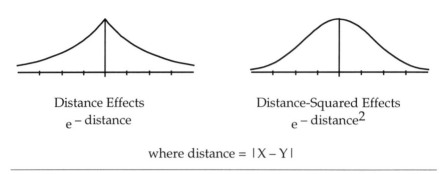

Distance Effects	Distance-Squared Effects
$e^{-\text{distance}}$	$e^{-\text{distance}^2}$

where distance $= |X - Y|$

Figure 5.3
Attenuation of Scatter as a Function of Distance
from the Central Tendency, $Y = X$

to be excavated and removed as quickly as possible. Therefore, data are often examined secondhand, only *after* they are cleaned-up by statistical screening. The statistics extract the pure form, usually assumed to be a line, describing it with summary statistics. Having let the statistics find our pure form, we seize upon it intellectually. We may not "see" the line (in a graph), but we've found it and may proceed like any other science.

Scatter analysis reverses this posture, re-directing attention to the scatter. Without doubt, scatter creates problems. But "scatter" is also a rich source of information. There is strength in these "weak" data, information of which our pampered colleagues with well-behaved data might well be jealous.

Generally, data do not simply "miss" the general tendency, they scatter quite systematically and one clear component of the scatter is, often enough, a distance function: The data "miss," but they tend to be close, and their frequency diminishes quite systematically as a function of distance from the center. And, often enough, the attenuation with distance works as if the data were following one or the other or both of two patterns.

One pattern is shown, schematically, at the left of Figure 5.3. In this pattern the data concentrate around the central tendency, where $Y = X$ and attenuate exponentially. At some distance away from the center, in either direction, the density of scatter falls off by half. At twice this distance it falls off by half again. At three times that distance it tends to fall off to one-eighth of the original frequency, and so forth.

The other pattern is shown schematically at the right. It is almost the same equation except that, here, the governing number is the square of the distance, not the distance itself. This is the pattern usually referred to as a "bell-shaped curve" and matches the basic pattern of Gaussian, or "normal," scatter.

While the difference between these two shapes may seem subtle, perhaps too subtle for the current state of the art in social science, the difference is quite easily detected when it works itself into the data. In Figure 5.4, the table at the top shows a pure case of simple exponential decay, 512, down to 256, down to 128, . . . , decaying from the "diagonal" of perfect correlation. By contrast, the table at the bottom shows a pure case of exponential decay with respect to the squared distance, 512, down to 256, down to 32, ... The difference is not that the latter decays faster — that is data dependent, and may or may not be true. The observable difference is actually in the odds ratios, within the pattern of contrasts localized within the sub-tables of the tables. In the first case you get large local correlations for sub-tables crossing the central tendency, $Y = X$. In the example, the sub-table with frequencies 512, 256, 256, and 512 has an odds ratio of 4 while elsewhere the local correlations are 0, with odds ratio 1. For example, the sub-table with frequencies 256, 128, 512, and 256, has an odds ratio of 1.

In the distance-squared prototype these ratios are quite different and are, in fact, uniform throughout the table: On the diagonal, for example, with frequencies 512, 256, 256, and 512, the odds ratio is 4, while off the diagonal the frequencies 256, 32, 512, and 256 again yield 4.

Do such things occur in practice? That is a matter for hypotheses and testing, although things roughly like this are probably common. The distance-squared effect, with its uniform values of odds ratios, matches the correlations specified by the Gaussian, or "normal," distribution that serves as a common statistical model for correlation. The simple distance effect, with its special odds ratios, is probably more characteristic of phenomena in which the central idea "$Y = X$" really means "the same," like the relation between a father's occupation and his son's occupation. The distance-squared effect seems to fit a less demanding idea of

112

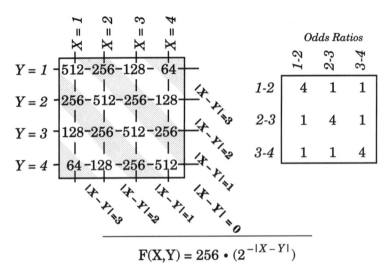

$$F(X,Y) = 256 \cdot (2^{-|X-Y|})$$

Pattern of Exponential Decay With Respect to Distance

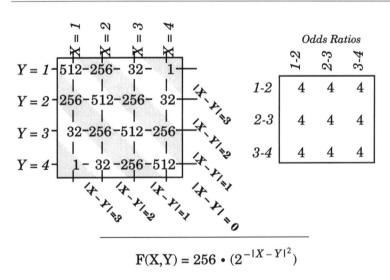

$$F(X,Y) = 256 \cdot (2^{-|X-Y|^2})$$

Pattern of Exponential Decay With Respect to Distance-Squared

Figure 5.4
Patterns With Respect to Distance and Distance-Squared

512	128	256	64
128	512	256	256
256	256	512	128
64	256	128	512

Table 5.1
Simple Distance, Interchanging Middle Categories

correlation — *this* education corresponds to *that* education, subject to considerations like average levels of income and education, monetary inflation, and so forth. The simple distance effect, with its special odds ratios, seems to require a strong meaning for "equal" — parent does manual labor, child does manual labor, parent is a professional, child is a professional — where "equal" is relatively well defined, whether or not it is achieved in practice.

The use of these two patterns is conceptually straightforward: Consider a simple case following the prototype pattern of simple distance, in Figure 5.5. Were these real data, inspection would confirm the distance function: The maximum frequencies, "512," appear at the center of the XY relation, where $Y = X$, and $X - Y = 0$. The lower frequencies, "256," appear where Y is unequal to X (where $|Y - X| = 1$), and so forth. But suppose I had failed to report the X's and Y's, 1, 2, 3, and 4. Suppose that the X's were unknown, suppose that the Y's were unknown, and suppose that even the order of the X's and Y's were unknown. Even if this information were withheld, the pattern of the scatter would allows us to figure it out. If, for example, the data were jumbled and unlabeled as in Table 5.1, and if you had reason to guess, as a working hypothesis, that they could be described by the function $Ae^{-B|X-Y|}$, then you could quickly reconstruct the "unknown" order for both the rows and the columns. Then, with the order restored, you could quickly reconstruct the relative sizes of the intervals, equal in this case. And then, finally, you could test the working hypothesis that you used in the process of restoring the X and Y. The working hypothesis helps us to analyze the data, and the data help us to verify the hypothesis, initially assumed to be true: Yes, the equation fits the data.

The use of distance-related scatter is just that simple, but the data are usually more complex. Usually you have to dig for the relevant information. And, as usual, my all-purpose digging tool is the logic of contrasts. Consider, for example, the odds ratios associated with the "data" of Figure 5.4. The distance function generates large odds ratios near the diagonal of the table and small odds ratios elsewhere. These odds ratios are generated by the distance function and I will accept any table showing these same odds ratios as a table with the same underlying distance function. For example, if everything in the table is multiplied by 2, the odds ratios do not change — they detect the same pattern, shown by the odds ratios in Table 5.2.

And, if everything in row 1 is multiplied by 2 then, once again, the odds ratios do not change — they detect the same pattern, shown in Table 5.3.

And, similarly, if everything in column 1 is multiplied by 2 then, again, the odds ratios do not change and they have detected the same pattern, shown in Table 5.4.

The logic of contrasts extracts the same X intervals and Y intervals from all of these cases. Thus, instead of writing the equation either as $A*2^{-|X-Y|}$ or as $A*2^{-|X-Y|^2}$, I will write it in a form that automatically includes all tables that share the odds ratios determined by the distance, writing it in the form:

$$F(X_i, Y_j) = Ar_i c_j e^{-p_1 \delta_{i,j} - p_2 \delta_{i,j}^2}$$

[5.1]

where "A", with no subscript, corresponds to a multiplier for the whole table, where r_i, with a row subscript, is generic for any row multiplier, where c_j, with a column subscript, is generic for any column multiplier, and where δ_{ij} is short-hand for $|X_i - Y_j|$, the distance of the $x_i y_j$ combination from the central tendency where $X = Y$.

p_1 and p_2 are included as a convenience that combines the two distance functions: $p_1 = 1$ and $p_2 = 0$ yields the distance model, while $p_1 = 0$ and $p_2 = 1$ yields the distance-squared model, and any non-zero combination of the two merges the two models in one equation. A little algebra will show that the non-distance constants in this general formula "cancel" in terms of correlation.

1024	512	256	128			
				4	1	1
512	1024	512	256			
				1	4	1
256	512	1024	512			
				1	1	4
128	256	512	1024			

Table 5.2
Modified Simple Distance Table Plus Odds Ratios
(All table values multiplied by two)

2048	1024	512	256			
				4	1	1
512	1024	512	256			
				1	4	1
256	512	1024	512			
				1	1	4
128	256	512	1024			

Table 5.3
Modified Simple Distance Table Plus Odds Ratios
(All table values multiplied by two, first row multiplied by two)

4096	1024	512	256			
				4	1	1
1024	1024	512	256			
				1	4	1
512	512	1024	512			
				1	1	4
256	256	512	1024			

Table 5.4
Modified Simple Distance Table Plus Odds Ratios
(All table values multiplied by two, first row multiplied by two, first column
multiplied by two)

$$\frac{F(X_{i'},Y_{j'})/F(X_{i'},Y_j)}{F(X_i,Y_{j'})/F(X_i,Y_j)} = e^{-p_1(\delta_{i'j'}+\delta_{ij}-\delta_{i'j}-\delta_{ij'}) -p_2(\delta^2_{i'j'}+\delta^2_{ij}-\delta^2_{i'j}-\delta^2_{ij'})},$$

[5.2]

The one equation relates the scatter, F, to the variables, and to the central tendency $X = Y$. If it appears simple, it is. It is almost as simple as a straight line, except that this equation also describes the frequencies of events that do not fit the line, falling above it or below. The familiar linear analysis persists, hidden in the exponent. What we've added to it is a description of the scatter.

Even when it works, a derived interval scale can not specify that X is a person's weight in pounds and "Y" is a person's height in inches. Interval scales are not that specific, but all the solutions will give the same relatively-sized intervals and the same central tendency, $X = Y$. And we cannot, of course, extract such information from just any scatter of data. Reality is a powerful constraint on the analyst: Sometimes the analysis works, it fits the data. Sometimes it doesn't. And sometimes you can't be sure.[2]

Computation Comments

The programs used to implement the distance models are new and special purpose. I have no objection to standard programs, GLIM, for example, and various programs with names like GAUSS and NEWTON, but I have not found them useful in practice. Programs like GLIM

---

2. Chapters 6 and 7 provide two examples of failure, where it doesn't work. In Chapter 7, failure with the data for political preference (Strong Republican, Republican, Independent, . . .) and income reflects the absence of a relation between these two variables. In Chapter 6, failure with the first analysis of the data and height and weight indicates that something more complex governs the relation between the variables. The failure is detected by attempting to estimate interval scales, then generating the frequencies for each combination of height and weight *as they would be* if the interval scales were correct, and then analyzing the differences between these predicted frequencies and the facts.

(General Linear Model) have found such wide use that people have begun to think that, if you are clever enough, then it should be possible to use these programs to solve any version of a table-fitting model that involves logs. That may even be true, in theory. But in practice it is false because computing time still has a cost. It is several orders of magnitude cheaper than a decade ago, but if you're not careful you can come up with a computation that is several orders of magnitude longer and get right back where you started.

That's what's going on here or, rather, that is what I have worked carefully and deviously to avoid. To give an example, those who are familiar with the "crossings model" know that if you already know the order for your categories, if you are looking for a one-dimensional solution, and if your row categories are the same as your column categories, then GLIM can fit, or attempt to fit, the crossings model to your data with an answer that comes back almost instantaneously.[3] But if you relax just one of those assumptions, the assumption that the order is known, *a priori*, then you get into deep trouble. If you had only 5 categories to work with, then you could try all of the 60 distinct orderings, $(5*4*3*2)/2 = 60$, each one of which could be solved "instantly," except that the amount of work would be creeping up by two orders of magnitude — because you would have to do it 60 times. Go up to 9 categories, a perfectly reasonable number for a variable like "occupation" and the straightforward approach would give you 181,440 of these "instantaneous" computations, creeping up on five orders of magnitude. If "instantaneous" means 1 second, then 181,440 instantaneous computations are going to take you 50 hours.

So, of course, you don't do it in a straightforward way. You become devious. But the trouble with "devious" is that it introduces a bit of uncertainty and cleverness in a place where scientists don't like it. A result is supposed to be a result, and anybody is supposed to be able to duplicate it. We save mysteries for the research problem — they're not supposed to lurk around in the methods themselves. Still, I know of no way around it: If I have to check the possible solutions, finding the best fit of a model to the data, I'm probably not going to check all the solutions one at a time. I'm going to find some way of connecting the

---

3. For a general introduction to this class of models read Michael Hout, *Mobility Tables*, Sage, Beverly Hills, 1983, pp. 27-37.

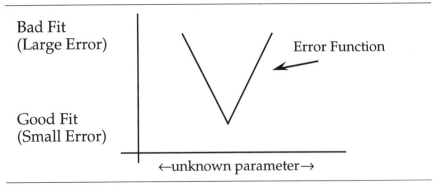

Figure 5.5
Fit, or Error, Varying as a Function of the
Unknown Parameter, Simple Case

solutions, usually in some sort of continuum, and then move through the continuum of solutions looking for a best result. If I am lucky, a plot of the "badness" of the results will look like Figure 5.5.

If I start by simply guessing the value of the unknown parameter, I'll be wrong. But if the guess is too low, somewhere at the left side of the graph, then "how good" will get better if I try a larger value, something a little further to the right. So I "move" a little further to the right, measure again, and sure enough the error will get smaller again, down to a limit. Then eventually, when I pass the middle of the graph,

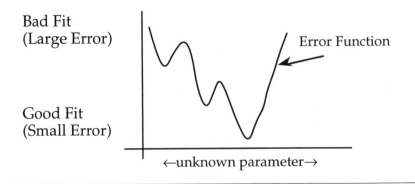

Figure 5.6
Fit, or Error, Varying as a Function of the
Unknown Parameter, More Realistic Case

"how good" will begin to get worse, and the estimation will be done. That's the way we would like things to work when we have to check a whole range of possible solutions to a problem, finding the best solution. Unfortunately, in practice, error may not be that well behaved and, even when it is, you may not know it because you can't step back and "look" at the graph. In practice, with some models, you start at a point, trying one value, and all you know is that in the immediate neighborhood of that point one direction makes things better. But if the curve looks like the curve in Figure 5.6 (were we able to see it) then the simple step-by-step procedure won't always work. It can get stuck at a so-called local minimum, a value that is locally best, but not *the* best. And, since you can't step back and "look" at the curve, you won't know that your "best" effort is a local minimum — not until you've published your answer and a year later someone else has found a better one.

There is no all-purpose general answer to this problem, but you do get better at it. Experience is another thing that we would rather do without in the scientific method, but you get "experience" with models and, in fact, since we are human beings with some knowledge of the real problem behind the numbers, we have some idea of what "should be" the right answer. In effect then, you can get close to "seeing" the curve. You still can't guarantee a minimum, but you get better at it. This is where general-purpose "optimizers," software with names like GAUSS and NEWTON, help but don't help too much.[4] They are programs that are very good and efficient at starting somewhere on a curve like the one above and moving "downhill" to a minimum. But they too are subject to local minimum problems, in which the solution depends on the starting point. "Generally" you solve that problem by repetition, starting again and again from lots of different starting points. If the unknown curve is not too erratic, then that will do the job. If you run the program one hundred times and get only three different answers, then the best of the three is probably the best of all — probably: You never know for certain.

---

4. These are software packages built on estimation procedures bearing these names. For a generic reference on the types of algorithms, see Forman Acton, *Numerical Methods That Work*, Harper & Row, New York, 1970.

But even if the curve is well behaved, left to right, it is usually not "one-dimensional." We have to find the best values for each category relative to all of the others — simultaneously. Each of those numbers has to be varied, separately and in combination, and each different combination gives a slightly different "fit" to the data. The computation remains simple, in theory, but in practice we may have to repeat it so many times that it becomes impractical. And, of course, for this model we also have to find the best multipliers and, perhaps, the best weighting of the two terms in the exponent. When I tell my physics and mathematics friends that I am trying to "optimize" error as a function of 31 parameters (for a 9 by 9 table of occupations), they shudder (and probably think evil thoughts about sociologists). In fact the only reason we are able to find solutions at all is that the surface (which we can't see) is probably extraordinarily well behaved.

To give you some idea of the computing time involved here, I think nothing of starting up a computation for, say, a 9 by 9 table, and simply walking away for the day, letting the computer run. So I get very touchy about "little" changes that might make the program a little slower (and very happy about changes that make it faster). That's also why I'm fairly narrow-minded about the error criterion. For log-linear models in the general literature, it is often appropriate to maximize something called the likelihood function. Why not use it? Why not use the error function that some people expect? Answer: It may in fact be better, but it is non-trivial to switch to a function that may take twice as long to compute, not when computations are measured in days.[5] So, all hands are welcome in solving the computation problems, but changes of this sort are non-trivial matters and their consequences are likely to be small in comparison to the first issue that must be settled. The first issue is "Does the model, do the various models, 'work'?"

---

5. The likelihood function is the product of the predicted probabilities of "events," in this case the predicted probabilities of people being found in various cells of the data tables. Thus each number, and each parameter, occurs in both the numerator and the denominator of the likelihood ratio (you have to divide by a sum that guarantees that all the predictions are "probabilities" (i.e., that they range between 0 and 1 and sum to 1). That appears to be a more costly computation, as compared to chi-square.

There is at least one saving grace in this complexity: In a very real sense it does not matter where the solution comes from or how the computer did it. What counts is the fit. If I found an oracle, preferably one less cryptic than the tease that was said to inhabit Delphi, and the oracle said, "Levine, the solution to problem number one is $x_1 = 3$, $x_2 = 7$, . . . , then that would suffice. That solution is reproducible in the sense that, wherever it came from, I can test it: Do the oracle's numbers fit the model to the data? If they do, then the model fits. It would be nice to do without the oracle, and to do without random elements in the computer programs, but if the results can be verified, then even the use of an oracle, or an inspired guess, would be a perfectly acceptable method, if somewhat unorthodox.   The point is, keep your eyes on the equation: Do these "distance" equations match/fit the data? Do they tell me something about the real world? All the rest is detail.[6]

---

6. And I truly hope that somebody, using perhaps wholly new tactics — but the same equations — will find ways of reducing these computations to "instantaneous" results.

6

Big Folks and Small Folks: The Relation Between Height and Weight

The presence of correlations among events keeps social scientists in business: If the world were random then we, and everyone else, would be in big trouble. But the step from informal notions of correlation, "X is related to Y," up to a specific mathematical model for the relation requires a great increase in specificity. Linear models are one rendering of the idea saying, specifically, that for every additional unit of X you get "m" more units of Y.

$$y = m x + b \qquad\qquad [6.1]$$

Linear models are one of the more useful tools we have for describing data. Part of their advantage is that they match our human capacities: We humans are pretty good at spotting a straight line on a piece of graph paper but, beyond that, our visual repertoire is limited. Another part of their advantage is that straight lines are not nearly so limited as they appear. If a relation between two variables is (in one form) exponential,

$$u = A e^{mv}, \qquad\qquad [6.2]$$

then a straight line can capture the same relation in terms of logs:

$$\log u = m (\log v) + b , \text{ where } b = \log(A) . \qquad\qquad [6.3]$$

Or, if a relation is quadratic in one form,

$$u = m\,v^{\,2} + b\,v,$$ [6.4]

then the straight line can capture the same relation in the form

$$u/v \;=\; m\,v + b\;.$$ [6.5]

With good reason we deem linear analysis worthy of students' attention and dedicate a considerable amount of their time to the machinery for "fitting" these lines to data. This chapter is a warm-up, linear analysis "by the book," as compared to linear analysis using the scatter. The analysis "by the book" uses means, standard deviations, and correlations as summary statistics; the analysis using the scatter uses the detailed frequencies for all of the observed combinations of x and y, both on the line and off the line. "By the book," this is literally a textbook example using *a priori* physical measures of "x" and "y," as compared to the scatter analysis that knows nothing, *a priori*, of these physical intervals.

The data for this warm-up describe height and weight for 4,995 British women, using the example from Kendall and Stuart's *Advanced Theory of Statistics*.[1]   Everyone knows the relation between height and weight: Generally big people are taller and they weigh more, small people are shorter and lighter. Everyone knows the answer, so it's a good place to practice technique.

I'm going to treat these data in three passes, "by the book," using the scatter, and then critically — because it turns out that the relation between height and weight is not simple. Looking ahead, the first pass, "by the book," establishes a rough statement of the correspondence between pounds and inches (about 8 pounds per inch, on the average). The second pass, using the scatter analysis, reconstructs intervals that differentiate between common body weights, below 140 pounds, and heavy body weights, above 180 pounds. Within the lower, more "normal" range, body weight is correlated with height, whereas, within the higher, heavyweight range, weight and height are unrelated.

---

1. Sir Maurice Kendall and Alan Stuart, *The Advanced Theory of Statistics*, Volume 2, 4th Edition, Griffin & Company, London, 1979, p. 300. Original source, "Women's Measurements and Sizes," H.M.S.O., 1957.

Weight	5	33	254	813	Column Sums 1340	1454	750	275	56	11	4	Totals 4995
278.5 lbs						1						1
272.5 lbs												0
266.5 lbs						1						1
260.5 lbs							1					1
254.5 lbs												0
248.5 lbs					1	1						2
242.5 lbs							1					1
236.5 lbs							1					1
230.5 lbs					2				1			3
224.5 lbs					1	2	1					4
218.5 lbs			1		2	1		1				5
212.5 lbs				2	1	6		1	1			11
206.5 lbs				2	2	3	2		1			10
200.5 lbs			4	2	6	2						14
194.5 lbs				1	3	7	7	4	1			23
188.5 lbs			1	5	14	8	12	3	1	2		46
182.5 lbs			1	7	12	26	9	5		1	2	63
176.5 lbs			5	8	18	21	15	11	7		2	87
170.5 lbs			2	11	17	44	21	13	3	1		112
164.5 lbs		1	3	12	35	48	30	15	5	3		152
158.5 lbs			8	17	52	42	36	21	9			185
152.5 lbs		1	7	30	81	71	58	21	2	2		273
146.5 lbs		2	13	36	76	91	82	36	8	1		345
140.5 lbs		1	6	55	101	138	89	50	8			448
134.5 lbs			15	64	95	175	122	45	5			521
128.5 lbs		1	19	73	155	207	101	25	3			584
122.5 lbs		3	34	91	168	200	81	12	1	1		591
116.5 lbs		3	24	108	184	184	50	8				561
110.5 lbs		5	33	119	165	124	22	4				472
104.5 lbs	1	3	33	87	95	35	6					260
98.5 lbs	2	5	29	59	45	16	3					159
92.5 lbs		6	10	21	9							46
86.5 lbs		1	5	3								9
80.5 lbs	2	1	1									4
Height	54in	56in	58in	60in	62in	64in	66in	68in	70in	72in	74in	

Reproduced from Kendall and Stuart, *op. cit.*, p. 300.

Figure 6.1

Distribution of Height and Weight for 4,995 Women, Great Britain, 1951.

Separating the two groups, the line for the "normal" group, using the scatter, is somewhat lower than the conventional line, "by the book." The third pass is a kind of methodologist's nod to the data, critical of both approaches: These height-weight data are supposed to sit back and behave, letting us use them to illustrate technique. But there's life in these data yet, still resisting the simplifications assumed by technique. In fact, their detail carries an unexpected message, a challenge perhaps, and a small warning for the broader log-linear literature in the social sciences.

First Pass: Summary Statistics

The data describe weight in 6-pound intervals and height in 2-inch intervals for 4,995 women. Beginning the first pass through these data, "by the book," where x is height and y is weight, a standard procedure would tell us:

$$\widehat{\mu}_x = 63.06 \qquad\qquad \widehat{\mu}_y = 132.82 \qquad\qquad [6.6]$$

$$\widehat{\sigma}_x^2 = 7.25 \qquad\qquad \widehat{\sigma}_y^2 = 507.46 \qquad\qquad [6.7]$$

$$\widehat{\rho}_{xy} = 0.332 \qquad\qquad \widehat{\rho}_{xy}^2 = 0.1037 \qquad\qquad [6.8]$$

$$x = 0.0385y + 57.96 \qquad\qquad y = 2.292x - 36.96 \qquad\qquad [6.9]$$

This is straight out of the book, a *statistics* book (Kendall and Stuart), and the first warning that a presentation like this should signal to a scientist is that we are on somebody else's turf: It is replete with Greek letters, italics, subscripts, and four- or five-digit numbers, but not a word about pounds and inches. As prestigious as symbols may be to the general population, especially Greek letters in italics, and as necessary as these symbols are to the statistician, such things are less scientific, not more so, than statements using the units of analysis which are, in this case, pounds and inches. Pounds and inches are what we, as scientists, would be studying with these data. In context, here's what the numbers mean. Translating 6.6 and 6.7:

Mean height = 5-feet 3-inches,   standard deviation = 2.7 inches   [6.10]

Mean weight = 133 pounds,   standard deviation = 23 pounds   [6.11]

For these British women, circa 1951, the average height was 5-feet 3-inches, perhaps a little short by 1991 U.S. standards, with a "standard deviation" (root mean squared deviation) around the mean of 2.7 inches. Very roughly, this standard deviation implies that approximately 70% of the women were within 2.7 inches (above or below) the mean.   Their average weight was 133 pounds, with approximately 70% of them falling within the broad range between 110 and 156 pounds (23 pounds above or below the mean).

The two linear equations in x and y, 6.9, called regression lines, would be used for the specific purpose of predicting weight from height or height from weight. Predicting weight from height:

Weight = (2.6 lbs/in) x Height − 37 lbs,   [54in ≤ Height ≤ 74in] .   [6.12]

The equation tells you to predict weight from height by allowing 2.6 pounds per inch and subtracting 36.96 pounds. (Hypothetically, a woman with no height would have a weight of *negative* 36.96 pounds, but the equation is explicitly limited to the range of heights, from 54 inches to 74 inches, for which we have data.)

Conversely, predicting height from weight,

Height = (.0385 in/lb) x Weight + 58.0 in,

[80lbs ≤ Weight ≤ 279lbs]   [6.13]

The equation tells you to allow .04 inches per pound and add 58 pounds.

Finally, giving us some estimate of how good these *best* lines are, the expression "$\rho_{xy}^2 = .1037$," line 6.8, tells us that Height "explains" approximately 10 percent of the variation in Weight and vice versa.

The use of these two equations is quite precisely circumscribed: Under a precise specification of the word "best," these equations give the best prediction of y from x, or x from y. If you accept certain premises, then these are the mathematically best equations. All quantitative social scientists study the "math" of these things and know the limits under which they are appropriate. But, in practice, it is rarely understood just how narrow these limits are and how easy it is to slip beyond them. Most important, neither of these lines can be used as an objective description of reality, the facts and nothing but the facts, free from the interventions of the observer. If there is any doubt about the non-descriptive nature of these lines, it can be verified by converting both of the slopes into units, as statements about pounds per inch. On conversion, one says 2.7 pounds per inch while the other, at .0385 inches per pound, translates to 26 pounds per inch, almost ten times the number used in the first equation. This warns you, quite clearly, that regression lines are not descriptive (nor do they claim to be). Neither can claim to be free from the interventions of the observer, not when we, the observers, have to choose between 2.7 pounds per inch and 26 pounds per inch using criteria external to the data. Any positivist would blush at the act of using a regression line as a description of "what happened."

But even in context, sticking to the business of "best" prediction, it is surprising how little these equations help. Consider a case of pure prediction: You are the star of a carnival sideshow. Your job is to guess women's weights. But this is a statistician's sideshow with unusual rules: You are going to do your sideshow in two acts, with and without regression. In Act I your prediction is particularly difficult: Your job is to guess the weight without any knowledge whatever about the women. You don't even get to look at them. Under these difficult circumstances, if you know the average, then your best bet is to use it. For "Woman Number 1," you guess "133 pounds," for "Woman Number 2," you guess 133 pounds, and so on. In the absence of any specific information about these women, the average is your best answer. Not surprisingly, your best under these circumstances will be none too good. You will be off by an average (root mean squared error) of 22.52 pounds.

For Act II, we bring *STATISTICS* to your rescue. Now let's see what you can accomplish. In this act I'll tell you the height, then you will pull out your calculator and predict the weight, using the regression line. For woman number one the height is 5-foot-3. To guess her weight you multiply by 2.7 pounds per inch and subtract 36.96 pounds to predict about 133 pounds. Now, knowing height and using the statistics of regression, how big are your errors? Now you are off by "only" 21.29 pounds. Congratulations, that's it: 22.52 pounds "average" error knowing only the average weight, 21.29 pounds knowing their height and using regression. The standard deviation of the residuals is reduced by 5.5%. With a correlation of .32, which is pretty strong by current social science standards, that's as well as you can do.[2]

Even if the correlation were stronger, with a correlation equal to .45, the magnitude of correlation we associate with things like "the rich get richer and the poor get poorer" (correlations between the incomes of parents and their children), you would have an "average" error of 20.12 pounds.

This is not necessarily bad news. In the real world, outside my carnival sideshow, errors have costs: If a school system has more students than were predicted, then you pay the cost in the classroom. If a hospital has more patients than beds, or a city has more office space than tenants, then the cost of error is high and even these barely helpful predictions will be worthwhile. If that's your business, if you are in social science strictly for short-term practical benefits, if you want to predict numbers of students in schools, numbers of hospital beds, average income, life expectancy (and, perhaps, dimensions for women's clothes), then use regression. And you always have the option of improving your prediction by adding more variables. (But good luck to you: You will need a total R greater than .87 to cut the standard deviation of the error by even fifty percent.)

Fortunately (considering the weakness of our present ability to predict), most social scientists are not in the business of producing predictions as the first and immediate result of their research. Most of us are not, not immediately, policy oriented. It's something of a mystery to me, therefore, why regression is, nonetheless, used so frequently. Perhaps it is nervousness about the professional standing of our science: You prove your profession is a science by making quantitative predictions, not by comfortable verbal explanations. So we predict,

---

2. For the skeptics, follow the reasoning with the data for height and weight: The original variance of the weight is 507.46. With correlation "r," the variance of the residuals is $(1 - r^2)$ multiplier by the original variance. Numerically, the quantity $(1 - r^2)$ is equal to .89316 which, when multiplied by 507.46, yields 452.243 for the variance of the residuals. Therefore the standard deviation of the residuals is the square root of 452.243, which is equal to 21.2895.

which is necessary, but go one step too far by insisting on this very particular type of least squares prediction. Perhaps it is a kind of Gresham's law for statistics: Precise statements, bristling with probability theory, drive out the alternatives, not-withstanding the fact that, as in the case of height and weight, they are precise statements about very small effects, much ado about (practically) nothing. Perhaps it is a kind of desperation, strong statistics for weak data, unaware of alternatives.

OK, you're convinced. But what should you do? The statistical repertoire is hardly exhausted by simple regression. My best general advice is to pick up John Tukey's textbook on *Exploratory Data Analysis*,[3] but for this occasion let me come up with one specific suggestion. Following my own advice in the previous discussion of lines, one solution for the descriptive line, solving the problem of asymmetry, x to y or y to x, is the "SD line."[4] In effect, the SD line ignores direction, predicting neither height from weight nor weight from height. Instead, it extrapolates to the line that would hold if there were a perfect linear relation between height and weight: If there were a perfect linear relation then a person of average height would have average weight and a person with average height *plus* one standard deviation would have an average weight *plus* one standard deviation — which implies the equation

$$\bar{y} = m\,\bar{x} + b \ .$$
[6.14]

where the slope, m, is the ratio of the two standard deviations and

$$y = \left(+\frac{s_y}{s_x} \right) x + \left(\bar{y} + \frac{s_y}{s_x}\bar{x} \right)$$ (assuming a positive slope). [6.15]

For height and weight that leads to the SD line:

---

3. *Exploratory Data Analysis*, John Tukey, Addison Wesley, 1977.
4. *Statistics*, David Freedman, Robert Pisani, and Roger Purves, Freedman, Norton, 1978.

Weight = (8.4 lbs/inch) × Height − 395 lbs
  [where   54″ ≤ Height ≤ 74″,
  80.5 lbs ≤ Weight ≤ 278.5 lbs, and r = .322]   [6.16]

The central tendency in pounds and inches has a slope of 8.4 pounds per inch.

Second Pass: Analyzing the Scatter

If you insist on a summary line for these data, using summary statistics, then these three lines, the two regression lines and the SD line will do. Two are useful for prediction, one is useful as a description of the height-weight relation. You could improve them a bit by resorting to non-linear relations using, for example, the cube root of weight. But the truth is that in pounds and inches or even cube-root pounds and inches, no line is going to be "close" to these data and if your curiosity is limited to "the" line that describes these data you are going to be disappointed.[5]

Analyzing the scatter can not fix the situation, but it can extract information of another sort. And, although the scatter is not about to go

---

5. The weight distribution is skewed toward the high end, which generally implies that something like the square root or the log will improve the correlation. In this case, the generalization applies, but it doesn't improve the correlation by much. The maximum correlation occurs for the negative fourth power of weight: That doesn't help much and it evades any plausible interpretation I can think of.

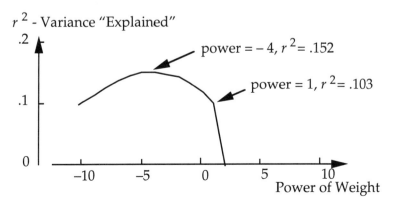

r^2 - Variance "Explained"

power = − 4, r^2 = .152

power = 1, r^2 = .103

Power of Weight

away, the scatter analysis can at least describe it and, in a sense, "predict" the observed combinations of height and weight.

Earlier I introduced two pure models for the scatter. By one model the logs of the frequencies "fall off" in proportion to their absolute distance from the central linear tendency where $y = mx + b$. Data conforming to this model have large log odds ratios near the line and zero-valued log odds ratios away from it. By the other model the logarithms of the frequencies fall off in proportion to the square of their distance from the central tendency. Data conforming to this second model have non-zero log odds ratios throughout the table.

Which pattern is exhibited by the data? Figure 6.2 shows a sketch of the largest and smallest log odds ratios, marking the largest ones "#" and the smallest ones "=." The pattern, if any, is not clear. There may be a line of #'s one standard deviation of weight below the SD line and parallel to it, suggesting the first power of distance (relative to a lower estimate of the line) — but there is also a substantial scattering of both large and small odds ratios elsewhere. Faced with ambiguity, let me combine both models (at the cost of estimating one extra constant for the equation). I now feign ignorance of the physical measures for height and weight and treat these two variables as unknown-interval scales. I assume that the relation between these two unknown scales is linear and analyze the scatter — inferring the unknown interval scales from the scatter.

Table 6.1 shows the whole range of numbers associated with the model, let me take them one set at a time. First, the inferred interval scales: Figures 6.3 and 6.4 show the graphs relating these inferred intervals to the physical measures.

The inferred interval scale for height, drawn in Figure 6.3, is an increasing function of physical height, well approximated by a line, but non-linear (examined in the range between 58 and 68 inches for which the frequencies are large).[6] By contrast, the relation between the inferred scale for weight and the physical weight is not so simple. Drawn in Figure 6.4, the relation appears to have two pieces: Between 80 and, perhaps, 140 pounds the relation bends. The bend is sharp, sharper than would be predicted by the cube root of weight (which might, on *a priori* grounds, be expected to a simple function of height).[7] Above 180

---

6. At $r = .988$ the residuals with respect to the regression line appear to be small. Nonetheless, the regression line does not "fit" because the pattern of the residuals, shown here, clearly indicates that the function is non-linear.

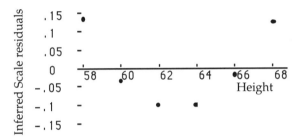

Residuals from the Regression Line Predicting the
Inferred Scale from the Physical Height

7. The sharpness of the bend is confirmed by attempting to predict the inferred scale from the cube root of weight and then inspecting the residuals: It fails.

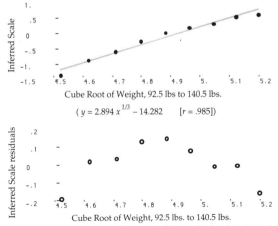

Graph of Cube Root of Weight and of Residuals Against Inferred
Scale of Weight, for Weights Between 92.5 Pounds and 140.5 Pounds
(The residuals suggest departure from linearity with the cube root.)

pounds the relation turns flat.   These two pieces suggests that *if* the weight is between 80 and 140 pounds, then greater weight corresponds to greater height. But *if* the weight is above 180 pounds, then extreme weight is not related to height. The implication is asymmetrical: In one direction, greater height implies greater weight. In the other direction greater weight (over 140 pounds) does not imply greater height: Tall people tend to be heavy, but heavy people are not necessarily tall. Thus, the inferred scales suggest that there is an asymmetrical correlation and that there are at least two "types" of people in the data. For one, but not the other, weight corresponds to height.

With the model, as formulated, it is hard to estimate the constants governing the relation between height and weight within the "correlated," lighter, population. If I attempt to fit a power function of height, I get something close to the negative-fourth power. This makes no sense. More likely the curvature is created by the gradual shift from a population whose height is, for the most part, responsive to weight (at the low end) to a population whose height is not (at the high end). (Few of the 140-pounders are in the heavy population, few of the 180-pounders are "light.")   Nonetheless, it is worth sketching the curve. Figure 6.5 shows the height-weight matches (where inferred "height" minus inferred "weight" equals zero) superimposed on the table of log odds ratios, together with other lines for comparison.

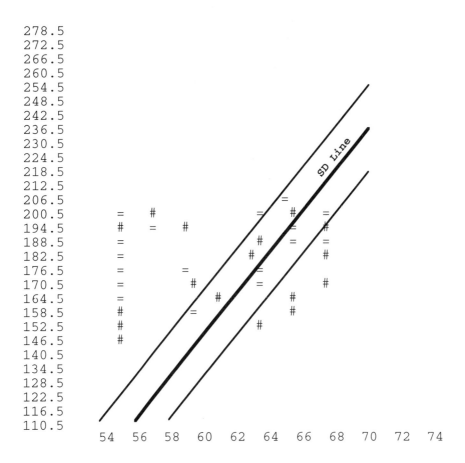

Log odds ratios were computed using each pair of adjacent rows and each pair of adjacent columns, restricting the computations to the sixty-seven four-cell tables for which all frequencies exceeded 5. Among these the largest 25% of the log odds ratios are marked "#" and the smallest 25% are marked "=." Lines show the approximate location of the SD line as well as a reference line one standard deviation above the SD line and another reference line one standard deviation below.

Figure 6.2
Schematic Diagram of Log Odds Ratios

Estimated Scale and Multipliers for Weight

(Light to Heavy, using the 32 Weights with Non-Zero Frequencies.)

Weight (lbs)	Scale	Multiplier	Weight (lbs)	Scale	Multiplier
80.5	−3.812	1.228	182.5	.723	.047
86.5	−1.628	.007	188.5	.722	.034
92.5	−1.386	.018	194.5	.770	.018
98.5	−.909	.032	200.5	−1.625	.010
104.5	−.622	.046	206.5	.724	.008
110.5	−.266	.096	212.5	.712	.010
116.5	−.004	.142	218.5	.480	.004
122.5	.163	.183	224.5	.388	.002
128.5	.303	.214	230.5	.929	.005
134.5	.538	.274	236.5	.665	.001
140.5	.596	.255	242.5	.665	.001
146.5	.602	.198	248.5	−.118	.001
152.5	.509	.137	254.5	omit	omit
158.5	.666	.120	260.5	.665	.001
164.5	.669	.097	266.5	.071	.000
170.5	.655	.071	272.5	omit	omit
176.5	.786	.067	278.5	.071	.000

Estimated Scale and Multipliers for Height

Height (in)	Scale	Multiplier	Height (in)	Scale	Multiplier
54	−1.835	.023	66	.321	.102
56	−1.340	.054	68	.830	.043
58	−.986	.208	70	2.970	2.120
60	−.789	.456	72	2.970	.688
62	−.491	.465	74	3.845	15.138
64	−.127	.302			

All Effect: 4995

Coefficients of the First and Second Power of the Distance: 1,   .5773

Chi-Square Error: 185.839

Table 6.1
Parameters and Expected Values for Height-Weight Data, One Dimension,
First- and Second-Order Polynomial

Expected Values

	54in.	56in.	58in.	60in.	62in.	64in.	66in.	68in.	70in.	72in.	74in.
278.5lbs.	.0	.0	.1	.3	.5	.6	.2	.0	.0	.0	.0
272.5lbs.											
266.5lbs.	.0	.0	.1	.3	.5	.6	.2	.0	.0	.0	.0
260.5lbs.	.0	.0	.1	.2	.5	.6	.5	.2	.1	.0	.0
254.5lbs.											
248.5lbs.	.0	.0	.2	.5	.8	.8	.2	.0	.0	.0	.0
242.5lbs.	.0	.0	.1	.2	.5	.6	.5	.2	.1	.0	.0
236.5lbs.	.0	.0	.1	.2	.5	.6	.5	.2	.1	.0	.0
230.5lbs.	.0	.0	.1	.4	.9	1.4	1.2	1.0	.6	.2	.2
224.5lbs.	.0	.0	.2	.6	1.2	1.5	.9	.2	.0	.0	.0
218.5lbs.	.0	.0	.3	1.0	1.9	2.5	1.6	.5	.1	.0	.0
212.5lbs.	.0	.0	.3	1.3	2.9	4.1	3.0	1.8	.6	.2	.1
206.5lbs.	.0	.0	.3	1.1	2.3	3.4	2.5	1.5	.5	.2	.1
200.5lbs.	.9	2.0	4.4	6.7	3.6	.9	.1	.0	.0	.0	.0
194.5lbs.	.0	.0	.5	2.1	4.6	6.8	5.1	3.6	1.3	.4	.3
188.5lbs.	.0	.1	1.2	4.6	10.1	14.6	10.7	6.6	2.1	.7	.4
182.5lbs.	.0	.1	1.6	6.3	13.8	19.8	14.6	9.0	2.8	.9	.6
176.5lbs.	.0	.2	1.9	7.5	16.9	25.0	19.0	13.9	5.1	1.7	1.1
170.5lbs.	.0	.3	3.0	11.4	24.5	34.3	24.3	12.6	3.3	1.1	.6
164.5lbs.	.0	.3	3.9	15.0	32.4	45.6	32.5	17.5	4.8	1.6	.9
158.5lbs.	.0	.4	4.9	18.8	40.4	56.9	40.5	21.7	5.9	1.9	1.1
152.5lbs.	.1	.8	8.8	32.3	65.9	86.8	57.0	20.3	3.8	1.2	.6
146.5lbs.	.1	.9	9.8	36.8	77.5	106.2	73.2	33.2	7.7	2.5	1.3
140.5lbs.	.1	1.2	12.9	48.2	101.3	138.4	95.1	42.4	9.7	3.1	1.7
134.5lbs.	.1	1.5	16.2	59.8	123.2	164.3	109.6	42.2	8.4	2.7	1.4
128.5lbs.	.2	2.4	23.4	82.1	156.0	188.6	107.5	23.4	2.6	.8	.3
122.5lbs.	.3	3.0	28.1	95.4	172.8	197.0	78.9	15.8	1.2	.4	.1
116.5lbs.	.4	3.6	31.7	103.5	176.9	187.9	49.4	9.0	.5	.2	.0
110.5lbs.	.5	4.6	35.8	110.2	172.2	123.9	22.3	3.5	.1	.0	.0
104.5lbs.	.7	4.6	31.0	88.0	93.5	37.0	5.5	.7	.0	.0	.0
98.5lbs.	.9	5.0	30.2	63.2	43.6	15.3	2.0	.2	.0	.0	.0
92.5lbs.	1.1	4.6	11.2	18.0	10.6	3.0	.3	.0	.0	.0	.0
86.5lbs.	.6	1.3	2.8	4.3	2.3	.6	.1	.0	.0	.0	.0
80.5lbs.	2.0	.8	.8	.7	.2	.0	.0	.0	.0	.0	.0

Table 6.1 — Continued

138

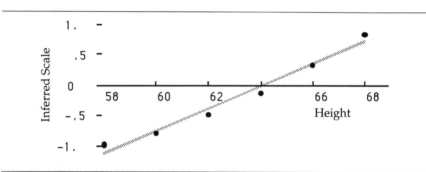

Figure 6.3
Graph of Height Against Inferred Scale for Height, for Heights Between 58 and
68 Inches, Showing the Regression Line, $y = .18\,x - 11.70$ $[r = .988]$.

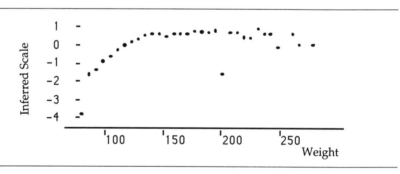

Figure 6.4
Graph of Weight Against Inferred Scale of Weight

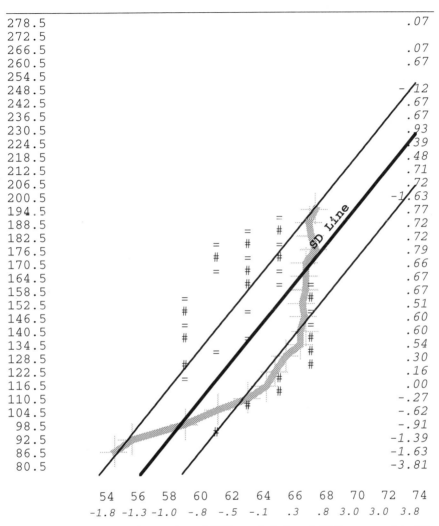

278.5	.07
272.5	
266.5	.07
260.5	.67
254.5	
248.5	-.12
242.5	.67
236.5	.67
230.5	.93
224.5	.39
218.5	.48
212.5	.71
206.5	.72
200.5	-1.63
194.5	.77
188.5	.72
182.5	.72
176.5	.79
170.5	.66
164.5	.67
158.5	.67
152.5	.51
146.5	.60
140.5	.60
134.5	.54
128.5	.30
122.5	.16
116.5	.00
110.5	-.27
104.5	-.62
98.5	-.91
92.5	-1.39
86.5	-1.63
80.5	-3.81

54   56   58   60   62   64   66   68   70   72   74
-1.8 -1.3 -1.0 -.8 -.5 -.1   .3   .8 3.0 3.0 3.8

Inferred line, in grey, where inferred "X" equals inferred "Y," compared to SD line. The line is superimposed on the grid of height and weight, with odds ratios marked as in Figure 6.2. Because the inferred scales are not linear functions of the physical scales, the inferred line does not appear "straight." Above 180 pounds the scale of weight "collapses" and is omitted from the graph.

Figure 6.5
Inferred Line for Height and Weight

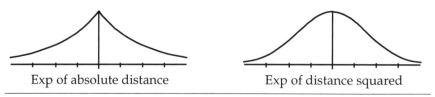

Exp of absolute distance   Exp of distance squared

Figure 6.6
Decay Curves for the Two Distance Models

Note three things about this inferred line in Figure 6.5, as compared to the SD line: One, it is generally lower than the SD line. Two, it is fairly smooth up to about 180 pounds. And three, it coincides, roughly, with the "ridge" of large odds ratios, marked +. Together these three things say something about the data: Because the inferred line is lower than the SD line and smooth, it suggests that the SD line (and the regression lines) are too high — presumably because the SD line and regression line are unable to separate the "normal" women from the extremely heavy — and then attend to the "normal." By collapsing the intervals for the groups above 130 to 140 pounds, the scatter model effectively separates the very heavy from the norm for whom the line is appropriate. Because the curve coincides with the "ridge" of large log odds ratios, it suggests consistency of all or part of the data with model 1, absolute distance, as compared to model 2. This is surprising, suggesting it is *not* the bell-shaped pattern that data analysts learn to expect. Recall the two curves shown in Figure 6.6. The cusp in the absolute distance function is more-demanding than the gentle curve of the squared distance function: The distance-squared correspondence says, to put words on it, taller is heavier. By contrast, the sharpness of the absolute distance function suggests a relatively specific matching of, for example, 65 inches to 110 pounds.

Finally, how good are these "best" estimates? The expected values are shown in Table 6.1. The evidence supporting these inferred intervals lies in their ability to regenerate the observed frequencies shown in Figure 6.1. For example, the "10" for 92.5 pounders who are 58 inches tall, in Figure 6.1, is predicted by combining constants according to the equation of the model:

$$F(x_i, y_j) = (All)\ r_i \cdot c_j \cdot e^{[-(distance(i,j)\ +\ a_2.distance(i,j)^2)]}.$$ [6.17]

For this weight and height, *All* is equal to 4,995, r_i is equal to .0176912 and c_j is equal to .207562. The coordinates are x_i equal -1.38639 and y_j equal -.985768, leading to a distance of .400622. Finally, using a_2 equal .577621, and combining all the numbers together, yields an estimated frequency of 11.1993.

$$11.1993 = 4995 *.0176912 *.207562 * e^{-\left[(.400622\ )+.577621*\left(.400622\right)^2\right]}$$ [6.18]

Altogether, comparing observed and reconstructed values by summing the values (Observed – Reconstructed)^2/Reconstructed, summing them throughout the table, leads to a chi-square value of 185.462. I hate to disappoint holdouts among you who may hope that here, at last, is a number that can be subjected to so-called "rigorous" (that is, probabilistic) analysis: How good is chi-square = 185? All I'm willing to say about 185 is "not too bad."[8]

Summarizing the indications of the scatter, to the extent that these errors are deemed "small" here's what we know about height and weight: First, let's not miss the forest for the trees. Given no information at all about physical height, just 11 categories with no numerical identity, the scatter analysis is able to solve for an interval scale of height that is, roughly, a linear function of the known physical measures (that were not used in the analysis). For weight, the result is more complicated. Up to about 140-150 pounds the estimated scale is monotone with physical

---

8. It is difficult to construct a statistical assessment of this chi-square: Many cells of the table show zero values and my experience with extreme cases of such tables (where the number of zeroes is so large that the number of cells in the table exceeds the number of people being distributed) suggests that ordinary means of counting degrees of freedom may not be valid for them. In addition, with many low frequencies combinations of height and weight the distributional properties of the chi-square are in doubt. And, to make matters much more difficult, significance testing is most-commonly applied to "null" hypotheses whereas, in this case, we are interested in the positive hypothesis. The switch from "null" to positive hypotheses, changes all the rules.

weight, showing a roughly curvilinear relation to physical weight. Above about 180 pounds the intervals are erratic (the frequencies are small), but there is no apparent trend. Implication: There are two different extremes, perhaps two different populations in the data, those for whom height and weight are correlated and those for whom additional weight bears no relation to height. More speculatively, it appears that the joint distribution itself may be more-sharply peaked than one would expect for a Gaussian/normal relation, implying, if true, that there is an unexpectedly sharp indication of the "correct" correspondence between height and weight ("correct" in the sense that that is what occurs).

Third Pass: Two Lines — Complications and Blemishes

It is sometimes fashionable in the social sciences to divide the activities of the sciences into two packages. One is the domain of "mind" — it builds theories, it intuits, it makes leaps of insight or outright guesses. We don't need to know the rules by which "mind" works, we need its results. The other is the domain of numbers — it accumulates facts and tests theories. It uses numbers and symbols and at least flirts with mathematical concepts of proof. We all live in both domains, but we tend to specialize, and all of us claim the prestige of science, with or without casting aspersions on specialists in the other domain.

I offer this aside on the state of the art in order to make it clear that the work does not fit this supposed framework for our science and you will, when you practice these analyses, feel uneasy if you are too well socialized into the popular, but wrong, idea of the way things are supposed to work.

You get closer to the mark if you adopt John Tukey's metaphor of the data analyst as detective. As "Sherlock Holmes" we are free to guess, to note events that have not happened, to use our experience. Our job is not to prove, our job is to penetrate to the heart of the matter quickly. When we've figured it out, however we managed that, we turn the dreary business of proof over to the lawyers and the courts. The detective/scientist is both intuitive and objective. But even Tukey's division of data analysis into "exploratory" work (for heroes like ourselves and Holmes) and "confirmatory" work (for lawyers) is a bit off the mark because it still allows the possibility proof. But proof is a certainty reserved for mathematics, not science. For science, the best we can hope for is a theory that is not yet known to be false, for a generalization for which there is no contrary evidence (not yet).

The work of statisticians, proving things beyond a (statistically) reasonable doubt, can not evade this fundamental limit on science. In skilled hands it makes no such claim, though it may appear to. That is why statisticians come up with convoluted phrases about disproving (or not disproving) null hypotheses — "proving," for example, that it is not the case that there is no difference between two groups.

What does this have to do with models for scatter and, in particular, models for the relation between height and weight? First it means that I cannot say that these models "fit." Is $\chi^2 = 185$ a large error? In truth, for positive hypotheses that is not a very important question. If by some chance the chi-square were truly close to zero, the most it would mean is that I had exhausted the information present in these data. And if I had had data for 49,950 women instead of 4,995, then subtle effects (not yet accounted for) would have become detectable by chi-square — effects due to age, nutrition, fashion, ethnicity and so forth surely exist.

The reason this is rarely discussed in the methodology texts is that, until very recently, particularly with log-linear models (a generic term for scatter analysis), we rarely came close enough for "fit" to be an issue. All that was claimed was that we had a linear estimate of the central tendency. For example, Figure 6.7 includes a plot of approximately 100 points governed by a theoretical Gaussian distribution with correlation $\rho = .32$, the correlation estimated for height and weight. Applying "statistics" to correlations of this order is not a matter of subtlety — it's a matter of dire necessity in order to assure the unaided "eyeball" that a correlation is, in fact, present among these data and that the correlation is in the positive direction. The accompanying plot, in the same figure, is governed by a stronger correlation $\rho = .80$. That would be a very strong correlation for social science data, but even here someone fitting a line to such data would claim only that the line is the central tendency. With the possible exception of proponents of something called "causal analysis," few social scientists would claim that linear equations were accurate indicators of the underlying mechanism.

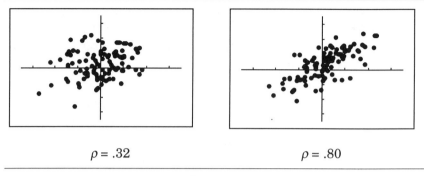

$$\rho = .32 \qquad\qquad\qquad\qquad \rho = .80$$

Figure 6.7
Random Samples of 100 Points from a Theoretical Gaussian
Distribution with $r = .32$ and $r = .80$

For positive hypotheses the carefully learned tools of significance testing, chi-square, r^2-variance explained, and probability levels have very limited and only informal applicability. This was always the case, it just wasn't an issue. Let me use another non-social science example from my favorite textbook. One of Tukey's examples fascinates me because it is easy to fit the data very closely and equally easy to see that the size of the error is almost irrelevant. Even a prediction that gets 99% of the table variation is demonstrably wrong. (I like non-social science problems — in our problems you are rarely confronted with the fact that the method may be inadequate, too many inadequate things are happening at the same time.) The example describes the plasticity of a fiber of wool as it is stretched, minute by minute, beyond its original length.[9] After 1 minute the fiber had stretched 32.1%, datum (1, 321); after 10,680 minutes it had stretched 65.4%, datum (10680, 654). Altogether 34 observations are provided.

If you try to predict percent stretch from time, you get

$$y = .030x + 378.199 \ . \tag{6.18}$$

---

9. John Tukey, *op. cit*, page 201, citing O. Ripman and J. B. Speakman, "The Plasticity of Wool," *Journal of Textile Research*, Volume 21, page 217.

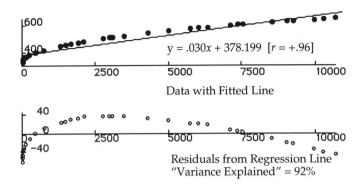

$$y = .030x + 378.199 \; [r = +.96]$$

Data with Fitted Line

Residuals from Regression Line
"Variance Explained" = 92%

Graphing minutes, left to right, by increased length, bottom to top, expressed as 100 times the percent compared to the original length. The top graph shows the data. The bottom graph shows residuals, comparing the data to a fitted line.

Figure 6.8
Plasticity of Wool

The correlation "explains" 92% of the variation in stretched length. Is that correct? No, it doesn't matter how good that r^2 is because the residuals make it clear that the pattern was not linear: The residuals show a nice systematic pattern of error. The magnitude of the residuals is quite small but, beyond any doubt, the linear model does not "fit."

Since the "error" is curved, let's try a quadratic fit:

$$y = .0567 \, x - .0000028 \, x^2 + 353.0894 \; . \qquad [6.19]$$

With this equation the unexplained variance is miniscule, on the physical scale of this graph all the points "touch" the line. But does it fit? No, again the residuals show a pattern indicating that the quadratic hypothesis is wrong.

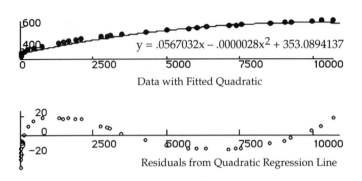

$$y = .0567032x - .0000028x^2 + 353.0894137$$

Data with Fitted Quadratic

Residuals from Quadratic Regression Line

Figure 6.9
Plasticity of Wool With Fitted Quadratic and With Residuals

Now the residuals look cubic. But try fitting a cubic to these data and the residuals will look quartic: Predictions using these equations would be wonderfully close, numerically, but quite clearly the ideas embodied in these curves miss the point of "what's going on" among these data.

Does this mean that you should abandon Tukey's style of exploratory data analysis or forsake models of the scatter because they cannot give answers? Not at all, because "turning the crank" as we used to call it, pushing the numbers through the computer doesn't work either. Many of the answers, the sure and clear answers to positive questions that you thought you were getting from mechanical application of conventional statistics were an illusion. You've got to think theoretically, even when you're using numbers.

The great-thought versus hard-data debate in social science is a false debate. Between those who think great thoughts, without hard rules of evidence, and those who handle data, without hard thought (as each would slander the other), you need not take sides: Data analysis, modeling, and theory building are a single activity.

Now, does the model fit the relation between height and weight? Of course not, that's not an interesting question. Does the model describe what these data have to tell us or does it fail in such a way as to indicate that there is something more in the data, more than is described by the model? Yes, it fails and this failure is interesting. We've used height-weight data as good servants to the methods, serving as means to the end of illustrating the technique. But these good servants still have a little spirit in them, defying analysis. First, even by conventional methods the weight distribution is "skewed," there are too many heavy people at the far end of the distribution. Actually, this is exactly what should happen if weight "should" be analyzed in terms of its cube root or square root instead of pounds. But in this case that doesn't explain the skew, it is too large: The necessary correction, to achieve symmetry and eliminate the skew, is too extreme, suggesting not the .5 power (square root), not the .33 power (cube root), not even the "0" power (log), but the inverse or –4 power. And, in non-statistical language, that doesn't make sense. In addition, the skew in these data defies my experience: "Experience" tells me that a variable that is skewed is going to be heteroscedastic, the standard deviation (of weight) for short people will be unequal to the standard deviation for tall people. But it isn't. The data are homoscedastic which, in context, is odd. The data resist.

And there are more peculiarities. Figure 6.10 is a table of large and small residuals, marked "R" and "r" with respect to the linear scatter model. The residuals suggest, to me, that they may be lined up in bands parallel to the SD line. Perhaps there are two body types, and at least two lines in the data, even within the "normal" range of height-weight combinations. Perhaps women's combinations of height and weight do not follow the "normal" distribution of a single population, or, perhaps, style has created two norms. And, just maybe, the manufacturers of women's clothes know what they are doing when they present clothes in two parallel ranges of sizes, odd-numbered sizes and even-numbered sizes, for two different physical proportions.

For me the most striking discrepancy, however close the fit, lies in an effect among the odds ratios — values that "shouldn't" be there in a simple relation between height and weight: Note the band of twenty-one frequencies shown in Figure 6.11, extracted from the full table.

148

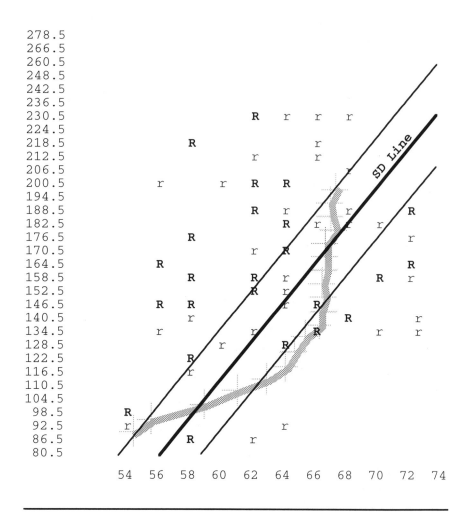

Figure 6.10
Largest and Smallest Residuals with Respect to the Inferred Line
(Residuals Computed as Contributions to the Overall Chi-Square)

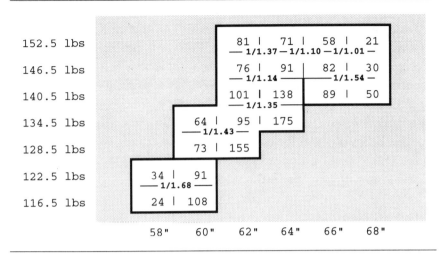

Figure 6.11
Data Isolated from the Original Data, Figure 6.1, Showing Sub-tables
in Which the Taller People Are More Likely to Be Light

Those numbers shouldn't be there: Everyone knows the relation between height and weight: Generally big people are taller and they weigh more — except that here, among these numbers, it isn't true. The eight log odds ratios (for each of the eight 2-row 2-column sub-tables marked by an odds ratio) are "wrong." For example, take the log odds ratio at the lower left: Among women fifty-eight inches tall the odds are almost 3 to 2 (34 to 24) that they will be heavy (122 pounds rather than 116). But for women two inches taller the odds are about 10 to 12, which is a change in the wrong direction: These taller women are less likely to be heavy. That isn't supposed to happen, but it does in this region of the data. The deviations vary in magnitude, and I can not test them for significance (for that I would have to decide what to test before I had looked at the table, not after) — but I find these contiguous "wrong" numbers disturbing: In these sub-tables, tables with large frequencies, extracted from the center of the main table, taller people have better odds for being light.

These features taken together may be attributable to the presence of two populations mixed together, two or more different "norms" mixed together in one population. In principle, it is at least possible for two relations, both of which are positive, to create a negative result (odds ratios in the wrong direction) when the two are combined.[10] With ordinary linear methods, based on means, I would be hard-pressed to test such a hunch or hypothesis: I would have to pre-classify people as one type or the other and divide the data, somehow, before I could talk about two mean weights for each height. But, using the scatter, I can hypothesize the presence of "ridges" running down the center of the distribution without any need to classify individuals. I simply switch from a distribution that looks single-peaked (in cross section) to one that looks double-peaked, from a distribution with one central tendency to a distribution with two "central" tendencies.

Accordingly I've modified the model, describing data as "falling off" from two different lines.

$$F(x_i, y_j)$$

$$= All \cdot r_i \cdot c_j \cdot Exp\{ \ [-a_{11}d_1(i,j) - a_{12}d_1(i,j)^2 \ ] + [-a_{21}d_2(i,j) - a_{22}d_2(i,j)^2]\},$$
$$|\!\!<\!\!\text{---line 1---}\!\!>| \qquad |\!\!<\!\!\text{---line 2---}\!\!>| \ [6.15]$$

where d_1 is the distance between the data point and the point on the simple line $y = x$, and where d_2 is the perpendicular distance between

---

10. For example, two tables with log odds ratios equal to 1.4 (log 4) can be added to yield one table with log odds equal to -1.85 (-log 6.4):

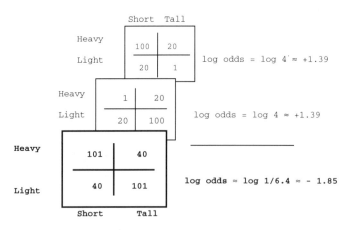

This double model could rescue the "simplicity" of a positive height-weight relation while accommodating some apparently negative effects.

the data point and a *second* line $y = mx + b$. The second line requires only 3 more numbers (for a total of 85). (It requires a slope and an intercept and the a_{21} parameter. Mathematically the effect of the a_{12} parameter and the a_{22} parameter are equivalent, although I have estimated them as if they were distinct.) In effect, I am laboring, with an equation, to express something that is well known outside the world of male data analysts: that proportions, as enshrined in manufacturers' clothing sizes, come in at least two styles, known in this country as "juniors" and "misses." The gain, using this double model and these three additional parameters, is a better fit, dropping chi-square from 194 to 155, a 20% decrease in the chi-square error. Results are shown in Table 6.2.[11]

Now, with this modification, does the equation describe the relation between height and weight? It's closer. It appears that the data allow at least two height-weight "norms" separated by roughly 12 pounds. Is that complete? Probably not: This two-population model is able to produce odds ratios in the direction of the ones that are "wrong." But the produced odds ratios may not be strong enough, and the distribution of errors continues to suggest "bands" of error, as did the residuals from the simpler model.[12] And there is an alternative two-population model, at least as credible, that works more or less equally well — combining the distributions outright.[13]

---

11. The estimates of these parameters prove to be unstable. For example, estimated slopes for the second line that are either greater or less than the slope of the first line (1.1 to .9) all yield χ^2's in the 155-165 range. So I have taken the "simplest" solution, slope = 1. Similarly, I have limited myself to the absolute distance term so that this model actually uses only one more parameter than the simpler one-line model.

12. Comparing odds ratios marked in the data to odds ratios generated by this particular two line model: 1/1.68 to 1/1.002, 1/1.43 to 1/1.001, 1/1.35 to 1/1.000, 1/1.14 to 1/1.001, 1/1.37 to 1/.999, 1/1.10 to 1/.999, 1/1.01 to 1/1.299, 1/1.54 to 1/.961. The Figure of residuals is added as an appendix.

13. $F(x_i, y_j) =$
$$\{r_i c_j \mathrm{Exp}[-a_1\, d_1(i,j) - a_{12} d_1(i,j)^2]\} + \{r_i' \cdot c_j' \cdot \mathrm{Exp}[-a_{21} d_2(i,j) - a_{22} d_2(i,j)^2]\}$$
$$|<\!\!\!-\!\!\!-\!\!\!-\!\!\!-\text{line 1}-\!\!\!-\!\!\!-\!\!\!-\!\!\!->|\quad |<\!\!\!-\!\!\!-\!\!\!-\!\!\!-\text{line 2}-\!\!\!-\!\!\!-\!\!\!-\!\!\!->|$$

which simplifies to

So, here's what we know, so far, as working hypotheses: These data for height and weight include women ranging from six-foot-two to four-foot-six, a ratio of about three to two, and weights ranging from two hundred and seventy eight pounds to eighty pounds, a ratio of more than three to one. The key to these data is, in a sense, non-numerical: The key is that the population seems to be twice divisible: First, there is a split between the heavy and the norm or, more precisely, between heavier people (above 180 pounds) whose weight appears to be unrelated to height, and lighter people whose weight is related to height. Second, the "norm" itself is split into two overlapping populations, perhaps corresponding to clothing manufacturers' distinction between "misses" size and "petite." Very roughly, "eyeballing" Figure 6.12, within each norm the central relation is about four pounds per inch, with much variance, while between the two there is a difference of about twelve pounds separating women of the same height.

$$F(x_i,y_j)=\{r_i \cdot c_j \cdot [\text{Exp}[-a_{11}d_1(i,j) - a_{12}d_1(i,j)^2] + \text{Exp}[-a_{21}d_2(i,j) - a_{22}d_2(i,j)^2]]\}$$

|<———line 1———>| |<———line 2———>|

To date, my efforts with this version yield almost exactly the same fit, chi-square approximately equal to 155, suggesting that, at least for now I have reached the end: perhaps exhausting the ability of these data to discriminate among alternative descriptions, alternative two-population models that may describe these data.

Estimated Scale and Multipliers for Weight
(Light to Heavy, using the 32 Weights with Non-Zero Frequencies.)

Weight (lbs)	Scale	Multiplier	Weight (lbs)	Scale	Multiplier
80.5	−4.068	.041	182.5	3.350	1.892
86.5	−1.474	.004	188.5	1.735	.108
92.5	−1.588	.018	194.5	1.224	.025
98.5	−1.137	.035	200.5	−.799	.003
104.5	−.772	.045	206.5	2.072	.041
110.5	−.374	.083	212.5	1.932	.041
116.5	−.004	.118	218.5	.538	.003
122.5	.129	.143	224.5	.379	.001
128.5	.415	.191	230.5	2.106	.023
134.5	.796	.279	236.5	.722	.001
140.5	1.007	.326	242.5	.722	.001
146.5	1.039	.262	248.5	−.118	.000
152.5	.824	.154	254.5	omit	omit
158.5	1.375	.237	260.5	.722	.001
164.5	1.396	.198	266.5	.276	.000
170.5	1.122	.098	272.5	omit	omit
176.5	3.261	2.178	278.5	.276	.000

Estimated Scale and Multipliers for Height

Height (in.)	Scale	Multiplier	Height (in.)	Scale	Multiplier
54	−3.030	.074	66	.142	.166
56	−2.243	.123	68	.538	.048
58	−1.379	.282	70	1.212	.010
60	−1.047	.593	72	1.155	.003
62	−.701	.663	74	3.551	.000
64	−.304	.479			

All Effect: 4995

Coefficients of the First and Second Power of the Distance:
First line	1,	(2nd power forced to 0)
Second Line	.856,	(2nd power forced to 0)

Coefficients of the second line:
Intercept −.579, slope 1 (slope forced to 1) (Inferred Height Scale as Function of Inferred Weight Scale)

Chi-Square Error   156.121

Table 6.2
Using Two Lines: Parameters and Expected Values for Height-Weight
Data, One Dimension, First Order Polynomial

Expected Values

	54in.	56in.	58in.	60in.	62in.	64in.	66in.	68in.	70in.	72in.	74in.
278.5lbs.	.0	.0	.1	.2	.4	.6	.2	.0	.0	.0	.0
272.5lbs.											
266.5lbs.	.0	.0	.1	.2	.4	.6	.2	.0	.0	.0	.0
260.5lbs.	.0	.0	.1	.2	.5	.7	.5	.2	.0	.0	.0
254.5lbs.											
248.5lbs.	.0	.0	.1	.5	.9	.8	.2	.0	.0	.0	.0
242.5lbs.	.0	.0	.1	.2	.5	.7	.5	.2	.0	.0	.0
236.5lbs.	.0	.0	.1	.2	.5	.7	.5	.2	.0	.0	.0
230.5lbs.	.0	.0	.2	.6	1.2	1.6	1.2	.6	.4	.1	.0
224.5lbs.	.0	.0	.2	.6	1.2	1.6	.8	.2	.0	.0	.0
218.5lbs.	.0	.0	.3	1.0	1.9	2.7	1.5	.5	.0	.0	.0
212.5lbs.	.0	.0	.4	1.5	2.8	3.9	2.8	1.5	.9	.3	.0
206.5lbs.	.0	.0	.3	1.2	2.3	3.1	2.2	1.2	.7	.2	.0
200.5lbs.	.0	.2	2.2	5.4	5.6	2.2	.4	.1	.0	.0	.0
194.5lbs.	.0	.1	.8	2.7	5.3	7.2	5.1	2.8	.9	.3	.0
188.5lbs.	.0	.2	1.5	5.2	10.2	13.9	9.1	5.4	3.1	.9	.0
182.5lbs.	.0	.2	1.9	6.8	13.3	18.2	12.9	7.1	4.1	1.2	2.0
176.5lbs.	.0	.3	2.5	9.1	17.7	24.2	17.2	9.4	5.8	1.6	2.0
170.5lbs.	.1	.4	3.5	12.6	24.6	33.6	23.8	13.0	3.0	1.0	.0
164.5lbs.	.1	.5	4.6	16.4	32.1	43.9	31.1	17.0	6.5	1.9	.0
158.5lbs.	.1	.6	5.7	20.4	39.8	54.4	38.5	21.0	7.9	2.3	.0
152.5lbs.	.2	1.0	9.0	32.1	62.6	85.6	60.7	23.2	2.9	1.0	.0
146.5lbs.	.2	1.2	10.8	38.6	75.3	102.9	72.9	36.2	7.0	2.3	.0
140.5lbs.	.3	1.5	14.1	50.6	98.7	135.0	95.6	45.6	8.3	2.8	.0
134.5lbs.	.3	1.9	17.0	61.0	118.9	162.6	115.2	42.5	5.1	1.7	.0
128.5lbs.	.4	2.4	21.5	76.9	150.1	205.2	100.2	26.4	1.9	.6	.0
122.5lbs.	.5	2.8	25.4	90.8	177.0	202.5	81.3	12.4	.9	.3	.0
116.5lbs.	.5	3.0	27.6	98.9	192.8	179.7	51.4	7.9	.6	.2	.0
110.5lbs.	.6	3.6	32.9	117.6	169.2	124.2	21.0	3.2	.2	.1	.0
104.5lbs.	.6	3.7	34.2	84.7	94.2	36.0	6.1	.9	.1	.0	.0
98.5lbs.	.9	5.2	31.7	63.4	40.7	15.5	2.6	.4	.0	.0	.0
92.5lbs.	.9	5.5	12.9	15.9	10.2	3.9	.7	.1	.0	.0	.0
86.5lbs.	.2	.9	3.1	3.8	2.4	.9	.2	.0	.0	.0	.0
80.5lbs.	2.0	1.0	.5	.7	.4	.2	.0	.0	.0	.0	.0

Table 6.2 — Continued

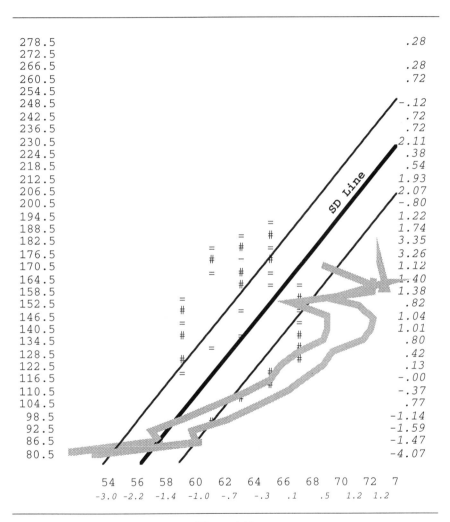

Figure 6.12
Inferred Lines, in Grey, Superimposed on the Grid of Height and
Weight, with Odds Ratios Marked as in Figure 6.2

Appendix 6.1

Largest and Smallest Residuals with Respect to the Two-Line Model

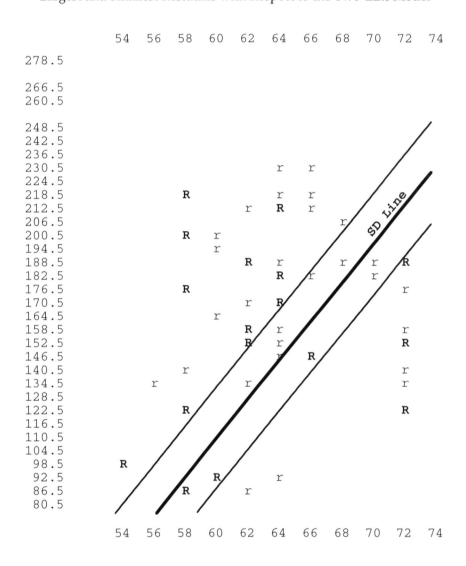

7

Democrats, Republicans, and Independents: What *Is* Party Identification?

I am convinced that the philosophers have had a harmful effect upon the progress of scientific thinking in removing certain fundamental concepts from the domain of empiricism, where they are under control, to the intangible heights of the a priori.

—Albert Einstein, *The Meaning of Relativity*[1]

In the world of self-evident assumptions, some assumptions seem safer than others. In sociology, common sense tells us the meanings of certain variables. We all know the meaning of Age, Race, Sex and so forth. And everyone knows that these "sociological variables" are reliable predictors of individual behavior. It's not exciting, but it is safe to assume that voting behavior, and other significant behavior, are predicted by a person's age, education, income, race, region of residence, religion, and sex. Everyone knows that Republicans are more likely to be wealthy. They are also more likely to be white, Protestant, and male. Race, sex, religion, and so forth explain nothing about behavior — for that you need a theory and a mechanism. But it is clear what it means to assert, as fact, that these attributes are correlated with behavior.

But are the meanings of these variables obvious and do the correlations exist? Are the safe assumptions correct? I submit the obvious: No social science variable has a Platonic existence, separate from the flow of events. And common sense may claim what it pleases about

---

1. Fifth Edition, Princeton University Press, 1956. Cited by Arthur I. Miller, *Imagery in Scientific Thought*, M.I.T. Press, 1986.

correlations, but it has no authority. In this discussion I am going to examine one key variable, "Party Identification," in several contexts. Operationally, party identification is simply the response to the question *"Generally speaking, do you usually think of yourself as a Republican, Democrat, Independent, or what?"*[2] That's it operationally. But what *is* Party Identification, what does it mean when someone says, "I'm a Democrat"? The variable has no mathematical definition. It has no properties subject to *a priori* specification. As a response, the statement, "I'm a Democrat" may or may not have the meaning intended by the person who asked the question.

In the U.S., Party Identification is usually considered to have three principal values, Democrat, Independent, and Republican, plus several intermediate values that form an ordinal scale. We all recognize that this is an over-simplification: Independents, for example, may have an identity of their own, and not all elections are two-party choices, even in the U.S. But few of us would hesitate to accept Party Identification as a five-point ordinal scale with categories "Strong Democrat," "Democrat," "Independent," "Republican," and "Strong Republican," and then examine its correlations — in that order — with age, education, income, race, religion, and sex.[3]

Is this "correct"? Maybe it is, maybe it isn't. Even if all sociologists were to agree, "*Let* Party be an ordinal variable," reality need not

---

2. Using 1986 data from *The General Social Survey*, National Opinion Research Center, Chicago, 1986. Updated U.S. national surveys by NORC and by the Survey Research Center at the University of Michigan in Ann Arbor are publicly available, often at nominal cost. Data from these sources and from tables in the U.S. government's *U.S. Book of Facts, Statistics, and Information* or *The Statistical Abstract of the United States* invite analyses parallel to the work presented here: In context, what are the inferred interval scales of occupation? In context, what is the "meaning" of ethnicity or religion?

3. The specific coding I've used for the NORC data includes "0" (Strong Democrat) as Strong Democrat. It combines "1" and "2" (Not very strong Democrat and Independent, close to Democrat) as Democrat, uses "3" (Independent) as Independent, combines "4" and "5", (Independent, close to Republican and Not very strong Republican) as Republican, and uses "6" (Strong Republican) as Strong Republican.

conform. Such questions are answerable only in context and the contexts I'll look at are eight of the usual reliable predictors: Race, Occupation, Age, Education, Religion, Region, Sex, and Income. In each case I will withhold the *a priori* assumption about Party and, instead, estimate the scale intrinsically, by estimation from the data. Unleashed from *a priori* constraint, unconstrained — except by the facts — Party blossoms forth with a variety of interval scales, suggesting different meanings. Call this distressing or call it rich, as you please. But it means, for example, that *if* you make the conventional assumption about Party and *if* you look for a correlation between Party and Age, then you will find very little because your assumption has filtered out the empirical relation and your correlation coefficient will miss it. But *if* you interpret Party as a statement of commitment (from Strong to Independent) then you will find the (relatively) strong correlation with Age that exists in the data.

That's what you find at the first level of analysis, a profusion of distinct scales of Party. But such wealth does not make a sociologist happy. Variety may be interesting and it may justify lots of publications, but if each context is unique we're in big trouble. If that's what truth demands of us, so be it, but too much variety would reduce our "science" to a well-stuffed catalogue of special cases. Fortunately, it appears that for Party there is both variety and order, a two-dimensional order. It appears, though not conclusively, that Party has a dimension of partisanship and a dimension of commitment. It is not one, or the other, but both: Age is correlated with Party *as commitment*, from Strong to Independent, while Race is correlated with Party *as partisanship*, from Strong Democrat to Strong Republican. And other variables, like Occupation, blend the two dimensions: Operatives and Craftsmen act as Uncommitted–Democrats. Sales people (e.g., real estate brokers) act as Committed–Republicans. "Party ID" can realize simplicity without resort to the forced simplicity of strong *a priori* assumptions.

Party in the Context of "Race"

The first of the eight contexts is "Race." Let me contrast self-identified Democrats, Republicans, and Independents with respect to Race and show how these contrasts are represented by the scatter

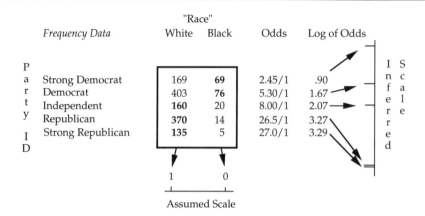

Frequencies Report Combinations of the two variables. For example, there were 169 "Whites" who identified themselves as Strong Democrats. Scales indicate the interval scale for Party Identification as the logarithms of the odds. Bold numbers indicate values that are greater than they *would be* under conditions of no correlation. Row multipliers are 147.154, 465.953, 264.985, 4545.783, 1741.686. Column multipliers are 1.081, .656. p_2 =.5. In standardized form the coordinates are .5611, .2235, .0327, −.4694, −.4729 and −.1500, 1.0085 while the multipliers are 146.136 for the "All" and 1.0569, 1.7490, .6239, 1.5418, .5623, and 1.8146, .5511.

Figure 7.1
Party Identification by Race

analysis. Bear with me because techniques embody concepts: I want you to understand the contrasts among Party ID groups *and* the equation.

The data for Race and Party ID are shown in Figure 7.1 and the important information is obvious: There is a sharp contrast between Strong Democrats, at the top, and Strong Republicans, at the bottom. Among Strong Democrats, Whites outnumber Blacks 2 to 1 but among Strong Republicans, at the bottom, the odds are 27 to 1, very different: The odds change by more than a factor of ten. This strong contrast is the evidence of a strong correlation between Race and Party ID. Between these two extremes, the odds ascend in traditional order, 5.3 to 1 for Democrats, 8 to 1 for Independents, and 26.5 to 1 for Republicans.

First question: Is this correlation "real"? True, the odds differ from row to row, but even unpatterned random numbers would show a little variation. So, is what we observe "real"? Using a simple-minded answer, a chi-square test says "Yes": The correlation in this table is statistically significant at the .05 level (chi-square = 98.90).[4] The correlation indicated by the odds is statistically present. Were it not, I would be very uneasy about pushing forward with an analysis of what we observe.

Suitably encouraged by chi-square, or not discouraged, the interval scale for Party ID (distance-squared model) is simply the logs of those odds, as sketched in Figure 7.1.[5] You can verify this by direct computation: For the distance-squared model the log odds ratio is supposed to equal two multiplied by "p_2" multiplied by the product of the intervals.[6] Using log odds as the scale and p_2 equal to .5, that's exactly what we get (where p_2 is the coefficient of the distance-squared term). For Democrats

---

4. The lowly chi-square test and its meaning are decidedly non-trivial matters, but that's another issue. See for example, Randall Collins' chapter "Statistics Versus Words" in *Sociological Theory*, Randall Collins (Ed.), Jossey Bass, 1984, p. 329.

5. In larger tables any two columns would work "in theory." That is, any two would work if the model fit the data perfectly. That is extremely unlikely, introducing relatively complex computations, but no new concepts, in order to average-out the estimate using the table as a whole.

6. Where $F(x_i, y_j) = A r_i c_j e^{-p_2 |x_i - y_j|^2}$ the log of the odds ratio effects a cancellation of the A and the r and c factors

$$\left(\frac{F(x_i, y_j) / F(x_i, y_{j'})}{F(x_{i'}, y_j) / F(x_{i'}, y_{j'})} \right) = \left(\frac{e^{-p_2 |x_i - y_j|^2} / e^{-p_2 |x_i - y_{j'}|^2}}{e^{-p_2 |x_{i'} - y_j|^2} / e^{-p_2 |x_{i'} - y_{j'}|^2}} \right)$$

Taking the logarithm of the odds ratio, and simplifying, this yields

$$\log(\kappa) = 2 p_2 (x_i - x_{i'})(y_j - y_{j'})$$

showing that the log of the odds ratio is theoretically equal to two multiplied by p_2 multiplied by the product of the x-interval and the y-interval.

and Strong Democrats the interval is .77. The interval, White to Black is 1. And, therefore, the product $p_2\Delta x\Delta y$ is equal to .385, matching the log odds ratio in the data. The scale gives the categories a visual spread corresponding to the correlations: Big contrasts between odds are visually coded as big distance between corresponding categories.

If we were content to look at the scales, then we would be done: Contrasted with respect to Race, Party ID groups fall on a scale from Strong Democrats to Strong Republicans, in the traditional order. Sociologically, we would be finished with these data. But in most cases models will not fit the data, not exactly, and it becomes necessary to predict specific frequencies, cell by cell. Then, comparing "predictions" to facts, cell by cell, we can use the predictions to assess the scales. Predictions, cell by cell, are the product of the All effect times the row effect times the column effect times the negative exponential of p_2 times the squared difference of coordinates. For Strong Democrats who are White we would "predict"

$$F(StDem,W) = All * Row_{StDem} * Col_W * Exp\,[-.5(1-.90)^2\,] = 169, \qquad [7.1]$$

using numbers recorded in Figure 7.1.[7]

For Race by Party that gives us "predictions" (that are, for two columns, perfect and therefore uninteresting). Conventionally there is one more matter to attend to on Race. I've assigned numbers to the scales but remember that an interval scale is the *same* interval scale if you add something to it or multiply it — under any non-zero linear transformation. So I have to pick one example of the scale when I want to write it. Here I used numbers from the log odds for the obvious reason that they showed the connection between the data and the scale. But generally I will shift the scale, adding or subtracting a little from each scale to make both averages "zero." And I will multiply the x's and y's so that the two scales have roughly the same visual range, giving both scales the same standard deviation. Beyond that I will force $p_2 = 1$. This limits the product $p_2\Delta x\Delta y$: Without the assumption about p_2, I could

---

7. The multipliers are whatever numbers do the job of getting the predicted table to be as close as possible to the observed table. For this two-column case we can generate them by a mechanical and otherwise uninteresting process, sketched in the Appendix 7.1.

accommodate any change of the intervals by an appropriate p_2. Now, I multiply the scales to get $p_2 = 1$. In addition, I will standardize the multipliers: Note that the multipliers I used in Figure 7.1 show "big" row multipliers and "small" column multipliers. This is a happenstance of the way I estimated the numbers. That's OK, but generally I will clean them up by giving them a geometric mean equal to 1 and absorbing the "big" multipliers into the All effect.

(The absolute-distance model creates similar standardization problems, with this exception: Where the distance-squared model leads to two interval scales, the absolute distance model fixes both variables together on a single interval scale.[8] So I will set the combined mean, not the separate means, to zero. In each case, you should be able to verify the model using the numbers as given: Multiply 'All' times 'Row' times 'Column' times the negative exponential of distance or distance squared. That should give you the numbers predicted by the model.)

Now, suitably standardized, I can't even give you a new figure to illustrate the final result because the scales "look" just like the old ones. The new numbers, in standardized form, are included in the legend to Figure 7.1.

Now, back to sociology: Having found it, let's actually look at the interval scale for Party ID that was sketched in Figure 7.1. Comparing Party ID groups with respect to "Race," the intervals are consistent with tradition, adding detail. They estimate Strong Republicans, Independents, and Strong Democrats as a three-point scale with Independents squarely in the middle. But Republicans are almost identical to Strong Republicans with respect to "Race," while Democrats assume an intermediate value between the Independents and the Strong Democrats. So, Party ID as an inferred-interval scale offers no surprises and some detail.

---

8. You can verify this algebraically by adding a constant to just one of the sets of coordinates in the absolute-distance model. You will find that the addition changes the predicted log odds ratios — a tip-off that you have done something that is not allowed. Add the same constant too all of the coordinates and nothing changes. Multiply all of the coordinates by a constant and you will find that you have changed the coefficient of the distance term, but the log odds ratios are unaffected. That is, in the absolute distance case you are dealing with one common interval scale.

Party in the Context of Income

For the remaining variables I can proceed more quickly, estimating six more interval scales and then concentrating on what I claimed to be analyzing, concentrating on Party ID. But there is one more delay: One of the variables has to be eliminated because, comparing Party ID's with respect to Income, the relation fails the first test: There is no statistically significant correlation between Party ID and Income. I can't use it. The income relation is one that "Everyone knows": Republicans are rich, and rich people are Republicans. Democrats are poor — or poor*er* — on the average. Maybe, but the data do not support this gem of common knowledge and, if there is a relation, it is hard to detect. The chi-square, at 17.12 is **not** statistically significant at the .05 level. Table 7.1 shows the data, restricting the data to reports for *men* reporting their *own incomes*, (anticipating the reasonable criticism that a weak result would be "explained" by failure to "control" for sex and for respondent's own

PARTY				INCOME	
	<$4,000	$4-13,000	$14-$34,000	$35,000+	
Strong Rep.	3	4	**23**	**10**	
Weak Rep.	**13**	26	70	**36**	
Independent	**9**	**21**	32	13	
Weak Dem.	9	**46**	73	24	
Strong Dem.	4	11	**28**	8	
	Frequencies				

PARTY				INCOME	
	<$4,000	$4-$13,000	$14-$34,000	$35,000+	
Strong Rep.	8%–	4%–	**10%+**	**11%+**	9%
Weak Rep.	**34%+**	24%–	31%	**40%+**	31%
Independent	**24%+**	**19%+**	14%–	14%–	16%
Weak Dem.	24%-	**43%**	32%	26%–	33%
Strong Dem.	11%	10%–	**12%+**	9%–	11%
	Percentages				

Data for 463 men. Source: *General Social Survey*, NORC, 1986
chi-square = 17.12, with 12 degrees of freedom

Table 7.1
Party Identification by Income (Frequencies and Percentages)

income (as compared to family income). There are, of course, some bumps: A few larger-than-expected values at the upper right of Table 7.1, in bold letters, and a few elsewhere. But, wherever they are, they are not big enough to tip the scales of the chi-square test. The chi-square test is not necessarily the last word on such matters, but failing chi-square or even an obvious non-significant pattern, I will not estimate interval scales from these data. (The data are explored in more detail in Appendix 7.2.)

The Overview of Party Identification

Now, at last, I'm ready to look at Party ID. Dropping any *a priori* assumption of order and estimating interval scales from the data I get seven scales (omitting the Income context). Two are best fit by the absolute-distance model Figure 7.2. Five of the relations are best fit by the distance-squared model, Figure 7.3. ("Fit" statistics are in Appendix 3.)

The most obvious feature of these scales is what they are not: They are not a rousing affirmation of the "obvious" meaning of Party ID. Only three of the seven yield a scale consistent with *a priori* expectation. Among the "deviant" patterns, the one that seems clear is the pattern of contrasts with respect to age: "Party" in the context of Age is a commitment variable. The older group, 60-plus, is relatively committed, 41 percent are either Strong Democrats or Strong Republicans compared to 17 percent of the young, 20-39. The middle-aged are in the middle. (And the very few teen-aged non-voters who made it into the survey, 1 percent of the survey, follow the pattern of their middle-aged parents.) In this context the *a priori* meaning of Party misses the point by assuming, in advance, that the salient feature of Party is Republican versus Democrat. For the pollster it may be, for the age groups it is not. The differentiation among age groups is by commitment, in the order Strong, Weak, Independent — ignoring party.

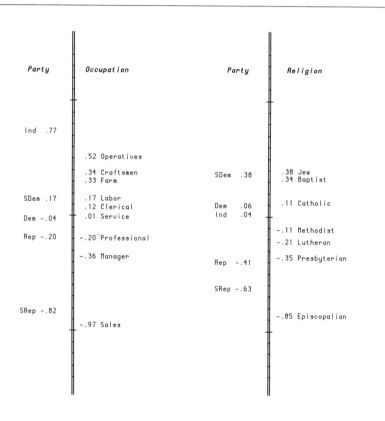

Figure 7.2
Interval Scales Using Distance Model

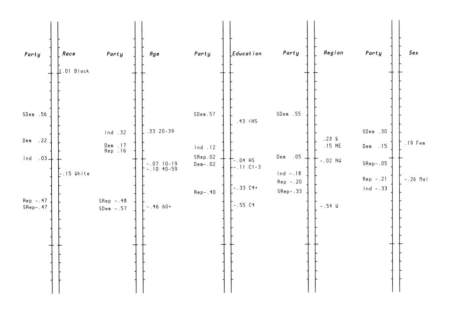

Figure 7.3
Pairs of Distance Scales Using Distance-Squared Model

Beyond this clear case we have not clarity but detail: For Religion, the strong contrast is the traditional one, Strong Democrat to Strong Republican. Among Strong Democrats, Episcopalians plus Presbyterians plus Lutherans and Methodists combined are outnumbered by Catholics plus Baptists and Jews, 3 to 1, as compared to 2 to 1 in the full table and 1.2 to 1 among Strong Republicans.

Contrasting Party ID with respect to Region, principally it is Strong Democrats who are differentiated as a Party and the West that is differentiated as a Region. The contrast says, in effect, that Strong Democrats are not in the West or, conversely, that the West is (relatively) not Strong Democratic territory.

For Education, tradition sets us up with clear and contradictory expectations: Education makes you liberal and therefore (maybe) Democratic. Education makes you wealthy and therefore (maybe) Republican. Education makes you fact oriented and therefore (maybe) Independent — so much for the folk lore of education. Estimating the scales from the data, the scale shows no clear indication. The most visible feature is the polarization of Strong Democrats at one end and Republicans (not Strong Republicans) at the other, plus the paired separation of the least educated with the Strong Democrats.

For Occupation, tradition is again rich and contradictory. Estimating the scales from the data, what we get is a clear progression: With respect to Occupation, Independent is one extreme, Republican is the other. Sales, Professionals, and Managers are predominantly Republican. Operatives (get that, education snobs, *Operatives*, not Professionals) are the most highly Independent. Farm and Other Blue Collar are the more Democratic. ...

Now, if you're like me, your eyes are beginning to glaze over as I wallow in the wonderful rich detail of these data — one case does this, another does that, and so on. That's the proper response if I push it too far: Science is not a collection of detail, it's a balance of detail and order. And the reason that these particular details are important is that they contradict the order that would have been imposed by the usual *a priori* assumption.

	Less than High School	Four Years of College			Less than High School	College Plus
Republican	74	61		Strong Republican	44	10
Strong Democrat	105	11		Strong Democrat	105	14

$\kappa = 7.87, \Delta^2 = 2.06, Q = .79$ $\kappa = 1.70, \Delta^2 = .53, Q = .26$

Figure 7.4
Extremes of Party Versus Extremes of Education: Inferred
Order, Left, Versus Traditional Order, Right.

Do I believe this denial of the *a priori*? I certainly do. Look at the extreme corners of the data tables: Taking the Education data as an example, the extreme corners of the Education table, in inferred order, show an odds ratio of almost 8, on the left of Figure 7.4. The odds that a Republican will have completed College are almost 8 times greater than the odds for a Strong Democrat. By contrast, in *a priori* order the extreme corners of the Education table show an odds ratio of only 1.7 (on the right of Figure 7.4).

The most extreme example of the effect of inferred scales on apparent correlation is shown by the data for age: Improvising a comparison by means of the ordinary product moment correlation, the product moment correlation between the inferred scales for Age and Party is .217. By contrast, the correlation between rank order of Age and the conventional rank order for "Party" is $r = .048$. Using the conventional comparison for two r's, using r^2's, that is a 2,000 percent improvement. (See Appendix 7.5.) Granting that I have selected these cells and intervals *post hoc*, the stronger correlations, using the inferred order, are not likely to be explained away — leaving tradition unscathed. That's why I'm interested in this detail.

Hypothesis

But, having used the detail let loose by estimating scales directly from the data, what do I do with it? My mind rebels at limp relativism: "Sometime's a variable means one thing, sometimes it means another. Each instance is special." I can't prove it, but there may be a way to salvage order from this diversity, without denying the diversity: The detail suggests that another order, a two-dimensional concept of Party ID, may be able to synthesize the detail.

Consider, for example, the hypothetical case in Figure 7.5. It shows how two dimensions can be consistent with various one-dimensional views. If Republican, Democrat, and Independent form a triangle, in two dimensions, then any one dimensional order, RID, the traditional order, Republican, Independent, Democrat, or RDI (comparable to the scale of Occupation), or DRI (comparable to the scale for Sex) can be "explained"

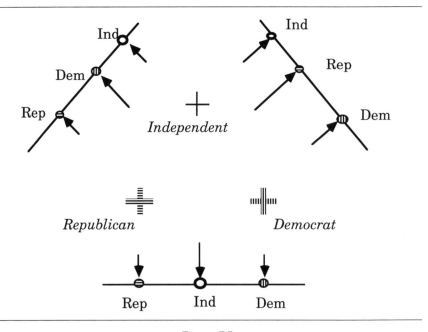

Figure 7.5
Hypothetical Relation Between Separate
One-Dimensional Orders (Circles with Normal Text) and
a Two-Dimensional Structure (Crosses with Italics)

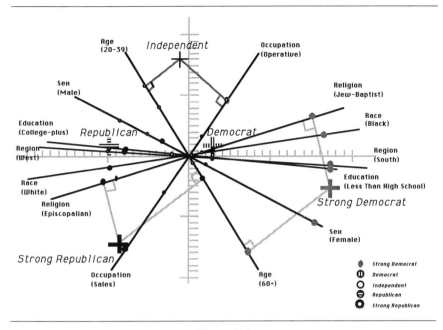

Figure 7.6
Two-Dimensional Approximation to the 7 Interval Scales

as a one dimensional projection of a two dimensional structure.

Figure 7.6 shows the map obtained by placing all 7 variables into a principal components analysis.[9] Principal components analysis is a little bit of an overkill for this kind of problem: There is no sense in which these seven scales are a representative sample of all the scales that might be obtained for this variable. Nor does it take into account the varying strengths of the separate correlations or reliability of the separate scales or the varying reliability of individual values. But generically, the principle components question is: Can these seven scales be "derived" as linear combinations of a small number of underlying components?

It appears that they can, the two-component analysis "predicts" the seven scales with multiple correlations ranging from .893 ("deriving" either Sex or Education) to .997 ("deriving" Religion). And, looking back

9. For an elegant introduction to factor analysis, a closely related technique, read Stephen J. Gould's *The Mismeasure of Man*, Norton Press, 1981.

at these scales in two-dimensional context, we get the overview: Contrasts by Race and Religion parallel the line between Strong Republican and Strong Democrat. These two will look the most traditional. Region and Education, and to a lesser extent Sex, as well as Race and Religion, establish a direction most salient for separating Strong Democrats from everyone else. Age contrasts have a strong component of Strong versus Independent, with the Young "tilted" toward the Republicans, while Occupation too has a strong component of Strong versus Independent, with Operatives tilted toward Democrats.

The two-dimensional hypothesis, if good, allows infinite variation but not all variation: Certain things are impossible. There are 10 logically possible polar pairs, the graph suggests that only 4 of the 10 will occur (and have occurred), 6 will not. For example, strictly speaking (which means that I am still not allowing for variability), Democrats and Republicans are not in symmetrical positions. The Democrats are (slightly) closer to Independents. If true, then it should be impossible for Democrats to appear as a pole of a one-dimensional contrast, while Republicans can (and do).

How "deep" is this underlying structure, how far will it generalize? These individual scales may change from year to year, between surveys. We might be very lucky and find that the underlying space stayed constant. If the military draft were to become a partisan issue once again, we might find the Age scale of Party ID rotating to increase its component of partisanship. If we were very lucky we might find that the underlying space stayed constant while the individual scales moved. If the draft became a partisan issue, we might find the age rotating to increase its component of partisanship. If the U.S. educational system became more targeted to vocational training we might find the Education scale of Party ID rotating toward occupation, increasing its component of participation. It is at least possible that there is order to this small piece of the sociological world, an order which becomes accessible only after abandoning the forced simplicity of an assumed order for Party ID.

Appendix 7.1

To estimate multipliers for the two-column case, suppose that the All-effect and all the multipliers were equal to 1. Then for Strong Democrats who are White we would "predict"

$$F = 1*1*1*Exp[-.5(1-.90)^2] = .995$$

I multiply the all effect times the row effect times the column effect times the negative exponential of $|x_i - y_j|$ and get .995. Repeating for all 10 cells yields a table of estimates, using the correct scales but the incorrect multipliers. You can verify that these 10 numbers

		Sums	Multipliers	
.995		.670	1.664	1
.800		.249	1.049	1
.558		.115	1.049	1
.075		.005	.080	1
.072		.004	.076	1
Sums	2.500	1.042		
Mults	1	1		

have the right log odds ratios. But clearly they have the wrong row and column sums, as should be expected with these "dumb" estimates (1's). So we repair them, estimating multipliers as we go. In this table the first row sums to 1.664, it should sum to 268. So I fix the multiplier, dividing it by 1.664 and multiplying by 268, (using 268/1.664 = 143.021), which gets the right sum. Doing the same for each row, I get new "predictions":

			Sums	Multipliers
	142.247	95.753	238	143.021
	365.391	113.609	479	456.786
	149.243	30.757	180	267.246
	361.451	22.549	384	4801.476
	132.943	8.057	140	1840.521
Sums	1150.270	270.725		
Mults	1	1		

This is still another table with the correct log odds ratios (the correct interactions) and, still, the wrong multipliers. But this one is close to what we want. Still the columns could be better. 1237 is the correct first column sum, not 1150.27 and 184 is the correct second column sum, not 270.725. So I fix the column multipliers, using $1237/1150.270 = 1.075$ as the new estimate for the first of the two column multipliers.

		Sums	Multipliers
152.972	95.079	218.051	143.021
392.940	77.215	470.155	456.786
160.495	20.904	181.399	267.246
388.703	15.325	404.028	4801.476
141.891	5.476	147.367	1840.521

Sums	1237	184
Mults	1.075	.680

The new "prediction" is closer again. It too has the correct log odds ratios (interactions) but we need to fix the row multipliers again. So I change the first multiplier by multiplying it by $(238/218.051)$. And so on ... The whole business converges to an answer pretty quickly, but I wouldn't ordinarily try it without a computer, and this specific procedure does not generalize easily to larger tables. (See W. E. Deming's *Statistical Adjustment of Data*, 1943, Frederick Mosteller's "Association and estimation in Contingency Tables," Jrnl. American Statistical Association, 1968, and Bishop, Fienberg, and Holland's *Discrete Multivariate Analysis*, 1975.) For this table the five row multipliers converge to approximately 157.154, 465.953, 264.985, 4545.783, and 1741.686, while the two column multipliers converge to approximately 1.081 and .656.

Appendix 7.2
Income by Party Identification

Since this *non*-correlation comes as a surprise to most people, let me digress for a brief look at these data: Perhaps the "problem" lies in the specification of categories; that was my explanation. After all, to some of my Dartmouth students the high income category, $35,000+, is not really high. They might consider *starting* at $35,000 in 1988 dollars, but they would not think of it as "High." And $60,000+ would be just beginning to get interesting.

Perhaps they're right. Perhaps the truly wealthy are not detectable in these data because there are too few of them while those few who are present have been averaged-in among the more numerous incomes close to $35,000. Maybe. The conjecture is plausible, but the data do not support it. Table A5 gives the most-detailed view available for these data. The highest income that NORC records is $60,000+. Sure enough, among the 24 men in this highest category, 5 men are Strong Republicans and only 1 is a Strong Democrat, supporting the conjecture. Perhaps, but look at the $1,000-$1,999 group: The people in this low income category are also Strong Republicans, 3 to 0, which is not dramatically different from the high income group.

The data as a whole do not support this explanation, and as I persist in following this line of reasoning I am beginning to use strong means to preserve common sense in the face of hard evidence. If there is a relation, it is not the sure-fire thing of folklore. When we count-up the exceptions, the "working class" Republicans and the wealthy liberal Democrats, the exceptions may nicely balance the rule.

One interesting rebuttal to this has been, essentially, "No, no, you got it wrong. It's not that the wealthy are Republicans, the wealthy are *conservative*." Nice try, but the evidence is only moderately better: The relation between "Political Views" and Income is, in fact, statistically significant. But, and this is a big "but," that only tells us there is a relation. It does not tell us that the relation is, specifically, that the wealthy are conservative. The big statistical bump in the table is a relative absence of Conservatives in the $3,000 to $13,000 group, whatever that means. Examining the odds ratios, whose sign is order dependent, suggests that the correlation, whatever it is, is not the one we are looking for: The mean log odds ratio, with categories in *a priori* order, is .47 while the standard deviation of the log odds ratios (in *a priori* order) is .72. Because this mean is less than one standard deviation away from zero, the odds ratios *in the relevant direction* are not sufficiently positive to be taken seriously. There is something going on here, but it is not simple. Next time someone tells you about wealth and political identity ask for the evidence. And when they cite wealthy Republicans and wealthy Conservatives as evidence, pull out the chapter on correlation as contrast and ask them: Compared to what?

Frequency Table: Income by Party Identification
(for Males Reporting their Own Incomes)

			Party Identification					
Income Range in $1,000	Strong Dem	Weak Dem	Indep Leaning Dem	Indep	Indep Leaning Rep	Weak Rep	Strong Rep	*Sum*
<1	2	2	1	5	2	0	0	12
1 - 2.9	0	1	0	2	2	4	3	12
3 - 3.9	2	1	4	2	1	4	0	14
4 - 4.9	2	1	1	4	0	0	0	8
5 - 5.9	1	3	2	2	0	2	0	10
6 - 6.9	0	0	1	0	1	1	1	4
7 - 7.9	1	1	0	0	0	1	0	3
8 - 8.9	2	6	2	3	4	0	0	17
10 -12.49	4	10	5	7	2	6	1	35
12.5-14.9	2	9	5	5	4	5	2	32
15 -17.49	3	7	3	6	4	4	2	29
17.5-19.9	4	11	1	8	2	10	4	40
20 -22.49	6	6	4	7	9	5	3	40
22.5-24.9	6	5	2	6	2	7	3	31
25 -29.9	4	13	8	1	5	12	5	48
30 -34.9	5	9	4	4	5	5	6	38
35 -39.9	3	5	2	6	6	4	3	29
40 -49.9	2	5	5	2	2	8	2	26
50 -59.9	2	1	2	1	3	3	0	12
60+	1	3	1	4	5	5	5	24
Sum	52	99	53	75	59	86	40	464

Appendix 7.3
Chi-Square Values

	Null-Model	d.f.	X^2/d.f.	First Power	Second Power	d.f.	X^2/d.f.
Religion	54.13*	24	2.26	9.22[b]	36.41	14	.66
Occupation	65.86*	32	2.06	22.96[b]	32.66	20	1.15
Race	98.90	4	24.73	n.a.	n.a.	0	
Sex	13.89	4	3.47	n.a.	n.a.	0	
Age	71.55*	12	5.96	4.03	3.43[b]	5	.69
Region	33.14	12	2.76	6.28	4.49[b]	5	.90
Education	67.39*	16	4.21	18.43	14.28[b]	8	1.79
Income	17.12*@	12	1.43	n.a.	n.a.	n.a.	

*-includes low frequencies; @-not statistically
significant; n.a.-not applicable; [b] best fit

Appendix 7.4
Data

Rows and columns of the tables are ordered as indicated by the interval scales. Bold characters indicate frequencies that exceed the expected values for their cells. Thus, a strong correlation will correspond to a diagonal band of bold characters.

All data are from the *General Social Survey* for 1986, NORC, Chicago.

Party Identification by Race

	White	Black	*Sums*
Strong Democrat	169	**69**	*238*
Democrat	403	**76**	*479*
Independent	**160**	20	*180*
Republican	**370**	14	*384*
Strong Republican	**135**	5	*140*
Sums	*1237*	*184*	*1421*

Party Identification by Sex

	Male	Female	*Sums*
Strong Democrat	88	**157**	*245*
Democrat	190	**304**	*494*
Strong Republican	**61**	80	*141*
Republican	**181**	210	*391*
Independent	**93**	94	*187*
Sums	*613*	*845*	*1458*

Party Identification by Religion

	Epis	Presb	Luth	Meth	Cath	Bap	Jew	*Sums*
Strong Democrat	4	8	12	22	67	77	11	*201*
Democrat	11	11	42	47	147	102	16	*376*
Independent	0	5	10	18	47	28	3	*111*
Republican	15	20	37	43	88	62	8	*273*
Strong Republican	7	6	14	14	26	24	0	*91*
Sums	*37*	*50*	*115*	*144*	*375*	*293*	*38*	*1052*

Party Identification by Region

	W	NW	NE	S	*Sums*
Strong Democrat	23	65	57	100	*245*
Democrat	87	129	106	172	*494*
Independent	40	61	30	56	*187*
Republican	87	113	76	115	*391*
Strong Republican	37	34	29	41	*141*
Sums	*274*	*402*	*298*	*484*	*1458*

Party Identification by Age

	20-39	10-19	40-59	60+	*Sums*
Strong Democrat	68	2	77	97	*244*
Strong Republican	46	3	36	56	*141*
Republican	194	5	104	86	*389*
Democrat	247	6	133	107	*493*
Independent	99	3	52	31	*185*
Sums	*654*	*19*	*402*	*377*	*1452*

Party Identification by Education

	<HS	HS	C1-C3	C4+	C4	*Sums*
Republican	74	132	84	40	61	391
Democrat	137	165	94	45	53	494
Strong Republican	44	38	30	10	19	141
Independent	55	78	26	9	18	186
Strong Democrat	105	71	44	14	11	245
Sums	415	484	278	118	162	1459

Party Identification by Occupation

	Oper	Craft	Farm	Labor	Cler	Ser	Prof	Mgr	Sale	*Sums*
Strong Republican	7	8	3	4	1	1	10	14	11	59
Republican	12	34	11	7	9	16	42	38	9	178
Democrat	23	39	5	11	16	16	40	27	11	188
Strong Democrat	13	19	5	9	7	9	10	10	5	87
Independent	21	26	6	5	5	2	10	14	4	93
Sums	76	126	30	36	38	44	112	103	40	605

Appendix 7.5
Calculated *r*'s and *r²*'s Using Inferred Scales and Using *A Priori* Ranks

	Inferred Interval Scale		*A Priori* Rank Used as Interval Scale	
	r	r^2	r	r^2
Race	.255	(.065)	.250	(.063)
Age	.217	(.047)	.048	(.002)
Occupation	.198	(.039)	n.a.	n.a.
Education	.192	(.037)	.133	(.018)
Religion	.176	(.031)	n.a.	n.a.
Region	.139	(.019)	n.a.	n.a.
Sex	.098	(.010)	.074	(.005)

Appendix 7.6
Summary of Separate Solutions

Race by Party Identification

Chi-square, before and after standardization (rounding effects:
 2.01767e-2 before 3.00783e-2 after

Grand multiplier #1:   146.136

Item	Coord.	Multiplier
1	.5611	1.0569
2	.2235	1.7490
3	.0327	.6239
4	-.4694	1.5418
5	-.4729	.5623

Column	Coord.	Multiplier
1	-.1500	1.8146
2	1.0085	.5511

Polynomial coefficients: 0 1

Table of Observed and Expected Values

	White	Black
SDem	169	69
	168.4	69.6
Dem	403	76
	403.3	75.7
Ind	160	20
	160.4	19.6
Rep	370	14
	370.0	14.0
SRep	135	5
	134.9	5.1

Sex by Party Identification

Chi-square, before and after standardization (rounding effects:
 1.62404e-2 before 4.55029e-2 after

Grand multiplier #1:   142.994

```
Item       Coord.   Multiplier

SDem      -.3004      .9623
Dem       -.1538     1.8307
Ind        .0518      .5134
Rep        .2061     1.4776
SRep       .3299      .7483

Column     Coord.   Multiplier
Male       .2594      .8626
Female    -.1882     1.1593
```

Polynomial coefficients: 0 1

Table of Observed and Expected Values

```
           Male    Female

SDem        88      157
           87.7    157.3

Dem        190      304
          190.7    303.3

SRep        61       80
           60.9     80.1

Rep        181      210
          181.4    209.6

Ind         93       94
           92.4     94.6
```

Region by Party Identification

Chi-square, before and after standardization (rounding effects:
 4.40965 before   4.43362 after

Grand multiplier #1:   76.1764

```
Item        Coord      Multiplier
SDem        -.5474     1.1079
Dem         -.0511     1.7322
Ind          .1778      .6766
Rep          .2027     1.4147
SRep         .3324      .5444
```

Column coordinates and column multipliers:

```
W            .5379      .9118
NW           .0230     1.0503
NE          -.1465      .7919
S           -.2334     1.3185
```

Polynomial coefficients: 0 1

Table of Observed and Expected Values

	W	NW	NE	S
SDem	23	65	57	100
	23.7	64.1	56.8	100.4
Dem	87	129	106	172
	85.1	136.9	103.4	168.8
Ind	40	61	30	56
	41.4	53.0	36.6	57.3
Rep	87	113	76	115
	87.7	109.9	75.8	117.7
SRep	37	34	29	41
	36.2	39.4	26.1	39.8

Religion by Party Identification

Chi-square, before and after standardization (rounding effects:
9.21466 before 9.21466 after

Grand multiplier #1:   28.1375
1 dimensional coordinates. Composite multipliers

Item	Coord	Multiplier
SDem	.3837	1.0011
Dem	.0586	1.7246
Ind	.0425	.5214
Rep	-.4112	1.6363
SRep	-.6289	.6789

Column coordinates and column multipliers:

Epis	-.8541	.4946
Presb	-.3516	.4496
Luth	-.2131	1.0177
Meth	-.1110	1.2432
Cath	.1073	3.1798
Bapt	.3437	2.8169
Jew	.3772	.3969

Polynomial coefficients: 1   0

Table of Observed and Expected Values

	Episc	Presb	Luth	Meth	Cath	Bapt	Jew
SDem	4	8	12	22	67	77	11
	4.0	6.0	15.7	21.5	67.7	76.2	11.1
Dem	11	11	42	47	147	102	16
	9.7	14.5	37.7	50.9	146.8	102.3	14.0
Ind	0	5	10	18	47	28	3
	3.0	4.5	11.5	15.7	43.9	30.6	4.2
Rep	15	20	37	43	88	62	8
	14.7	19.5	38.4	42.4	87.0	61.3	8.3
SRep	7	6	14	14	26	24	0
	7.5	6.5	12.8	14.1	29.0	20.4	2.8

Occupation by Party Identification

Chi-square, before and after standardization (rounding effects:
 22.9633 before   22.9633 after

Grand multiplier #1:   18.0705
 1 dimensional coordinates. Composite multipliers

Item	Coord	Multiplier
SRep	.8210	.7218
Rep	.2005	1.3999
Dem	.0396	1.4533
SDem	-.1702	.6632
Ind	-.7677	1.0267

Column coordinates and column multipliers:

Oper	-.5161	1.4441
Craft	-.3374	2.1415
Farm	-.3291	.5376
Labor	-.1746	.5661
Clerica	-.1165	.5852
Serv	-.0100	.6684
Profess	.1980	1.6113
Manager	.3551	1.6793
Sales	.9662	1.0041

Polynomial coefficients: 1   0

Table of Observed and Expected Values

	Oper	Craft	Farm	Labor	Clerica	Serv	Profess	Manager	Sales
SRep	7	8	3	4	1	1	10	14	11
	4.9	8.8	2.2	2.7	3.0	3.8	11.3	13.7	11.3
Rep	12	34	11	7	9	16	42	38	9
	17.8	31.6	8.0	9.8	10.8	13.7	40.8	36.6	11.8
Dem	23	39	5	11	16	16	40	27	11
	21.7	38.5	9.8	12.1	13.1	16.7	36.1	32.0	10.4
SDem	13	19	5	9	7	9	10	10	5
	12.2	21.7	5.5	6.8	6.7	6.8	13.3	11.8	3.8
Ind	21	26	6	5	5	2	10	14	4
	20.9	25.8	6.4	5.8	5.7	5.8	11.3	10.2	3.3

Education by Party Identification

Chi-square, before and after standardization (rounding effects):
 13.8244 before 14.1921 after

Grand multiplier #1:   56.2797

```
Item   Dim  1 Multiplier
Rep    -.3971    1.5515
Dem    -.0177    1.7252
SRep    .0171     .4987
Ind     .1232     .6733
SDem    .5660    1.1126
```

Column coordinates and column multipliers:

```
<HS      .4325    1.7114
HS      -.0426    1.7270
C1-C3   -.1138    1.0011
C4+     -.3288     .4602
C4      -.5460     .7344
```

Polynomial coefficients: 0 1

Table of Observed and Expected Values

	<HS	HS	C1-C3	C4+	C4
Rep	74	132	84	40	61
	75.0	132.8	80.5	40.1	62.7
Dem	137	165	94	45	53
	135.5	167.5	96.5	40.6	54.1
SRep	44	38	30	10	19
	40.7	48.3	27.6	11.5	15.0
Ind	55	78	26	9	18
	58.7	63.7	35.6	14.1	17.7
SDem	105	71	44	14	11
	105.3	74.4	39.6	13.0	13.3

Age by Party Identification

Chi-square, before and after standardization (rounding effects):
 3.37371 before 3.37371 after

Grand multiplier #1:   46.325

Item	Coord	Multiplier
SDem	-.5668	1.0745
SRep	-.4801	.5802
Rep	.1619	1.3571
Dem	.1692	1.7239
Ind	.3222	.6856

Column coordinates and column multipliers:

20-39	.3273	3.1648
10-19	-.0659	.0878
40-59	-.0958	1.8062
60+	-.4623	1.9921

Polynomial coefficients: 0 1

Table of Observed and Expected Values

	20-39	10-19	40-59	60+
SDem	68	2	77	97
	70.8	3.4	72.2	98.2
SRep	46	3	36	56
	44.4	2.0	41.8	53.5
Rep	194	5	104	86
	193.1	5.3	105.9	84.8
Dem	247	6	133	107
	245.3	6.6	134.5	106.6
Ind	99	3	52	31
	100.5	2.4	48.4	34.0

8

Friends and Relations

J ohn loves Martha, Martha loves Erik, John shoots Erik . . . . Such are the themes of soap opera, family gossip, and one type of sociology: To structural sociology this is what's real and interesting about people. People love and people hate, people make things, break things, shoot their enemies and make peace. That's life. Structural sociologists begin with who does what to whom, attempting to work out the rules of behavior from the ground up.

Compared to standard sociology, this structural sociology is something new. To us, as structuralists, the big variables of standard sociology are phantoms: No gender ever loved anyone, no race can hate. No religion ever had an abortion. No "socio-economic status," the big causal engine of standard sociology, ever held a job. Using such categories, standard sociology attempts to predict what people in one economic status, or religion, or race, or gender will do, on the average. And, in point of fact, the phantom categories work — but they don't work well. Even supposedly obvious predictions like "Educated people will make more money" are so tenuous that it takes statistics to prove they work at all. Moreover, the intellectual standard for "explanation" in standard sociology is, from the structuralist perspective, a very hard won but a very short step removed from the bigotry of ethnic, gender-based, and racial explanations: "Jews do this, Catholics do that. Blacks do this, whites do that — that explains it."

By contrast, structuralists attempt to work out the rules of behavior from the ground up, observing real connections among real people. Consider, for example, a typical college yearbook: Aside from the smiling faces, the senior yearbook is a source of "structuralist" information. The picture of the football team, with names attached, shows a set of people who know each other and work together and few of them, if any, will be found in the picture of the drama club. The yearbook tells

Figure 8.1
A Simple One-Dimensional Structure

you clubs, politics, fraternities and sororities, majors, dormitories, job plans, and home towns. Where overlaps exist, they tell you something about key individuals and ties among groups. Where overlaps do not exist, they tell you about divisions on campus. Structuralists should be able to assemble such data into a map of the campus, a social map marking-out its cliques and key players, who counts and who doesn't.

But we're not very good at that kind of thing, not yet. Structuralists intend to talk about the big stuff. We intend to talk about hierarchies and dominance, about cliques, social systems, and markets. These are some of the *structures* of structuralism. But we start from the ground up. In this chapter I want to examine some of this ground-level "stuff," looking at friendship, antagonism, and a few simple relations among individual people: The question is, if these relations are the "ground," then how do you work "up" to rules of behavior and to the structures of groups? That's the agenda for this chapter.

What I mean by structure is hard to define. That's the way it is in science — you can't start out by *defining* the thing you are trying to discover. But what we have in mind is something like cliques and hierarchies, or structures suggested by terms like "centralized" and "decentralized." If a group were divided into two antagonistic cliques, that would be a simple structure, ordering the person by person likes and dislikes. If a group were not divided but joined by the connecting lines in Figure 8.1, that would be a simple structure.

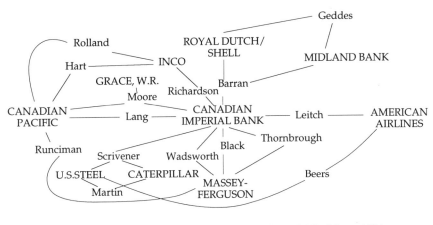

From *Levine's Atlas of Corprate Interlocks, Volume I,* Worldnet, 1984.

Figure 8.2
Real Connections of Ten Corporations and Fifteen Directors.

The structure would organize who likes whom and who doesn't, both what happens and what doesn't among the five persons and ten potential friendships in this group. Similarly, in a real-world example, the tangle of connections among ten corporations and fifteen directors, shown in Figure 8.2, masks a fairly simple "structure." (The data describe ten corporations and fifteen people who were directors of the ten corporations, circa 1979: Geddes, at the upper right, was a director of both Shell and Midland Bank.) Re-organizing the data, it seems relatively clear that the structure is a wheel-like structure, with Canadian Imperial at the hub, and with a periphery that shifts from an American group at the top to a Canadian group at the bottom, with a British group at the right, Figure 8.3.[1]

---

1. This example is meant as a visual illustration of a "structure." But for those who don't like things that are shown but not explained, this is a map obtained by the methods I am pursuing single-mindedly throughout these chapters: The ten corporations' data were arranged into a ten-row ten-column table counting the number of directors common to each pair of corporations, two in the case of Shell and Midland Bank. The table was analyzed in two dimensions using the absolute distance inferred from the frequencies.

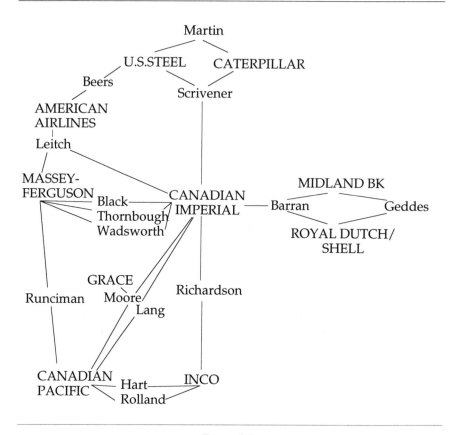

Figure 8.3
Re-organized Data for Connections of Ten Corporations

What we structuralists have in mind for "structure" is that primitive, at least for now. The question is, if simple relations, likes, dislikes, and various sorts of links are the "ground," then how do you work your way "up" to rules of behavior and to discovering the structures of groups?

That's the agenda for this chapter. How do you do it? How do you find rules of behavior, other than just listing who likes whom? How do you find hidden structures, if they exist? One thing structuralists know for sure is that you don't find rules of behavior and find structures by adopting standard sociological thinking: The data we work with are different from the stuff of standard sociology and require all-new thinking. The contrast between Tables 8.1 and 8.2 shows the difference: Table 8.1 is a standard cross-classification, Religion by Party, while Table 8.2 is a friendship relation. The cross-classification shows frequencies, while the friendship relation identifies pairs, pairs of people who were friends and pairs of people who were not. A cell of the cross-classification indicates that four people were cross-classified as both Strong Democrats and as Episcopalians, while a cell of the relation indicates only that two people, Allen and Taylor, were friends. The cross-classification represents data for 1,052 people, while the friendship relation represents data for exactly 9 men. The cross-classification aggregates people into categories, using two variables, while the friendship relation uses no aggregation and no variables.

Whatever it's going to take to "do" structuralism, we're on our own: The data we work with are different and the methods developed for standard data will not be much help.

. . . a few decades later . . .

Now: If you're with me so far, then you've survived a quick but fairly standard introduction to structuralism, a statement that might have been written at anytime in the last thirty years. Structuralism thrives by criticizing standard sociology, but we've accepted our own challenge and have been hard at work, for a few decades, trying to find the right

	Epis	Presb	Luth	Meth	Cath	Bap	Jew	Sums
Strong Democrat	4	8	12	22	67	77	11	201
Democrat	11	11	42	47	147	102	16	376
Independent	0	5	10	18	47	28	3	111
Republican	15	20	37	43	88	6	8	273
Strong Republican	7	6	14	14	26	24	0	91
Sums	37	50	115	144	375	293	38	1052

From *The General Social Survey*, NORC, 1986

Table 8.1
Standard Cross-Classification, Party Identification by Religion

	Allen		Donov		Hasul		Stein		Wind
		Cermak		Green		Ober		Taylor	
	I1	S4	W4	W9	W7	W8	S1	W3	W1
Allen (I1)	—	.	.	.	.	.	.	F	.
Cermak (S4)	.	—	.	F	.	F	.	.	.
Donovan (W4)	.	.	—	.	.	.	F	F	F
Green (W9)	.	F	.	—	F	F	.	.	.
Hasulak (W7)	.	.	.	F	—	F	F	.	.
Oberleitner (W8)	.	F	.	F	F	—	.	.	.
Steinhardt (S1)	.	.	F	.	F	.	—	F	F
Taylor (W3)	F	.	F	.	.	.	F	—	F
Windowski (W1)	.	.	F	.	.	.	F	F	—

From the Bank Wiring Room data, Homans, *The Human Group*, Harcourt Brace, 1950. Also see Roethlisberger and Dixon, *Management and the Worker*, Harvard University Press, 1939. The table shows the friendships for nine of the original fourteen men. (The remaining five men had no friends.) "W1" refers to Wireman 1. "S1" refers to Solderman 1. "I1" refers to Inspector 1.

Table 8.2
Friends

methods and the correct theories implied by these differences.[2] But I am suspicious of the premises from which we conclude that this "stuff" is different and I suspect that part of the difficulty in the few decades of work we have attempted is that we too, like standard sociology, have been colonized by benevolent mathematicians — deflected and distracted by a culture that doesn't understand science. *If*, as they are accustomed to saying, friendship is all or none, then we can pull out the mathematics of graph theory and draw out the consequences of various all-or-none assumptions. *If* social relations are all-or-none, then the mathematical concept of a "relation," a well-defined mathematical object, is a good model for real-world relations among people.

If . . . , then . . . It's an interesting game, but it's a colonists' game — their rules, not ours. You don't get too far in science by simply assuming the "obvious" about the stuff you are supposed to be analyzing. And that's what you let me do if you accepted my assertions that our data are unique, requiring a whole new way of thinking. So, the agenda is still to find rules that govern relations like friendship and to look for some sort of "structure." That's the agenda, but let's begin by dispensing with the myth of difference, working with real data.

The real data I'm going to use are called "the bank wiring room data." The wiring room itself was a shop in the Hawthorn plant of Westinghouse, circa 1932. Within the walls of the wiring room, fourteen men spent their days twisting wires around metal posts and then soldering them in place (to form *banks* of wires) — and also joking with each other, playing games, arguing, and generally going about the business of being human. I doubt that anyone has an enduring interest in wiring rooms, in general, or in the work lives of the fourteen individuals who labored there at Westinghouse sixty years ago. We study the bank wiring room because it was also a laboratory for observers from the Harvard Business School. The Harvard observers watched the fourteen men's friendships and battles, month after month, recording data that are now, sixty years later, the data on which structuralists learn their trade. The data preserve six relations: We know *Friends* (men who were

---

2. For a good introduction read *An Introduction to Structural Analysis: The Network Approach to Social Research*, by S. D. Berkowitz, Butterworths, 1982 or the revised edition forthcoming from Westview Press.

friends), *Games* (men who played games together), *Antagonists* (pairs of men who antagonized each other, *Windows* (men who argued about the opening and closing of windows), *Help* (men who helped each other with their work), and *Trade* (men who temporarily traded jobs). These are our who-did-what-to-whom data for the bank wiring room.

Now, with data, let's dispense with some myths that tell us how we're supposed to proceed with such data: First, is it true that friendship was all-or-none, you're friends or you're not, and therefore different from ordinary data? For the bank wiring room the answer is a clear "No." When the Harvard observers reported that Allen and Taylor were friends they were not pulling it out of the air. They had watched these fourteen men month after month. They had recorded interactions, one by one, and they had classified the nature of each interaction. The observers were reality oriented, and they knew how to count. And, thus, when they reported that Allen and Taylor were *friends*, as reported in Table 8.2, that report was a conclusion, not data. It was a conclusion based on counts of things that Allen did to Taylor and Taylor to Allen. The friendship table, you're friends or you're not, is a conclusion derived from counts.

Continuing with the myth of difference, is it true that data for individuals are intrinsically different from data for categories? True, individuals like Taylor, Allen and Windowski do not come with numbers or general labels attached. But that's a distinction that makes no obvious difference: For individuals, as for categories, the validity of the analysis depends on the pattern of the data. Whether we are assigning numbers to categories or assigning numbers to people, a long interval must correspond to some great difference and a small interval must correspond to some small one. And within these data there is evidence of great differences and small ones. Windowski and Green show a great difference: They were not friends and they had no friends in common. Looking at what they do, and with whom, these two men were distant, Table 8.3.

By contrast, Windowski and Donovan show a small difference: They were friends and had two friends in common. Looking at what they do, and with whom, these men were close, Table 8.4. And, peeking ahead at the results for these data, re-organized in Table 8.5, there is good reason to suspect a scale for the group as a whole.

Windowski (W1)	.	.	F	.	.	.	F	F	—
Green (W9)	.	F	.	—	F	F	.	.	.

Table 8.3
Windowski's Friendships Contrasted with Green's

Windowski (W1)	.	.	F	.	.	.	F	F	—
Donovan (W4)	.	.	—	.	.	.	F	F	F

Table 8.4
Windowski's Friendships Contrasted with Donovan's

	I1	W3	W1	W4	S1	W7	W8	W9	S4
Allen (I1)	—	F							
Taylor (W3)	F	—	F	F	F				
Windowski (W1)		F	—	F	F				
Donovan (W4)		F	F	—	F				
Steinhardt (S1)		F	F	F	—	F			
Hasulak (W7)					F	—	F	F	
Oberleitner (W8)						F	—	F	F
Green (W9)						F	F	—	F
Cermak (S4)							F	F	—

Table 8.5
Friends Re-organized

So much for the myth and for what's "obvious" about relational data. If I've confused you, that's good. If you're not confused: If you look at such data and say "Ah, a structure: Let's look for cliques (using so-and-so's computer program)." Or, "Let's look for centrality (using so-and-so's centrality index)." If you feel confident in such things, then your confidence is suspect. It all depends on the data: All bets are open and you clarify the situation by analyzing data, constructing working assumptions, and then testing them. If your intuition leads you to other working assumptions, other than mine or other than those that are standard, then the same rules apply.

Now, to work: For these data I make the working assumption that the data are counts, or can be treated like counts, and I make the working assumption that there is an interval scale that organizes the apparent diversity of these counts, the opposite of both myths. I think our mathematical forebears in this profession committed one oversight for which they may kick themselves: Reality (at least for these data) is simpler than they had supposed. Here, at least, the hypothesis of a one-dimensional structure, rather like Figure 8.1, within which men are simply "close" to their friends seems to do the job.

$$\widehat{F}(i,j) = M_i M_j \, e^{-\left[\begin{array}{c} distance \ and/or \\ distance\text{-}squared \end{array}\right]} \qquad\qquad [8.1]$$

Invoking the standard model as a working hypothesis, Equation 8.1, and comparing person i to j, if the distance between them is zero, then the expected frequency of friendly exchanges, $\widehat{F}$, will be large. I leave it open whether it is the simple distance or the squared distance that governs their behavior (or neither, if the equation doesn't work). I'll try both. In addition, if person i has a large multiplier, M_i, then person i will be friendly with everyone, having large $\widehat{F}$, across the group. And thus, combining structural and individual attributes, combining distances with individual multipliers, i and j can be friendly for different reasons: They may be friends because they are friendly, with large M_i and M_j, or they may be friends because they are close.

If that looks simple, you understand it: The working hypothesis is that these men act as if they were standing in a line. On that line they are friendly with their neighbors, depending on distance, and individually their circles of friendship may be either broad or narrow, depending on their different *M*'s. The basic structure is simple.

Now, with the equation in one hand and the data in the other, I invoke the familiar rituals: Typing the data for *Friends* (and the data for a second relation, *Games*) into my home computer, running the program that attempts to find *M*'s and *x*'s that "fit," and preparing the results for inspection.[3] Inspecting the results in Figure 8.4, the results for *Friends* in the bank wiring room and the results for *Games* support my one-dimensional working assumptions.

The first question is "Does it work? Is it reasonable to think of these workers as if they were standing in a line, being friendly with their neighbors?" If it doesn't work there is no reason to look at what else the analysis may say about the group. But it does: The histogram at the bottom left shows that non-friendships have been matched with small numbers (0 to about .2), as they should have been, and the adjacent histogram shows that friendships have been matched with large numbers (.7 to about 1.1), as they should. Comparing the two sets of numbers, small and large, there is no overlap. The estimated scales and multipliers match friendship with large values of $\hat{F}$ and non-friendship with small values.

The lines in Figure 8.4 show the inferred structure, the "line" within which these values were generated, the whole within which the individual friendships are parts: On this line the positions are consistent with cliques reported by the original observers, but more detailed. (The observers included W1, W3, W4, S1, and I1 in "Clique A," and W6, W7, W8, W9, and S4 in "Clique B." Other men were in no clique or were difficult to classify.) The detail puts Steinhardt and Hasulak at the adjacent boundaries of their sub-groups while it puts Allen and Cermak at the Extremes.

---

3. I do not mean to be too brief about the computer program and the exact method by which the numbers are estimated, but neither do I wish to dwell on these things: In a very real sense, they don't matter. What matters is whether or not there is a fit that's good enough. If I can find it, then the evidence will stand up whether I've estimated the numbers on my little hand calculator, or on my neighborhood supercomputer, or received them from a Greek oracle with a penchant for numbers. I worry about such problems a great deal, but they have to be kept in their place.

200

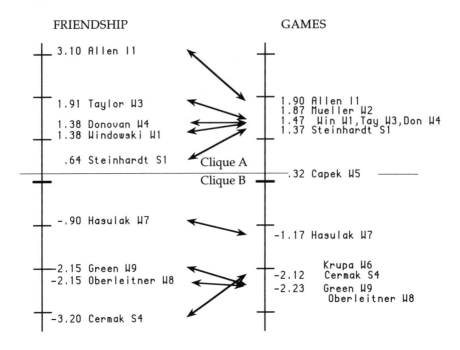

Figure 8.4
Friendship and Games:
Inferred Scales Compared, Re-Ordered Data, and
Distributions of Expected Values Using Distance Squared

The distributions of expected values show that, in every case, the presence of the friendship or game relation corresponds to large expected values while absence of the relation corresponds to low expected values.

Expected values are generated from the intervals and the multipliers. For Friendship the "All" multiplier is 2.67 and the nine multipliers are W1:.52, W3:1.09, W4:.52, W7:2.73, W8:.62, W9:.62, S1:1.42, S4:1.76, and I1:1.25. The chi-square is .43. For Games the "All" multiplier is 1.44 and the twelve multipliers are W1:.91, W2:.92, W3:.91, W4:.91, W5:2.63, W6:.66, W7:2.47, W8:.92, W9: .92, S1:.78, S4:.66, and I1:.80. The chi-square is 1.34. Thus the expected value for the "Friendship" between W1 and W3 is (2.67)(.52)(1.09)Exp(-.27), where the distance from W1 to W4 is .52 and the squared distance is .27.

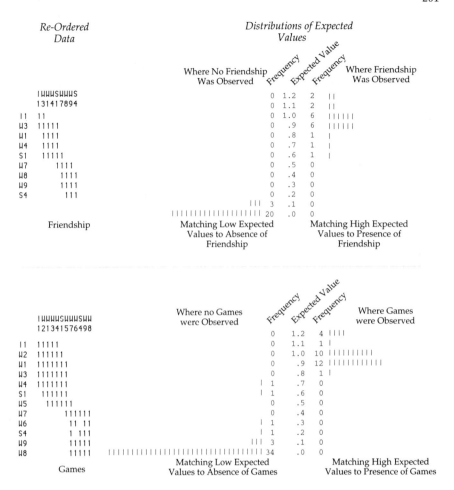

Figure 8.4: Friendship and Games (Continued)

In the same figure the reprint of the friendship data (upper left) and of the games data (upper right), shows the pattern of the data as ordered by the inferred scale. Both show the familiar pattern of high correlation, with large "frequencies" close to the diagonal, where $x_i = x_j$, and small frequencies elsewhere.[4]   The equations fit and the inferred structure of the group makes sense.[5]

Beyond the Obvious: Antagonism and Arguments

That completes my agenda.   I treated the data as if they were frequency tables and I inferred intervals. In turn the intervals generate numbers consistent with the data, showing that the assumptions are consistent with the reality. What we know, or affirm, about the nature of friendship is that you have it with people who are close, a not-quite-trivial statement.   And what we know about the structure of closeness in

---

4. The "frequencies" on the diagonal were ignored in both cases: We have no data for self-friendship nor, for that matter, do we have a relevant definition of the concept, so the diagonal cells were simply omitted from the computation.

5. I have used the distance-squared model in preference to the simple distance model because it produces the smaller chi-square in both cases: For Friendship, using the distance-squared distribution, the chi-square is .43, compared to .92 using simple distance. For Games, using the distance-squared distribution, the chi-square is 1.34 compared to 2.64 using simple distance.   For both Friendship and Games, the simple distance model, first power, comes close and the distance-squared model comes closer.   But I do not consider the difference conclusive, even for the bank wiring room: Both distributions produce expected values that match high values to the observed friendships and games while matching low values to the non-friendships and non-games. That is, both are good enough.   Further, chi-square is hard to interpret for such data and the data sets are small.   Moreover, the clearest difference between the shape of the distance distribution and the shape of the distance-squared distribution is at the point where the distance is equal to zero — and there we have no data at all. (As noted, for fitting the equation to the data I have not used the cells that would require either an assumption or data of "friendship" or "game playing" with one's self and, for that matter, a definition of the concept.) Chi-square values for different relations and different models are reported in Appendix 8.1.

the bank wiring room is that it is one dimensional, like a line. The results are consistent with the working assumptions. Moreover, when you look at the data, in order, you see the familiar pattern of a perfectly ordinary correlation between variables with data concentrated near a line running through the diagonal of the table. So much for the assumption that the data we structuralists work with are different — that is an unnecessary assumption. I find that pattern exciting because it means that even with the simple friendship data, there is a little more here than meets the eye. Or, perhaps I should say a little less: If I analyze these data as a simple relation, just the data, then I have to keep track of thirty-six facts to "summarize" the data. (There are *thirty-six* pairs of workers, Allen with Cermak, Allen with Donovan, Allen with Green, and so forth, among the nine workers who have friends within the wiring room.) But if you count up the number of numbers used in the analysis that matches the data there are fewer, only seventeen.[6] That says something about order, order in the sense of simplicity: Comparing thirty-six to seventeen, comparing what we observed to the smaller number (from which they can be derived or predicted) the implication is that reality is simpler than it might have been. Logically, the data might have been complex; empirically, they are not. And it is the distributional analysis that makes it possible to make that statement. This means that *anything* I can do with these friendship data — something simple, like combining them to find friends' friends, or something exotic, like counting the number of "transitive" threesomes for whom if A likes B and B likes C then A likes C — *anything* I might extrapolate from these friendship data is implicit in the seventeen numbers. No more is required.

Such simplicity needs to be explained: How is it that they behave as if they were standing in a line? With the evidence at hand I can only speculate. Perhaps nine men are too few to maintain a complicated pattern. More likely, perhaps *friendship* is not what we have been taught to think it is, not in the bank wiring room. We've been taught that

---

6. For Friends, using nine people, there is one all effect, plus nine multipliers of which eight are independent, plus eight intervals for a total of seventeen parameters required to predict the thirty-six "0" or "1" observations. For Games, using twelve people, the ratio of the two numbers is improved with twenty-four numbers required to predict sixty-six "0" or "1" game-playing observations.

friendship is an egalitarian relation: Friends are equals, friendship is a behavior that is supposed to stand apart from hierarchies and competition. Maybe that's true and maybe it isn't in the bank wiring room: Perhaps the one-dimensional scale that describes the group is related to a hierarchy, high to low. [7] Perhaps it is an underlying status order that constrains friendship toward the one-dimensional simplicity that has been detected.

Now let's go one step further: The one equation works for both *Friends* and *Games*. More interesting, it does not work for *Antagonism* or for *Arguments* — if it did, I would not have hesitated to show the results. That's not much of a surprise: If the friendship equation says friends are close, then you wouldn't expect the same equation to work for negative-sounding things like antagonism, saying enemies are close too. That would be unreasonable and suggests an obvious fix: If friends are close, then enemies should be far — so change the sign of the friendship equation, switching from the first distribution in Figure 8.5 to the second. That would be nice and it would be plausible — friends are close, enemies are far. But empirically that doesn't work either and that's where "antagonism" gets interesting: The change of sign doesn't help much and isn't even much of an improvement over the positive model. That's the trouble with putting plausible ideas into testable form — sometimes they fail the test.[8]

What works is something almost equally simple, but just complicated enough to be interesting. For a moment, speculate about antagonism: Who can you have a good fight with? It's not someone too close, like a friend. But neither is it someone too far, you don't fight with

————————————

7. While not referring specifically to friendship, the original observations described the cliques in terms of status, A is high, B is low. A includes the experienced workers and the highest producers. B includes the less experienced and less accomplished.

8. Using distance squared, as for friendship, realizes chi-square equal to 8.78. Changing the sign from positive to negative gives chi-square equal to 8.46. But using both distance and distance squared, with opposite signs, as described below, leads to chi-square equal to 2.31, a serious improvement. See Appendix 8.1.

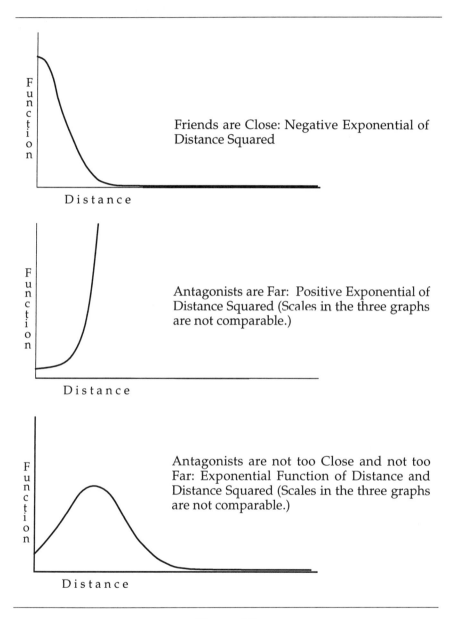

Figure 8.5
General Forms for Three Type of Distance Functions

strangers. You have a good sustained fight with someone who is not too close and not too far. Your antagonists are people you can't stand, but can't get away from either. One of my anthropologist colleagues calls this idea, "not too close and not too far," the sorcery phenomenon: In a society that believes in magic, who gets accused of witchcraft and sorcery? It's not a spouse — that's asking for trouble. But neither is it a stranger. The person you accuse of witchcraft is an in-law: My mother-in-law is a witch, my father-in-law uses magic. There is a balance point with negatives, not too close and not too far.

Mimicking this concept with mathematics, if you combine distance and distance squared in the same equation, you can get an equation that has a "bump," illustrated by the third distribution in Figure 8.5. Balancing the effect of distance with the effect of distance squared, using opposite signs, you can place the optimal distance for antagonists at an intermediate distance, not too close and not too far.

This works. Looking at the results for both *Antagonism* and *Arguments* in Figure 8.6, again the first question is "Does it fit?" — without that the discussion of bumps and "not too far" would degenerate into plausible speculation. The histogram at the bottom left shows that non-antagonism has been matched with small numbers (0 to approximately .4, with one exception). By contrast, the adjacent histogram shows that antagonism was matched with large numbers (.6 to 1.2). The high numbers and the low numbers are separate, with one error. The reprint of the data, re-ordered, shows the pattern of antagonism, with the data running in parallel bands on either side of the diagonal. The bump matches high $\hat{F}$ with antagonism and low $\hat{F}$ with its absence. The same pattern, with different numbers, works for Arguments. In each case there is one error.

Again there is less here than meets the eye, the sixty-six antagonisms and non-antagonisms are described by twenty-four numbers (with one error).[9] And, allowing for the one error, any combi-

---

9. The twenty-five numbers are not linearly independent of each other. There are twenty-four independent numbers: eleven for the intervals, twelve for the multipliers, and one for the distance-squared coefficient (standardizing the distance coefficient to negative one).

nation of friendship and antagonism should be predictable from the (relatively) few numbers used by the model.[10]

Now we know a little more about the nature of friendship, games, antagonism and arguments. Friendship and Antagonism are proximity relations. But Antagonism and Arguments are not direct opposites. Instead, Antagonism and Arguments are mediate relations, experienced with someone who is not too close and not too far. These are four relations with two distinct forms, reasonably well verified by results and the concept itself, "not too close and not too far," would be difficult to express without the interval scales. Speculating, for a moment, perhaps what we have observed in the bank wiring room is a tension between two kinds of forces. If the positive force pulls people closer, while antagonism does *not* drive them apart (not so far apart as to fracture the group), then the implication would be a human group in tension, one that does not unite and can not dissolve.

---

10. The chi-squares give a rough indication of the differences in fit among the different models:

	Positive Distance Squared	Negative Distance Squared	Negative/ Positive	
Antagonism	8.78	8.46	2.31	
Fights About Windows		4.80	4.14	2.60

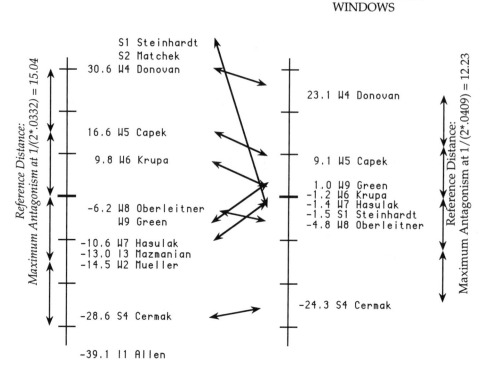

Figure 8.6
Antagonism and Arguments About Windows:
Inferred Scales Compared, Re-Ordered Data, and Distributions of Expected
Values using Displaced Affect, Combining Distance and Distance Squared

The distributions of expected values show that, with one exception for each relation, the presence of the relation corresponds to large expected values while absence of the relation corresponds to low expected values.

For Antagonism the "All" multiplier is .00023 and the twelve multipliers are W2:16.62, W4:.06, W5:40.28, W6:.50, W7:9.42, W8:.51, W9:.51, S1:.06, S2:.06, S4:.04, I1:2.99, and I3:14.72. The distance coefficient is -1 and the distance-squared coefficient is .03324. The chi-square is 2.31. For Arguments about Windows, the "All" multiplier is .04309 and the eight multipliers are W4:4.47, W5: .01, W6:4.43, W7:3.59, W8:.32, W9:.71, S1: 3.40, and S4:1.47. The distance coefficient is -1 and the distance-squared coefficient is .04309. The chi-square is 2.60. Thus the expected value for the "Antagonism" between W2 and W4 is (.00023)(.253)(.001)Exp(45.07-(.00324)(2031.30)), where the distance from W1 to W4 is 45.07 and the squared distance is 2031.30.

209

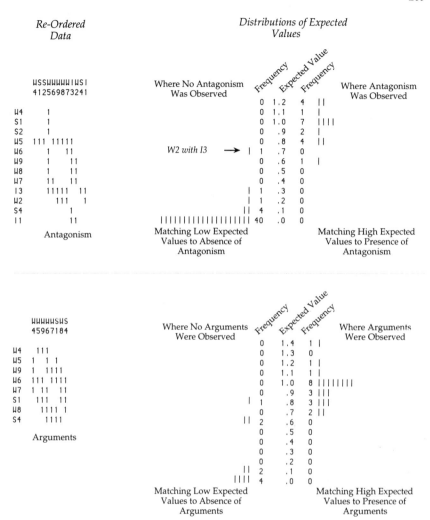

Figure 8.6: Antagonism and Arguments about Windows (Continued)

Giving and Taking: Help
(Split-role Models)

So far, I have used four of the six relations available for the bank wiring room. The remaining two are Help and Trade. *Trade* can be dispensed with immediately: Few of the workers trade jobs, and these few form a network that the distributional analysis can not help but fit, perfectly, making the fit uninteresting.[11] So we're left with one recalcitrant relation, *Help*. This one is more of a challenge. And while it's a judgment call whether or not the previous equations fit, deciding when "some errors" are "too many," I judge that *Help* does not work without one more twist of the basic model.[12] The necessary twist seems to be

---

11. The Trade data provide actual counts, shown below. (The 2 in W1's row and S1's column means that W1 initiated two trades with S1.) For Trade, the data seven people form one connected network, while two people form another. Among the seven, the pattern is too simple: If it were graphed, the workers would fall in the order W1, S1, W2, S4, and then W5, W7, and W8 together.

	W1 W2 W5 W7 W8 S1	S4		W6		S2
W1	2		W6	2		
W2	12 4		S2			
W5	7					
W7	2					
W8	20					
S1						
S4						

12. The chi-square using the best fit of the previous models is 22.32, but I am making my assessment more on the subjective visual evidence of overlap between the two distributions of expected values — shown here using the displaced relation model, with a negative coefficient for distance and a positive coefficient for distance squared.

Expected Value	Count		Expected Value	Count
1.6	0		1.6	0
1.5	1	|	1.5	0
1.4	0		1.4	0

non-symmetry: For the *Help* relation, one workman offered help, while another received it. One worker initiated the relation, the other concurred.[13] With this hunch in mind, the working assumptions I've used for these data split the roles, assigning one interval to Allen and Taylor as helpers and a different interval to Allen and Taylor, and all the rest, as helpees: Each person gets represented twice. (Operationally, that means each row gets a number and each column gets a number as well.) The result is another fit, good but not perfect (with two errors), Figure 8.7.[14] Aside from the usual inspection for results, the interesting thing about help is the lack of obvious correlation, positive or negative, between role positions of helpers and role positions of persons who get helped. As one who helps, Wireman 5, for example, ends up in the middle of the group. But as one who gets help he ends up at an extreme.

1.3	1	|	1.3	0	
1.2	1	|	1.2	2	||
1.1	2	||	1.1	3	|||
1.0	3	|||	1.0	2	||
.9	2	||	.9	2	||
.8	1	|	.8	2	||
.7	6	||||||	.7	3	|||
.6	7	|||||||	.6	2	||
.5	9	|||||||||	.5	6	||||||
.4	13	|||||||||||||	.4	2	||
.3	16	||||||||||||||||	.3	0	
.2	12	||||||||||||	.2	0	
.1	10	||||||||||	.1	0	
.0	2	||	.0	0	
(Observed Value = 0)			(Observed Value = 1)		

13. This lack of symmetry is not enough, by itself, to defeat the distributional model (non-symmetrical row and column multipliers may suffice) but it appears to be the culprit for helping.

14. There is reason to suspect that this "fit" exists simply because I've given myself an extra set of numbers to work with, increasing the complexity of the model. But not just any complicated model will do the job: For a check I have estimated the fit for an equally complicated model that says different things about the group. This comparison model uses two dimensions, again using two numbers for each person, but doesn't split the roles, using the same two numbers for Allen's "row" as for Allen's "column." The one-dimensional model, with split roles, is better, see Appendix 8.1. (For the one-dimensional model, with split roles, the chi-square is 5.06 while for the two-dimensional model, without split roles, the chi-square is 13.77.)

None of the obvious things seem to apply: Receiving help is neither the opposite nor the complement to giving help. One seems unpredictable from the other.

That pushes these simple data, all six relations, about as far as I dare, perhaps further than I should dare for only 14 men and crude data. Dropping the *a priori* assumption that structural data are "different" and then treating "friends" and the other relations as distributions of countable behavior yields results. The point is that treating the data as counts and estimating inferred interval scales yields information about these data. Inferring the nature of these data from the data, the results suggest that the five relations require only three, not five, abstract forms: There are proximate relations (*Friendship* and *Games*), mediate (displaced) relations (*Antagonism* and *Arguments*) and non-symmetrical relations (*Help*) in which the separate roles of giver and receiver are not only different but unpredictable, one from the other. I now know a little bit about friendship, friendship is "close," as expected. I now know something that was not obvious (to me) about antagonism, it's neither close nor far. And help shows a surprising asymmetry, unlike friendship and game playing. In each separate case the relation is, or is approximately one dimensional. And in each case the description is backed up by a testable statement which is, sometimes clearly, sometimes with errors, backed up by the data.

213

Distributions of Expected Values

Re-Ordered Data

uuuuususuuus
261792315844

U3
S2
S1
U8
U4
U5
U1
U6
U2
S4
U7
U9

Where Help
Was Observed

Frequency
Expected Value
Frequency

Where No Help
Was Observed

Matching Low Expected
Values to Absence of Help

Matching High Expected
Values to Presence of Help

Figure 8.7
Help:
Inferred Scales, Re-Ordered Data, and Distributions of Expected Values
Using Displaced Affect and Separating Role of Helper (Row) from Role
of Helpee (Column)

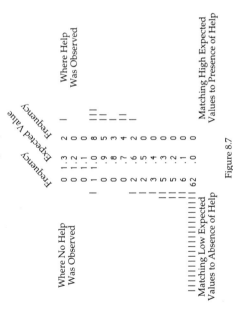
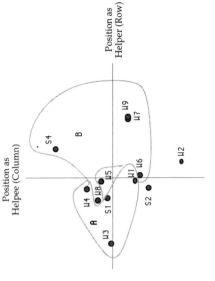

For Helper, row, the coordinates are W1:-.7, W2:3.2, W3:-13.0, W4:-2.2, W5:-1.1, W6:.6, W7:11.5, W8:-4.2, W9:11.8, S1:-4.3, S2:-7.1, and S4:5.7. For Helpee, column, the coordinates are W1:-4.2, W2:-13.2, W3:.8, W4:5.0, W5:2.4, W6:-5.1, W7:-2.2, W8:3.2, W9:-2.2, S1:1.0, S2:-2.1, and S4:11.6. The "All" multiplier is .100971. For Helper, row, the multipliers are W1:.93, W2:.99, W3:2.14, W4:1.05, W5:.41, W6:1.23, W7:1.43, W8:.90, W9:1.43, S1:.59, S2:.61, and S4:1.44. For Helpee, column, the multipliers are W1:2.90, W2:3.92, W3:5.76, W4:3.92, W5:.00, W6:5.22, W7:4.46, W8:2.82, W9:3.92, S1:2.94, S2:.00, and S4: 6.16. The distance coefficient is -1 and the distance-squared coefficient is .28072. The chi-square is 5.07.

Appendix 8.1
Summary of Chi-Square "Fits"

Relation	Coefficient of Simple Distance	Coefficient of Distance Squared	Chi-Square	Comment
Positive Relations (Friends and Games):				
Friend	Positive	None (zero)	.922	Symmetrical,
"Best"→	None (zero)	Positive	.435	9 people
Games	Positive	None (zero)	2.64	Symmetrical,
"Best"→	None (zero)	Positive	1.34	12 people

Displaced Relations (Antagonism and Arguments About Windows)

Antagonism	Negative	None (zero)	11.12	Symmetrical,
	None (zero)	Negative	8.46	12 people
	Positive	None (zero)	9.78	
	None (zero)	Positive	8.78	
"Best"→	Negative	Positive	2.31	
Arguments	Negative	None (zero)	4.35	Symmetrical,
About	None (zero)	Negative	4.14	8 people
Windows	Positive	None (zero)	6.23	
	None (zero)	Positive	4.80	
"Best"→	Negative	Positive	2.60	

Displaced, Two-Role Relations (Help)

Help	One Dimension — Without Role Division			
	Negative	Positive or Negative	23.82	Asymmetrical, 12 people
	Positive	Positive or Negative	22.32	
	Two Dimensions — Without Role Division			
	Negative	Positive	13.77	
	One Dimension — With Role Division			
"Best"→	Negative	Positive	5.06	

Appendix 8.2
Additional Data and Untried Applications

The study of social relations grew up with social psychology in the context of small group research, studying small face-to-face groups of people who had "feelings" about one another: Work groups, "T" groups, dormitories, and children's camps. An archive of such data, including the "classics" used by most researchers, is readily available as part of a software package known as UCINET, originally developed at the University of California at Irvine and now under the care of Professor Steve Borgatti at the University of South Carolina, Columbia, South Carolina.

Beyond these classical studies, as our capacity to study these things improves, there is no need to confine "relations" to individual people or to feelings or to small populations. It is possible to extend these studies outward into the "real world." I find that an exciting prospect because, scientifically, there is a problem with obscure examples, such as the bank wiring data: In the vernacular, "Who cares?" Ask yourself quickly — What was the relation between Windowski and Taylor? I myself don't remember. But ask me about the relation between the African National Congress and the National Party of South Africa, ask me about American politics or coalitions in the Middle East, or ask me about the politics of my university or my town: I care about these and I have expectations about them plus a great deal of informal knowledge (much of which is probably wrong). I feel no need to be *au courant* or fashionable in my choice of data; if obscure data provide the best opportunity for my agenda, then I'll use obscure data. But for the study of social relations current events data offer a distinct advantage — for the science. If I subject the coalitions and oppositions of current events and well-known people and major institutions to relational analysis and if I say something new, or something foolish, it will be noticed. That's good, for the science, because it creates a rough-and-ready form of falsifiability for our work.

Moreover, the technology of modern news services and electronic libraries has probably made it easier, today, to access who does what to whom, as current events, than to access who feels what about whom in the classical studies. Citation indices give us access to the developing structure of science and literature. Newspaper abstracts update the daily activities of political players on a world scale or in a community. Library indices connect world problems, international organizations, lobbyists, politicians, intellectuals, and business.

My own work has used networks, not of individuals, but of corporations, where the relation between them is not a "feeling" but a person. As in the Canadian Imperial example used earlier, this network makes some corporations "close" because they have one or two or more of the members of their boards of directors in common.[*]

Other workable examples should be readily accessible. I suggested earlier that a college yearbook is a source of structuralist information. For each student it describes his or her activities and thereby, indirectly, it tells you about connections among the groups.   Organizing and mapping the data should provide a social map of life on campus, placing prominent actors and organizations in position, showing which organizations and which people are central and who connects them.

For a more prominent set of fraternities, *The Almanac of American Politics* (published by Gambit Press, Boston), updated frequently, lists voting patterns of Senators and Representatives, thereby connecting issues (the coalitions who vote yes) in terms of the Senators and Representatives they have in common.

Creating the capability of a civilian intelligence agency, the monthly *TRANSDEX Index* (published by UMI, Ann Arbor, Michigan, for United States Joint Publications Research) indexes and translates "non-U.S. publications" including items relevant to military intelligence, international relations, business, politics, and science, listing prominent

------

[*]An early paper, using a dual network of corporations linked to banks by common corporate directors and, thus, indirectly to each other was described in "The Sphere of Influence: A Methodological Inquiry into U.S. Banking and Industrial Networks," *American Sociological Review*, February, 1972 (Reprinted in *Social Networks: A Developing Paradigm*, Leinhardt (Ed.), Academic Press, 1977).   The publication includes a copy of the data (which were obtained from public documents of the House Subcommittee on Banking).   More recent work, identical in technique to the methods used in this discussion, was published as *Worldnet 1980: Worldwide Corporate Interlocks (Volumes I and II)*, published by Worldnet, Inc., Hanover, New Hampshire, 1980 (with various data updates, prepared in 1985, 1986, and 1990).

actors and issues, sometimes providing, quite literally, the social relation "who is shooting at whom."

The *Science Citation Index* and *Social Science Citation Index* (published by the Institute for Scientific Information, Philadelphia) create the opportunity to map "science," or small subsets of scientists, with the potential for a map of "Who's Who" in a scientific specialty group — probably a useful exercise for a graduate student preparing to enter the professional fray and carve out a position, interpreting position quite literally.

9

Time and Money:
The Course of Human Events

The secret to getting rich in a gold rush is: Sell shovels.

— Anonymous

I f you are a data analyst with a streak of greed, or if you are just very
sure of your ability to go bravely where no data analyst has gone
before, then try analyzing what data analysts call "time series." That's
the polite name for it, "time series." Putting it more directly, try
predicting the stock market. Try predicting interest rates and unemployment and the gross national product. Try to predict the future — and
make yourself rich. This kind of analysis can be a bracing experience:
With this stuff you will know, beyond argument, when you were wrong.
Except that, well, . . . with a little better model, a little more data, a little
more time, . . . , it *should* work. If each profession has its occupational
hazards, then this invitation to madness is the occupational hazard of the
data analyst.

Economic data look predictable. Consider, for example, Figure 9.1,
a graph reproduced from Kondratieff's famous work on long cycles.[1]
The analyst looks at these graphs and says "cycles" while the skeptic
says "You mean: Sometimes it goes up and sometimes it goes down." I
put it to you: What do you see in this graph? Do you see cycles, and if
so, where? Kondratieff thought it was obvious, but which statement was
the "real Kondratieff"?

---

1. *The Long Wave Cycle,* by Nickolai Kondratieff, translated by Guy
Daniels, Richardson & Snyder, 1984. Chart 1: Indices of Commodity
Prices. The translation works from various sources dated between 1922
and 1928.

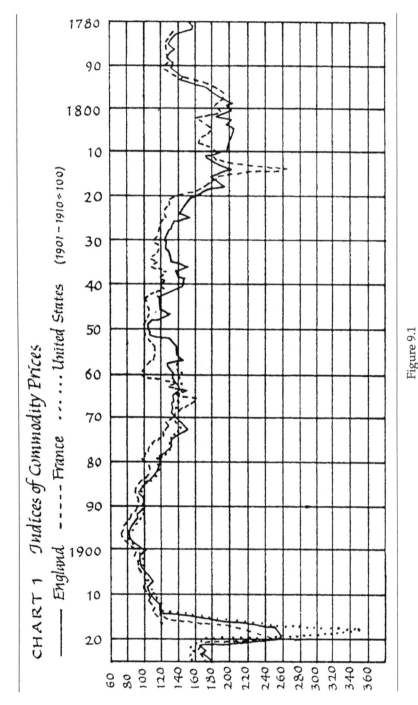

Figure 9.1

Indices of English, French, and U.S. Commodity Prices, Long-Term Movements
Reproduced from Kondratieff's *The Long Wave Cycle*, translated by Guy Daniels, Richardson & Snyder, 1984.

Was it:

The rising wave of the first cycle takes in the period from 1789 to 1814: that is, 25 years. The downward wave of the first cycle begins in 1814 and ends in 1849; that is, it lasts 35 years. . . . The rising wave of the second cycle begins in 1849 and ends in 1873: that is, it lasts 24 years. True, for the United States the prices peak in 1866. But this upswing is due to the Civil War; and the observed lack of coincidence between the turning point for . . . does not invalidate the general picture.

Or, was it:

The downward wave of the first cycle ends in 1805. The rising wave of the second cycle begins in 1805 and continues through 1897. The downward wave of the second cycle begins in 1897 and ends in 1919. . . . True, prices are level during the 1860's. But this interruption is due to the American Civil war; and the observed interruption in the cycle does not invalidate the general picture.

Which one is obvious? And for that matter, where are the peaks:

Do you see peaks in 1789, 1810, 1830, 1850, and 1897?

Do you see peaks in 1789, 1850, and 1898?

Or, is it that prices go up and prices go down?

To Kondratieff, the first statement was correct. And he seemed quite certain:

The index numbers plotted on Chart 1 have not been smoothed or processed in any way. Nonetheless, a mere glance at the chart shows that, despite all the deviations and irregularities of movement, the average level of commodity prices exhibits a series of long cycles. (*op. cit.*, p. 37)

Ah, now I see it — the human brain is a wonder at finding patterns, present or not.

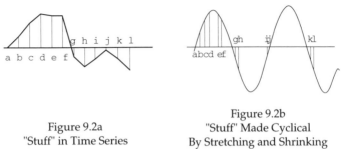

Figure 9.2a
"Stuff" in Time Series

Figure 9.2b
"Stuff" Made Cyclical
By Stretching and Shrinking
the Scale of Time

Figures 9.2a and 9.2b
Stretching and Shrinking to Produce the Appearance of Cycles

What's the problem with such statements? Re-read the Kondratieff statement: The cycle lasts 25 years, and then 35 years, and then 24 years — except for exceptions which, he claims, do not invalidate the claim. The problem with such statements is that they evade discipline: If I can stop the clock and start it, slow it down and speed it up, as I please, then I can make almost anything look "cyclical." If I can stop time, stretch it, shrink it, and mold it without limit then even the funny-looking sequence of Figure 9.2a conforms to the cycle of Figure 9.2b. And if the rules are so lax that anything looks cyclical, then making any *one* thing look cyclical proves nothing. There's the problem.

It's easy to ridicule time series analyses that evade scientific discipline. But the attempt to analyze these economic events should not be dismissed too quickly: There is nothing intrinsically ridiculous in the idea that a process varies in its speed, amplitude, or direction. Why assume *a priori* that the pace of human events will be regular with respect to a physical clock? Why assume that human development can not start and stop, speed up and slow down relative to a physical clock, pausing for weekends and holidays, flood and famine? If that is the way of human behavior, then it is presumptuous to dismiss the problem because our methods are not up to the task.

The reason that social scientists use the physical clock is depressingly practical, not theoretical. We use physical science methods because they're there and because we were trained by physical scientists and mathematicians. Now, foreign birth does not make these physical methods wrong for social science, but neither does it make them right.

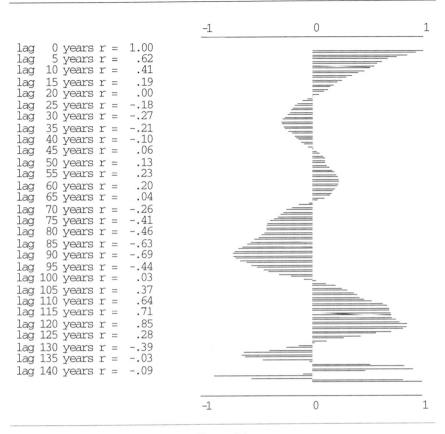

lag	0 years r =	1.00
lag	5 years r =	.62
lag	10 years r =	.41
lag	15 years r =	.19
lag	20 years r =	.00
lag	25 years r =	-.18
lag	30 years r =	-.27
lag	35 years r =	-.21
lag	40 years r =	-.10
lag	45 years r =	.06
lag	50 years r =	.13
lag	55 years r =	.23
lag	60 years r =	.20
lag	65 years r =	.04
lag	70 years r =	-.26
lag	75 years r =	-.41
lag	80 years r =	-.46
lag	85 years r =	-.63
lag	90 years r =	-.69
lag	95 years r =	-.44
lag	100 years r =	.03
lag	105 years r =	.37
lag	110 years r =	.64
lag	115 years r =	.71
lag	120 years r =	.85
lag	125 years r =	.28
lag	130 years r =	-.39
lag	135 years r =	-.03
lag	140 years r =	-.09

Figure 9.3

Autocorrelations Between English Commodity Prices and Previous Values of English Commodity Prices

The texts of physical science and mathematics offer a well-developed array of techniques, ranging from autocorrelation to Fourier series and spectral analysis, and they can be useful.

For example, Figure 9.3 shows the "autocorrelations" among Kondratieff's English commodity price data, comparing the correlations between current prices and historical prices. Reading from the first line, at the top, the correlation between prices and prices (lag 0) is 1, a mathematical necessity. Reading the next line, the correlation between current prices and prices as they were five years ago (lag 5) is .62, confirming the truism that this year's prices are pretty much like previous year's prices, at least on a historical scale. Many lines down, at a lag of 55 years, is where the autocorrelations among prices get interesting. Here, at 55 years, the correlations peak with *r* at .23. That means that commodity prices in any one year and the prices, as they were, *fifty-five years earlier*, are correlated. The prices varied up and down on a fifty-five year cycle. And that's interesting, although the 55-year autocorrelation is a definite none-of-the-above compared to Kondratieff's estimate of one 47-year cycle and one 60-year cycle.[2]

The availability of methods like autocorrelation is, in itself, good enough reason to give them a try: Here the autocorrelations are moderately interesting, giving a first-order approximation, a rough "overview" of the phenomenon. But when you transfer such things wholesale, away from their context of origin, you've got to be careful. In the original context, among physical phenomena, there is usually a good physical/theoretical base for the mathematics. There is good theoretical reason to expect physical oscillation to be sinusoidal and good reason to expect complex oscillations to resolve into sums of orderly harmonic sequences — matching the analytical base of Fourier methods. In context, the theory of the phenomena and the structure of the math are well matched. Out of context, the borrowed ideas become metaphor, not theory, and the method becomes description at best, not analysis. A vibrating string, or a pipe, or the pulse from an atom of hydrogen really has a frequency or a set of stable frequencies. If you talk about its frequency "± 20%," the phrase "plus or minus" refers to measurement error not to natural variability in the physical event. If you transfer methods from this context into a social context, a social context in which it is not obviously unreasonable for the period to vary, e.g., from 47 years to 60 years, then you're in trouble. It's not that you can't describe such things, you can wrap a Fourier analysis around just about any old data set, but the results will be misleading: If you use the wrong method, then a simple event will look complex, misleading the analyst. If an economic cycle exists and if it tends to long upswing followed by a sudden collapse, then the usual physical methods are going to make a

---

2. I am ignoring the much larger correlation that exists for lags, or cycles, of 120 years, *r* = .85. This correlation may be valid, and may be part of the same phenomenon, as 120 is approximately two times fifty-five. It is based on very few data points compared to the correlation for the shorter, 55 year interval.

mess of the description, describing it not as a funny-shaped cycle but as the sum of a whole set of different sine waves. Borrowed methods are not going to help us very much if we are tracking behavior whose period can vary by twenty percent, whose amplitude can vary, and whose clock can hesitate, advance, and, perhaps, turn backward — *if* that is our reality. So when a phenomenon looks complex, as most behavioral phenomena do, you're faced with a dilemma: You never know whether the phenomenon is really complex or simply misunderstood. You never know: Should I work harder or work smarter? You never know: Just maybe there's a better way.

For example, consider the problem of speech recognition by computer and let me speculate: Do you solve it by working harder or do you solve it by working smarter? It's a curious problem. As early as 1947 one version of the problem — recognizing speech from voice prints — was declared understood, in theory. To solve it, in practice, was a matter of putting the details together, working harder:

> The visible speech development shows that translation from speech to readable pictures is possible, and indicates principles that are essential. . . . The present situation is analogous in a way to the initial accomplishment of airplane flight. When the first plane left the ground for a brief journey through the air, it did not mean that these machines could immediately be made available for general use, but it did mean that man *could* fly and it established certain principles that were eventually built into machines that, after patient development, made possible aviation as it exists today. Similarly, we now know speech can be made visible in a meaningful form because patterns have been produced that people have learned to read. . . . In other words, principles for the translation of speech into meaningful patterns are established, but a considerable amount of work remains before the deaf will benefit by this result even though it does constitute a major advance.[3]

3. From *Visible Speech*, by Ralph Potter, George Kopp, and Harriet Green Kopp, pp. 287-288. Original copyright, 1947 by Bell Telephone Laboratories, quoted from the 1966 re-issue by Dover Publications, Inc.

Two generations later the speech recognition problem lives on. In our generation it is being tackled with computational power that was unimaginable in 1947 — and now the problem is beginning to yield. But you have to ask: Do we really understand the principles? Is it "really" that difficult? The answer, of course, is that no one knows. But there's the challenge, particularly for a scientist who is more interested in understanding the brain than in producing a machine. Consider the problem: If I speak my name, I can speak it slowly or I can blurt it out. If I adopt Fourier coefficients, sines and cosines (which were represented visually by the Potter *et al.* solution) as the description of the two sounds, then the two instances, fast and slow, are different, sorely challenging current models designed to detect what is constant, the sound of my name, amid the difference of sounds. But your brain knows they're the same word. Again, I can speak my name in a base voice or squeak it out in a high falsetto. If I adopt a Fourier description of the sound then the difference will wreak havoc with the coefficients that are supposed to describe it. But your brain suffers no confusion.

The problem looks difficult: What is the same about these sounds? And maybe it is difficult. But maybe the methods are making a simple problem more complex because they are measuring the wrong thing. Maybe the methods are making a simple problem more complex when they're supposed to work the other way around. Does the human brain work harder than our computers, doing Fourier analyses, pattern matching, and context checking at incredible speed, or does it work smarter, "knowing" something we don't?

Whether the problem is speech or social behavior, as it was for Kondratieff, we never know whether or not alternate theories exist (or will exist when we discover them). On the one hand, you have to be suspicious of "classical" techniques based on assumptions that are not obvious or not immediately compelling for human behavior. On the other hand, you have to walk away from analyses that abandon these assumptions without developing some other means of asserting scientific discipline.

So what do we do? If you can not rely on time — 1 year, 2 years, 3 years, 4 years — as a clock for behavior, then how do you analyze behavior that varies over time? With the demur that I am not obliged to answer that question — science tolerates doubt even in the absence of an alternative — I know of two major strategies for analyzing time series without the measure of time. One strategy is to "hide" time. The other is to analyze it. The first strategy makes the measure of time unnecessary by eliminating time from the equations. The second strategy gets the measure of time by inference from the data.

Briefly, lets look at the first strategy before examining the second strategy in detail. Suppose that human time exists but is perfectly free to expand or contract, stop or start, as compared to physical time. And suppose that variables we need to analyze are perfectly sinusoidal in human time except that we have no measure of human time — we have no way of observing this regularity. In this case some regularities can be detected by graphing one variable against the other, omitting time: We observe the combinations of X and Y and simply bypass the direct relation to time. In the simplest case, if X acts like the sine of human time and Y acts like the cosine of human time, then XY combinations

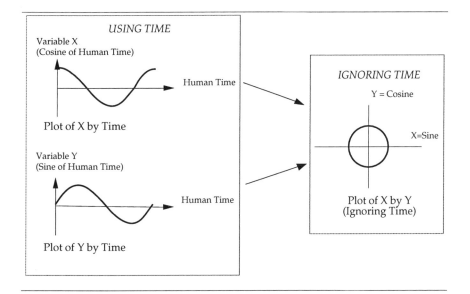

Figure 9.4
Finding XY Regularities, Ignoring Time

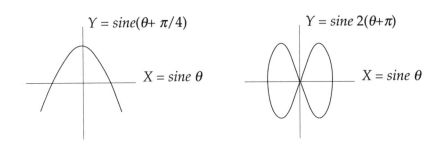

Figure 9.5
Examples of XY Time-Suppressed Plots

must trace the outline of a circle.[4]   If, for example, the mythical "Fu-index" of interest rates is a leading indicator of the "Fa-index" of industrial activity, in exactly the sense that a cosine "leads" a sine, Figure 9.4, then their relation can be verified by plotting Fu against Fa: Whatever "time" it is, the Fu-Fa combination will lie at a fixed distance from the center of the graph. You do not need to measure time.

More-complicated cyclical functions, more complicated than sine and cosine, can leave their characteristic traces in the XY plots, creating ellipses and figure-eights, and multi-lobed figures known as Lissajous figures, Figure 9.5.   The two-variable relations provide information, information that is more circumscribed than we might like, but information without explicit representation of time itself.

I leave it as conjecture that we could develop this first of two strategies into a "human time series" method — without measuring time. In this chapter I want to develop the second strategy: Instead of suppressing the measure of time I want to infer characteristics of time from the data. This requires no conceptual leap forward. It is more of a leap backward because you have to get out from under the cultural burden that tells you what time is, *a priori*. Behaviorally "age" is not a matter of the condition of my cells. Behaviorally "sex" is not a statement about chromosomes. And, behaviorally, "time" is not an astronomical

---

4. Because $X^2 + Y^2 = \sin^2\theta + \cos^2\theta = 1$. The circular plot would provide necessary, though not sufficient evidence of their relation.

statement about the movement of the planet around the sun. For the study of behavior you have to describe such things in the context of behavior. Here I will describe time with respect to behavior, following the same rule. Let me use U.S. stock market data as my behavior, abandoning Kondratieff's numbers.[5]

Table 9.1 records my "behavior" for this study of time series. The data indicate prices of forty-two stocks in sequence for twelve dates, June of 1986 through March of 1989. The forty-two are stocks of large companies in major industries, including many of the "Dow Jones Industrials."[6] Thus Row 1 of Table 9.1 tells you that the price of a share of AMR (American Airlines) started at $54.75 per share in June of '86, rose to $57.50 by June of '87, crashed in the fall of '87 (along with everything else), and then rose again in '88 and '89 (amid buy-out speculation). (These prices are adjusted for stock splits that occurred after June of '86.)

In the context of behavior, the difference between June of '86 and September '86 is the change of prices: AMR was up about 1%; Alcoa was down about 7%. Spread over these forty-two stocks, that's the difference between June and September. Working with all forty-two companies, the contrast is represented by the logs of the ratios, September to June, on the left of Figure 9.6. AMR is recorded at .011 (log of $55.375 divided by $54.75), Alcoa is recorded at −.068 (log of $39.125 divided by $41.875), and so forth. The interval, .079, between the two points indicates the relative rates of change for the two companies' stocks (where the anti-log of the interval .079 corresponds to an 8% relative change or to a ratio of 1.08 — which is the ratio of the two price ratios).

---

5. I set Kondratieff's numbers aside simply because they are not data. The numbers are highly processed derivatives of the data using smoothing functions, and fitted functions, and residuals from fitted functions. As a sociologist, but not an economist, and as a home owner, but not an investor, I can afford to be an agnostic, stating no opinion on the existence of Kondratieff's cycles.

6. Why these forty-two? I have no abstract justification: These are simply stocks that people who watch stocks tend to watch, I make no greater claim for their representativeness of the stock market as a whole. The dates run from June of 1986 to March of 1989, separated by three month intervals. (The price is the Friday closing price for the first week of the month.)

	6/2/86	9/2/86	12/1/86	3/2/87	6/1/87	9/8/87	12/7/87	3/7/88	6/6/88	9/6/88	12/5/88	3/6/89
AMR	54.750	55.375	57.750	58.500	57.250	57.500	29.125	41.250	47.500	46.500	53.875	61.000
Alcoa	41.875	39.125	34.625	44.750	50.875	61.000	45.750	44.625	50.500	50.750	52.875	61.375
AElPw	25.750	28.625	29.125	29.375	26.875	27.000	25.500	27.875	28.250	27.875	27.625	26.375
APresd	24.375	25.750	27.875	34.000	43.500	45.125	23.500	31.500	29.375	33.375	32.375	35.500
AT&T	25.000	24.750	27.375	23.375	25.625	33.000	27.375	28.000	26.500	25.500	29.500	30.500
BethStl	16.250	9.125	5.000	7.000	14.625	18.000	16.250	21.000	20.250	21.250	21.875	24.875
BrlNth	65.875	57.375	61.125	67.750	68.500	73.250	61.125	69.250	70.220	67.266	76.891	82.875
CSX	32.875	31.000	30.875	33.500	33.750	38.250	26.375	29.375	29.250	26.125	31.500	32.250
CdnPac	12.500	11.875	12.625	17.500	17.500	20.375	15.625	18.875	18.875	16.250	16.875	19.500
CaroFt	37.750	37.000	39.250	33.875	31.875	36.000	18.750	21.500	23.125	22.750	25.000	24.375
Chevrn	40.250	47.000	45.750	51.625	58.250	54.250	38.125	45.625	51.750	43.250	45.875	51.750
CitiCorp	59.875	54.750	54.500	53.125	29.125	29.938	17.250	19.750	24.125	24.500	26.375	25.750
CnsFrt	33.375	30.750	32.500	34.125	36.000	37.250	27.000	30.250	27.500	32.000	31.000	29.750
DeltaAr	43.625	41.625	49.750	62.500	55.000	54.375	34.125	46.250	52.125	48.875	49.875	57.625
duPont	87.000	86.875	89.750	105.250	114.625	118.250	80.375	85.750	87.250	81.500	82.375	98.125
EKodak	62.125	56.875	66.750	76.750	78.187	101.532	68.250	62.625	66.750	65.812	68.625	69.000
Exxon	60.125	70.375	69.250	81.500	87.250	95.750	78.500	84.250	91.750	90.250	89.250	89.000
FedExp	60.375	59.750	70.000	63.000	67.875	65.750	37.875	45.375	43.750	45.500	47.000	49.750
FstChic	34.500	28.750	32.250	32.125	29.625	29.000	18.500	23.125	29.125	33.000	29.750	36.125
GTE	34.094	38.531	39.688	40.750	37.750	41.625	35.375	38.375	37.750	42.500	45.375	46.250
GenEl	40.875	38.750	43.250	53.813	53.000	61.250	43.625	43.625	43.000	42.000	45.875	45.000
GMotr	77.375	70.750	71.000	77.500	85.875	86.125	59.000	71.750	78.250	73.250	86.500	84.750

Table 9.1

Goodyr	31.875	34.625	42.750	54.625	68.250	71.875	53.250	59.875	65.250	59.625	47.625	48.125
HouInd	30.000	34.875	36.000	37.500	32.375	32.625	29.250	30.500	31.750	29.000	27.500	27.125
IBM	149.875	140.375	126.625	139.375	160.000	161.125	110.125	115.500	116.000	114.375	120.375	118.250
Intel	25.750	22.500	22.000	36.000	40.266	54.282	36.375	45.750	51.000	42.000	33.000	39.562
IntPap	31.438	35.063	38.938	49.250	46.750	51.375	40.125	43.125	46.375	45.375	44.125	46.375
Merck	98.500	110.375	114.250	161.750	160.750	212.000	157.000	160.000	167.250	173.250	173.625	192.375
MMM	108.250	112.125	114.125	126.875	131.126	156.500	121.750	118.250	127.000	123.500	123.500	134.500
NWA	51.875	48.875	62.125	74.000	67.375	60.125	33.750	43.250	45.500	47.875	52.625	66.875
Navistr	9.500	8.000	5.625	7.000	8.250	7.875	3.750	5.625	7.000	5.375	5.000	6.250
Nflkso	29.469	27.250	28.844	31.813	31.250	35.000	24.500	29.500	27.875	28.750	31.875	34.500
PanAm	6.375	5.375	5.125	4.375	4.875	4.750	3.250	2.875	2.750	2.750	2.625	4.375
PhilMr	68.000	73.875	75.375	86.750	87.250	117.000	89.750	91.250	84.125	94.625	97.625	115.500
ProctG	77.750	76.500	77.750	88.875	92.375	98.500	83.500	79.875	77.500	78.250	84.000	88.000
Ryder	27.750	28.000	33.750	39.750	37.750	37.500	22.625	31.125	28.250	25.000	24.375	26.625
Texaco	33.125	34.375	34.625	34.625	38.000	40.375	35.875	45.250	51.875	45.500	50.125	52.375
USX	21.500	20.625	21.125	24.750	31.375	35.625	30.500	32.125	32.000	27.750	28.750	31.375
UCarb	22.375	22.500	23.000	27.000	29.125	28.500	20.500	24.625	20.500	23.125	25.750	31.000
UnPac	53.625	60.500	66.750	75.875	73.625	78.500	51.875	64.500	65.250	55.625	63.125	68.000
UnTech	49.500	45.750	44.875	53.250	46.000	55.750	31.625	39.875	38.875	36.500	40.000	44.375
WstgE	54.125	58.000	60.250	65.625	61.625	69.500	45.750	51.000	54.250	51.250	52.875	53.625
Intel	25.750	22.500	22.000	36.000	40.266	54.282	36.375	45.750	51.000	42.000	33.000	39.520

Price per Share of Stock for Forty-Two Companies at Twelve Dates

Two different dates can lead to similar results, a very roughly similar interval of time, or to different results, a different interval of time: As an example of similarity, the "line" for September '86 to December '86, in the center of Figure 9.6, yields a similar scale, which can be seen by directly observing the positions of the companies on the two lines or by numerical comparison with the coefficient r that I have maligned in previous lectures, $r = .59$. Thus, the interval June to September is similar to the interval September to December.

As an example of difference, the interval June '87 through September '87 yields a scale, on the right of Figure 9.6 that is unrelated to either of the other two ($r = -.10$ and $r = .10$).

Working with these data, two dates at a time, there is no challenge: You compute the scale and there it is. For any time interval there is a scale of change among stock prices. By contrast, working with these data, all dates combined, is a challenge because we don't know which model works best (distance, distance-squared, and so forth), we don't know whether any model works well, and we don't know whether a model that works well will be simple enough to be useful.

What I do at this point is straight forward. I apply the model in its various forms and see what fits. And what fits best for these data is the distance-squared model. Forgive the candor of these statements: A social scientist of this era is not supposed to be that straight forward. You're not supposed to say "I apply the model and see what fits." No, you're supposed to present an intellectual creation myth that leads inexorably from first principles to your model. You're supposed to present the kind of verbal patter that currently passes for theory in the social sciences, providing in this case a long story about companies and prices.

But that's not the way things work, that's not the way things should work (and, as you will see later, that's not my idea of theory). When you're serious about a calculus you do not start each problem *de novo* like a pleasant little five act fiction, complete with an introduction, a development of character, a crisis, a resolution, and a cleanup. Instead, you lean on your calculus. Consider: Suppose I were a physical scientist who wanted to use "velocity" as part of an equation. How would I think about what I was doing? I would not think about it as "the limit as delta-x approaches zero of the ratio between the change of my function and the

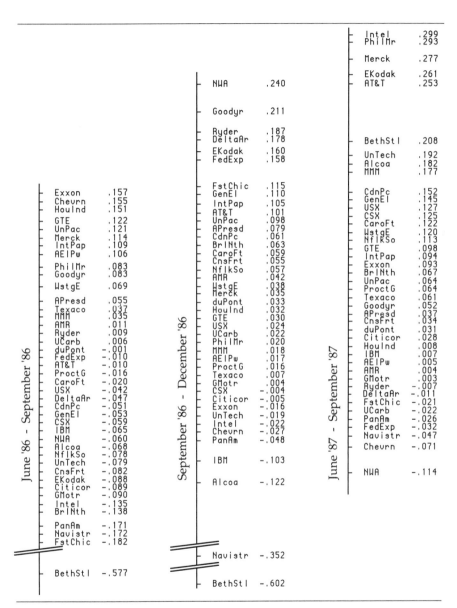

Figure 9.6
Three Examples of Scales Representing Differences Between Two Dates

change of *x* (if the limit exists)." That's what a velocity *is* in the calculus, but you don't have to think your way back to first principles. Instead, you lean on the calculus and think about "velocity." If I wanted to use "acceleration" as part of an equation, I would not think about it as "the limit as delta-*x* approaches zero of the limit as delta-*x* approaches zero of ... " — I don't even want to write that one out. No, you would think about "acceleration." The phrases in quotes are, in fact, what you're using when you use "velocity" and "acceleration," but the power of a calculus is that ideas are built in. If they are good ideas then you don't go back to first principles: You think your way forward to the next step.

So, when I say, "The version of the relational model that works best for stock market prices is the distance-squared model," that is what I'm thinking. I'll admit I'm hiding a little. I'm hiding experience that led me to expect distance-squared, but I tried simple distance — just in case. I'm hiding experience that lead me to a Euclidean definition of "distance," but I tried other definitions. Basically my line of reasoning is exactly what I've shown you: I'm checking whether or not I can tackle this problem within the conceptual framework, the calculus, that worked through previous examples. The version of the relational model that works best for prices is the distance-squared model. In two dimensions, it produces the map in Figure 9.7 and reconstructs the true stock prices with an average error of approximately eight percent.[7] [8]

---

7. I have shifted my error criterion. I used chi-square for the tables of frequencies, but for prices I used squared differences between the logs of the observed and expected values. Roughly, these squared differences of logs correspond to squared percent errors (but the calculations are much easier using logs). Using mean squared deviations of logs, a null model using row effects and column effects has a mean squared error of .02697. Using the same mean squared error of logs criterion, this model yields an error of .00563. In these terms, approximately 80 percent of the remaining error (remaining after the application of a null model) has been removed. I suspect, however, that the more convincing criterion for fit is the non-randomness of the placement of the date points on the graph.

8. The full set of parameters and expected values is presented as Appendix 9.1.

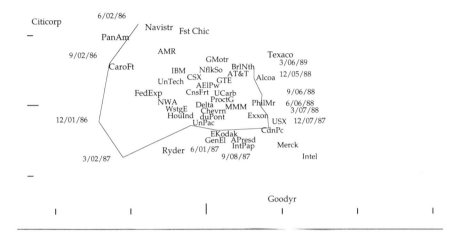

Figure 9.7
Two-Dimensional, Distance-Squared, Euclidean Map of Stock Market Time
Series (Labels Have Been Displaced to Reduce Overprinting of Text.)

What does this thing mean? To the extent that it works and can be credited with meaning anything, what does it say about stocks and time? When you're using the distance-squared model and when you're measuring distance with a Euclidean metric, the map "means" that all of the separate time lines, like the lines displayed in Figure 9.6, can be approximated by lines embedded in a relatively simple two-dimensional space.[9] If you extend the line from June '87 to September '87 in Figure 9.7, you get a line approximating the appropriate line in Figure 9.6, with Bethlehem still at/near one end and Citicorp at the other. Thus the two-dimensional graph characterizes time for *all* pairs of dates (to an approximation).

---

9. Technically, the class of models included under correspondence analysis (see *Metric Scaling: Correspondence Analysis*, by Susan Weller and A. Kimball Romney, 1990) is a special case of the general distance model, applicable for distance-squared with Euclidean distance.

That being said, Figure 9.7 is a remarkable graph, a remarkable description of three years of stock market activity: People who "play" the market can usually tell you a lot of detail about particular companies and particular industries, why they should go up or should go down. But the graph tells you that there is a bedrock of simplicity within the detail of the market. The market as a "whole" (for these stocks) resolved itself into only three directions (only two if you allow that the third direction is just the reverse of the first). For six months, June '86 through December '86 the market "moved" in approximately one direction. Later, for nine months from March '86 through December '87 the market "moved" in another direction. And then for fifteen months, December '87 through March of '88, the market "moved" in another direction, running backward in small steps that reversed the changes of 1986.

Table 9.2 shows the averages: For six months, June 1986 through March 1987, the twenty-one stocks that were high relative to the time line *fell* 3.85% while the twenty-one stocks below the line *rose* by 33.27%.[10] For six months, March 1987 through December 1987, the twenty-two stocks to the left relative to the time line *fell* by 35.4 percent while the twenty stocks to the right fell by only 3.08 percent. For fifteen months, December 1987 through March 1989, the twenty stocks that were low relative to the time line *rose* by only 16.83 percent while the twenty-two stocks above the line rose by 40.41 percent. (For comparison, during the same three periods the average for all forty-two stocks went up 13.20%, down 21.64% and up 28.64%.) The eleven time intervals (between the twelve pairs of consecutive dates) are two dimensional. Time grouped the stocks, or stocks grouped the time, into three broad movements, down, right, and up on the overall map.

---

10. Assuming initially equal investments in each of the twenty-one stocks.

Partition 6/02/86 – 3/02/89

Top (Falling Relative to Bottom)
21 Stocks, Mean Change = -3.85%

AMR	54.75	58.50	6.85%	GTE	34.09	40.75	19.52%
Alcoa	41.87	44.75	6.87%	GMotr	77.37	77.50	.16%
AElPw	25.75	29.37	14.08%	IBM	149.87	139.37	-7.01%
AT&T	25.00	23.37	-6.50%	Navistr	9.50	7.00	-26.32%
BethStl	16.25	7.00	-56.92%	NflkSo	29.47	31.81	7.95%
BrlNth	65.87	67.75	2.85%	PanAm	6.37	4.38	-31.37%
CSX	32.87	33.50	1.90%	PhilMr	68.00	86.75	27.57%
CaroFt	37.75	33.87	-10.26%	Texaco	33.12	34.62	4.53%
Citicorp	59.87	53.13	-11.27%	UCarb	22.37	27.00	20.67%
CnsFrt	33.37	34.12	2.25%	UnTech	49.50	53.25	7.58%
FstChic	34.50	32.12	-6.88%				

Bottom (Rising Relative to Top)
21 stocks, Mean Change = +33.27%

APresd	24.37	34.00	39.49%	IntPap	31.44	49.25	56.66%
CdnPc	12.50	17.50	40.00%	Merck	98.50	161.75	64.21%
Chevrn	40.25	51.62	28.26%	MMM	108.25	126.88	17.21%
DeltaAr	43.62	62.50	43.27%	NWA	51.88	74.00	42.65%
duPont	87.00	105.25	20.98%	ProctG	77.75	88.87	14.31%
EKodak	62.12	76.75	23.54%	Ryder	27.75	39.75	43.24%
Exxon	60.13	81.50	35.55%	USX	21.50	24.75	15.12%
FedExp	60.38	63.00	4.35%	UnPac	53.62	75.87	41.49%
GenEl	40.87	53.81	31.65%	WstgE	54.13	65.63	21.25%
Goodyr	31.87	54.63	71.37%	Intel	25.75	36.00	39.81%
HouInd	30.00	37.50	25.00%				

Table 9.2
Averages on Either Side of Two Partitions of
the Two-Dimensional Map

Partition 3/02/87 to 12/07/87

Left (Falling Relative to Right)
22 Stocks, Mean Change = -35.39%

AMR	58.50	29.12	-50.21%	FstChic	32.12	18.50	-42.41%
AElPw	29.37	25.50	-13.19%	GenEl	53.81	43.62	-18.93%
CSX	33.50	26.37	-21.27%	HouInd	37.50	29.25	-22.00%
CaroFt	33.87	18.75	-44.65%	IBM	139.37	110.13	-20.99%
Chevrn	51.62	38.12	-26.15%	NWA	74.00	33.75	-54.39%
Citicorp	53.13	17.25	-67.53%	Navistr	7.00	3.75	-46.43%
CnsFrt	34.12	27.00	-20.88%	PanAm	4.38	3.25	-25.71%
DeltaAr	62.50	34.12	-45.40%	Ryder	39.75	22.62	-43.08%
duPont	105.25	80.37	-23.63%	UnPac	75.87	51.88	-31.63%
EKodak	76.75	68.25	-11.07%	UnTech	53.25	31.63	-40.61%
FedExp	63.00	37.87	-39.88%	WstgE	65.63	45.75	-30.29%

Right (Rising Relative to Left)
20 Stocks, Mean Change = −3.09%

Alcoa	44.75	45.75	2.23%	IntPap	49.25	40.12	-18.53%
APresd	34.00	23.50	-30.88%	Merck	161.75	157.00	-2.94%
AT&T	23.37	27.37	17.11%	MMM	126.88	121.75	-4.04%
BethStl	7.00	16.25	132.14%	NflkSo	31.81	24.50	-22.99%
BrlNth	67.75	61.12	-9.78%	PhilMr	86.75	89.75	3.46%
CdnPc	17.50	15.63	-10.71%	ProctG	88.87	83.50	-6.05%
Exxon	81.50	78.50	-3.68%	Texaco	34.62	35.87	3.61%
GTE	40.75	35.37	-13.19%	USX	24.75	30.50	23.23%
GMotr	77.50	59.00	-23.87%	UCarb	27.00	20.50	-24.07%
Goodyr	54.63	53.25	-2.52%	Intel	36.00	36.37	1.04%

Table 9.2 — Continued

Partition 12/07/87 to 3/06/89

Top (Rising Relative to Bottom)
22 stocks, Mean Change = 40.41%

AMR	29.12	61.00	109.44%	FstChic	18.50	36.12	95.27%
Alcoa	45.75	61.37	34.15%	GTE	35.37	46.25	30.74%
AElPw	25.50	26.37	3.43%	GMotr	59.00	84.75	43.64%
AT&T	27.37	30.50	11.42%	IBM	110.13	118.25	7.38%
BethStl	16.25	24.87	53.08%	NWA	33.75	66.87	98.15%
BrlNth	61.12	82.25	34.56%	Navistr	3.75	6.25	66.67%
CSX	26.37	32.25	22.27%	NflkSo	24.50	34.50	40.82%
CaroFt	18.75	24.37	30.00%	PanAm	3.25	4.38	34.62%
Citicorp	17.25	25.75	49.28%	Texaco	35.87	52.37	45.99%
CnsFrt	27.00	29.75	10.19%	UCarb	20.50	31.00	51.22%
FedExp	37.87	49.75	31.35%	UnTech	31.63	44.37	40.32%

Bottom (Falling Relative to Top)
20 Stocks, Mean Change = 16.83%

APresd	23.50	35.50	51.06%	IntPap	40.12	46.37	15.58%
CdnPc	15.63	19.50	24.80%	Merck	157.00	192.37	22.53%
Chevrn	38.12	51.75	35.74%	MMM	121.75	134.50	10.47%
DeltaAr	34.12	57.63	68.86%	PhilMr	89.75	115.50	28.69%
duPont	80.37	98.12	22.08%	ProctG	83.50	88.00	5.39%
EKodak	68.25	69.00	1.10%	Ryder	22.62	26.62	17.68%
Exxon	78.50	89.00	13.38%	USX	30.50	31.38	2.87%
GenEl	43.62	45.00	3.15%	UnPac	51.88	68.00	31.08%
Goodyr	53.25	48.12	-9.62%	WstgE	45.75	53.62	17.21%
HouInd	29.25	27.13	-7.26%	Intel	36.37	39.56	8.76%

Table 9.2 — Continued

And what does *that* mean? For the first six months the direction is "down." The period is a movement toward Kodak, General Electric and Union Pacific and away from General Motors, GTE, and Burlington Northern, although I see no verbal gloss that describes stocks that rose relative to those that fell. For the next twelve months the market made a commitment to heavy industry in contrast to transportation: Alcoa, Bethlehem Steel, and General Motors versus AMR, CSX, Carolina Freight, Delta Air, Pan American and Ryder, although the verbal gloss (heavy industry in contrast to transportation) does not cover the large majority of these stocks. Then, tantalizingly, the third period is an almost exact reverse of the first, unwinding the relative advantages of the earlier period.

The numbers are frustratingly mute as to the cause of what they describe, but let me offer my own operationalist view of these graphs, a "theory" of the stock market that only a sociologist could offer: Negatively, I submit that you should not think of the market as some kind of giant scoreboard on the great game of capitalism. Instead think of it positively as a human institution which, like many things human, has two kind of players: big guys and the rest of us. The interesting players are the so-called "institutional investors," the handful of folks who manage 20 or 30 *billion* dollars or more. These are the people who move in a grand historical sweep, reallocating vast amounts of capital from one sector of the economy to another. You and I and a few million other investors may outnumber these players, but they're the ones to watch. And that, I suspect, is what we are watching on that map.

The guys at the top have a difficult job. In a sense they have less information than the rest of us because the manager of a few billion dollars can't shower as much love and attention on each of his dollars as one small player can give to his thirty dollar investment in AT&T. Moreover, even if the big guys could provide the same "attention per dollar" as the rest of us, they would not be free to act. Whatever their financial models tell them, they can't just sell a billion dollars worth of one company's stock because the act of selling would depress the value of the stocks they were trying to sell. The big guys have fewer choices. You and I can have tactics, shifting quickly, but the big guys need strategy, long term.

So, what do they do? What would you do? Are junk bonds dead? Should you retreat to proven performance? Is Detroit dead? Is military spending about to end? Perhaps there are economists, or futurists, who know the answers and aren't talking, but I doubt it. More likely, the ten or twenty biggest players in the market are as much in the dark as you or I. And, as if forecasting weren't tough enough by itself, the big guys can't take risks: By law, the managers of other people's money must be "prudent." And, operationally, "prudent" means that one manager of a billion dollars must act pretty much like every other manager of a billion dollars. They *must* operate within the consensus established by other people like themselves.

That, I speculate, is what we are seeing in these graphs: Lots of day-to-day changes but beneath it all a few large investors moving slowly, playing out their strategies over months and years. The graph traces the consensus, made visible by the long-term flows of capital. If these people believe in a scenario for the future then that scenario will be the dominant force. And, whatever they do, they do it slowly: In fact, these people seem to have New Year's resolutions just like the rest of us, but with considerably more effect. In the New Year of '87 they re-assessed their strategies and the line bent. In the New Year of '88 they re-assessed and the line bent again.

And now for the payoff: Does this method forecast the future? I submit that the answer is obvious, as perversely obvious as the cycles of Kondratieff: Look back at the time line of Figure 9.7. It doesn't take a particularly wild imagination to look at Figure 9.7 and speculate that these data witness three fourths of a cycle, down, across, and up. If these are three phases of a four-phase cycle, then put your money down and place your bet: The next move should be to the left. Buy Carolina Freight. But, of course, you might equally well read these data other-wise, suggesting that the market has one cyclical dimension, down, then up, and one forward-moving dimension, left to right. In this case, place your bet: The next move will be to the right. Buy Bethlehem Steel. And, of course, you might equally well anticipate that the immediate future will imitate the immediate past. In this case buy Bethlehem. The next move will be down. And, of course, you should not be surprised if the time line strikes out in a new direction. Personally, I'd recommend a dart board. Time series analysis makes no promises for the future, no promises expressed or implied.

Appendix 9.1
Numerical Detail and Expected Values for the Map of Figure 9.7

Coordinates and Multipliers

Sorted on first dimension

Corporation	1st Dimension	2nd Dimension	Multiplier
Citicorp	-3.53563	.90705	24.0971
PanAm	-2.07672	.79829	2.2001
CaroFt	-2.00810	.23871	22.858
FedExp	-1.44389	- .32524	29.5439
Navistr	-1.09808	1.23117	7.2417
NWA	- .96684	- .32438	29.4802
AMR	- .94289	.57610	28.9543
UnTech	- .86910	.12478	27.2962
Ryder	- .86177	-1.20522	23.3406
HouInd	- .72897	- .61704	23.9093
IBM	- .66698	.12558	38.8186
WstgE	- .61339	- .40091	30.0184
FstChic	- .57201	1.00542	23.1624
CnsFrt	- .40770	- .05925	24.0101
CSX	- .36303	.08174	23.8226
duPont	- .30162	- .48794	35.2395
UnPac	- .24092	- .72109	31.4314
AElPw	- .18831	- .10865	22.5314
DeltaAr	- .17651	- .37468	28.6099
Chevrn	- .09238	- .36598	28.258
NflkSo	.00591	.19316	23.4165
GenEl	.01460	- .82290	27.8774
UCarb	.01929	- .02950	21.3729
GMotr	.06509	.43954	33.2449
EKodak	.08589	- .77156	32.2664
ProctG	.08657	- .27199	34.1623
GTE	.19880	.11547	26.3817
MMM	.30688	- .32020	38.3557
APresd	.32172	- .71427	23.9714
AT&T	.39086	.19023	22.3747
BrlNth	.47658	.38271	32.0358
IntPap	.50622	- .91398	27.1719
Exxon	.81803	- .46437	33.9406
PhilMr	.89624	- .24928	34.8539
Alcoa	1.04519	.36844	28.2782
CdnPc	1.07751	- .57606	17.0311
Texaco	1.17112	.60499	26.6759
Goodyr	1.17382	-1.84214	29.1479
USX	1.31219	- .45169	22.6083

```
Merck                        1.39139   - .85883   40.5459
Intel                        1.89562   - .84540   25.3415
BethStl                      3.94138     3.30781   16.0361

12/01/86                    -1.98284   - .62560   11.6585
9/02/86                     -1.62838     .71344   11.5206
6/02/86                     -1.42478    1.87085   11.7332
3/02/87                     -1.21746   -1.06873   12.8341
6/01/87                    - .14685   - .47523   13.3013
9/08/87                       .33624   - .59656   14.1652
3/06/89                       .80636     .71458   13.1471
12/05/88                      .84045     .41452   12.2385
9/06/88                       .99488     .09852   11.8917
6/06/88                      1.02184   - .09340   12.1908
3/07/88                      1.15813   - .28372   11.9289
12/07/87                     1.21650   - .62560   10.4387
```

Twelve Observed Prices Followed by Twelve "Expected" Prices, Estimated From the Map

```
12/01/86 9/02/86 6/02/86 3/02/87 6/01/87 9/08/87 3/06/89
12/05/88 9/06/88 6/06/88 3/07/88 12/07/87

Citicorp 1st Coord:   - 3.5356
   54.50    54.75    59.87    53.13    29.12    29.94    25.75
   26.38    24.50    24.12    19.75    17.25
   55.81    54.88    57.79    46.42    35.62    32.52    28.21
   24.92    22.27    22.34    20.47    16.90

PanAm 1st Coord:      - 2.0767
    5.13     5.37     6.38     4.37     4.88     4.75     4.37
    2.63     2.75     2.87     2.87     3.25
    5.29     5.39     5.77     4.92     4.35     4.25     3.89
    3.46     3.17     3.20     2.99     2.50

CaroFt 1st Coord:     - 2.0081
   39.25    37.00    37.75    33.87    31.88    36.00    24.37
   25.00    22.75    23.12    21.50    18.75
   38.67    36.76    37.05    36.99    31.93    31.52    26.94
   24.38    22.73    23.17    21.92    18.66
```

```
FedExp 1st Coord:      - 1.4439
  70.00    59.75    60.37    63.00    67.87    65.75    49.75
  47.00    45.50    43.75    45.37    37.88
  67.98    61.30    58.69    69.39    61.47    62.69    51.20
  47.17    45.12    46.53    44.80    38.97

Navistr 1st Coord:     - 1.0981
   5.62     8.00     9.50     7.00     8.25     7.88     6.25
   5.00     5.37     7.00     5.62     3.75
   6.93     7.71     8.82     6.79     6.80     6.92     6.98
   6.16     5.65     5.66     5.33     4.41

NWA    1st Coord:      -  .9668
  62.13    48.87    51.88    74.00    67.37    60.12    66.87
  52.63    47.87    45.50    43.25    33.75
  61.74    56.59    54.68    65.25    60.69    63.26    52.80
  48.71    46.92    48.44    46.93    40.93

AMR 1st Coord          -  .9429
  57.75    55.38    54.75    58.50    57.25    57.50    61.00
  53.88    46.50    47.50    41.25    29.12
  55.40    57.01    60.87    56.46    55.40    57.21    53.49
  48.10    45.11    45.81    43.68    37.00

UnTech 1st Coord:      -  .8691
  44.87    45.75    49.50    53.25    46.00    55.75    44.37
  40.00    36.50    38.88    39.88    31.63
  47.92    46.67    47.47    50.05    48.22    50.24    44.54
  40.58    38.62    39.56    38.06    32.73

Ryder 1st Coord:       -  .8618
  33.75    28.00    27.75    39.75    37.75    37.50    26.63
  24.37    25.00    28.25    31.13    22.62
  35.53    29.21    25.66    39.27    35.13    37.17    27.92
  26.43    26.18    27.48    27.09    24.32

HouInd 1st Coord:      -  .7290
  36.00    34.87    30.00    37.50    32.38    32.63    27.13
  27.50    29.00    31.75    30.50    29.25
  35.32    31.44    29.55    38.45    36.04    38.12    30.99
  28.86    28.14    29.23    28.56    25.18

IBM 1st Coord:         -  .6670
 126.63   140.37   149.88   139.37   160.00   161.13   118.25
 120.37   114.37   116.00   115.50   110.13
 138.32   135.63   138.53   146.59   144.20   151.62   135.66
 123.69   118.05   120.98   116.72   100.47

WstgE 1st Coord:       -  .6134
  60.25    58.00    54.13    65.63    61.63    69.50    53.63
  52.88    51.25    54.25    51.00    45.75
  61.07    56.09    54.12    66.44    63.79    67.65    56.81
```

```
   52.59    51.04    52.81    51.48    45.09

FstChic 1st Coord:      -   .5720
   32.25    28.75    34.50    32.13    29.62    29.00    36.12
   29.75    33.00    29.12    23.12    18.50
   28.99    31.91    35.98    29.81    31.12    32.53    32.63
   29.02    27.01    27.24    25.90    21.68

CnsFrt 1st Coord:      -   .4077
   32.50    30.75    33.37    34.12    36.00    37.25    29.75
   31.00    32.00    27.50    30.25    27.00
   32.46    31.36    31.55    35.34    35.32    37.67    33.32
   30.57    29.45    30.30    29.43    25.52

CSX 1st Coord:      -   .3630
   30.88    31.00    32.88    33.50    33.75    38.25    32.25
   31.50    26.13    29.25    29.37    26.38
   31.36    30.89    31.59    34.04    34.46    36.76    33.16
   30.30    29.09    29.86    28.94    24.99

duPont 1st Coord:      -   .3016
   89.75    86.87    87.00   105.25   114.62   118.25    98.13
   82.38    81.50    87.25    85.75    80.38
   95.20    87.39    84.01   106.34   104.87   112.94    95.14
   88.38    86.39    89.62    87.84    77.30

UnPac 1st Coord:      -   .2409
   66.75    60.50    53.63    75.88    73.62    78.50    68.00
   63.13    55.62    65.25    64.50    51.88
   66.38    59.27    55.60    75.22    73.66    79.77    65.44
   61.22    60.31    62.84    61.90    54.91

AElPw 1st Coord:      -   .1883
   29.12    28.62    25.75    29.37    26.88    27.00    26.38
   27.63    27.87    28.25    27.87    25.50
   27.13    26.24    26.36    30.07    30.65    33.04    29.33
   26.97    26.10    26.90    26.22    22.81

DeltaAr 1st Coord:      -   .1765
   49.75    41.63    43.62    62.50    55.00    54.38    57.62
   49.88    48.87    52.13    46.25    34.12
   49.09    45.91    44.80    55.07    55.37    59.89    51.46
   47.67    46.52    48.18    47.20    41.41

Chevrn 1st Coord:      -   .0924
   45.75    47.00    40.25    51.63    58.25    54.25    51.75
   45.87    43.25    51.75    45.62    38.13
   46.70    43.85    42.90    52.69    53.46    58.04    50.11
   46.43    45.35    46.97    46.06    40.42

NflkSo 1st Coord:          .0059
   28.84    27.25    29.47    31.81    31.25    35.00    34.50
```

```
31.88    28.75    27.87    29.50    24.50
27.95    28.28    29.48    31.02    32.81    35.56    33.07
30.16    29.01    29.74    28.91    24.93

GenEl 1st Coord:              .0146
43.25    38.75    40.88    53.81    53.00    61.25    45.00
45.87    42.00    43.00    43.62    43.62
45.35    40.32    37.58    52.58    52.55    57.65    47.23
44.35    43.99    45.95    45.50    40.56

UCarb 1st Coord:              .0193
23.00    22.50    22.37    27.00    29.12    28.50    31.00
25.75    23.12    20.50    24.63    20.50
23.25    22.88    23.28    26.08    27.27    29.65    26.83
24.63    23.86    24.56    23.97    20.82

GMotr 1st Coord:              .0651
71.00    70.75    77.38    77.50    85.87    86.12    84.75
86.50    73.25    78.25    71.75    59.00
69.49    72.70    77.98    76.67    82.72    89.64    86.19
78.07    74.61    76.17    73.76    63.11

EKodak 1st Coord:             .0859
66.75    56.87    62.13    76.75    78.19   101.53    69.00
68.62    65.81    66.75    62.63    68.25
67.78    60.80    57.07    78.82    79.58    87.53    72.42
67.91    67.33    70.28    69.59    61.94

ProctG 1st Coord:             .0866
77.75    76.50    77.75    88.87    92.37    98.50    88.00
84.00    78.25    77.50    79.88    83.50
78.81    75.35    74.74    89.74    93.21   101.94    89.76
82.98    81.05    83.83    82.26    72.04

GTE 1st Coord:                .1988
39.69    38.53    34.09    40.75    37.75    41.63    46.25
45.37    42.50    37.75    38.38    35.37
35.92    36.22    37.57    40.56    43.56    47.67    44.28
40.50    39.16    40.23    39.26    33.97

MMM 1st Coord:                .3069
114.12   112.12   108.25   126.88   131.13   156.50   134.50
123.50   123.50   127.00   118.25   121.75
113.06   108.24   107.26   131.09   138.88   153.52   135.71
125.72   123.37   127.78   125.86   110.53

APresd 1st Coord:             .3217
27.87    25.75    24.37    34.00    43.50    45.12    35.50
32.38    33.37    29.37    31.50    23.50
29.30    26.69    25.33    34.58    35.88    39.87    33.58
31.46    31.25    32.60    32.35    28.78
```

```
AT&T 1st Coord:              .3909
  27.38    24.75    25.00    23.37    25.63    33.00    30.50
  29.50    25.50    26.50    28.00    27.38
  23.54    24.12    25.32    26.87    29.55    32.60    30.83
  28.16    27.24    27.96    27.32    23.60

BrlNth 1st Coord:            .4766
  61.13    57.37    65.88    67.75    68.50    73.25    82.25
  76.89    67.27    70.22    69.25    61.13
  57.49    60.55    65.05    65.51    73.49    81.20    78.97
  71.74    69.10    70.69    68.89    59.19

IntPap 1st Coord:            .5062
  38.94    35.06    31.44    49.25    46.75    51.38    46.37
  44.12    45.37    46.37    43.12    40.13
  38.85    34.71    32.34    46.87    49.00    55.04    45.58
  42.98    43.06    45.11    45.03    40.36

Exxon 1st Coord:             .8180
  69.25    70.37    60.12    81.50    87.25    95.75    89.00
  89.25    90.25    91.75    84.25    78.50
  67.98    65.00    64.03    82.31    91.12   103.30    91.76
  85.50    84.90    88.29    87.77    77.66

PhilMr 1st Coord:            .8962
  75.38    73.87    68.00    86.75    87.25   117.00   115.50
  97.62    94.62    84.13    91.25    89.75
  72.14    71.09    71.81    87.06    98.34   111.60   102.20
  94.66    93.50    96.87    96.02    84.40

Alcoa 1st Coord:            1.0452
  34.62    39.13    41.88    44.75    50.88    61.00    61.38
  52.88    50.75    50.50    44.62    45.75
  36.12    38.71    41.98    42.93    50.99    57.85    57.61
  52.45    50.97    52.23    51.29    44.23

CdnPc 1st Coord:            1.0775
  12.63    11.87    12.50    17.50    17.50    20.38    19.50
  16.87    16.25    18.88    18.88    15.63
  13.00    12.37    12.09    16.12    18.21    20.92    18.54
  17.34    17.35    18.09    18.08    16.08

Texaco 1st Coord:           1.1711
  34.62    34.37    33.13    34.62    38.00    40.38    52.38
  50.13    45.50    51.88    45.25    35.87
  29.85    33.11    36.95    35.45    43.23    49.19    50.74
  45.91    44.37    45.29    44.36    37.98

Goodyr 1st Coord:           1.1738
  42.75    34.62    31.88    54.63    68.25    71.87    48.12
  47.62    59.62    65.25    59.87    53.25
  43.70    35.47    30.22    57.56    61.12    71.56    54.37
```

```
 52.76     54.90     58.60     60.00     55.64

USX 1st Coord:              1.3122
 21.13     20.63     21.50     24.75     31.38     35.62     31.38
 28.75     27.75     32.00     32.13     30.50
 21.01     20.46     20.38     26.36     30.71     35.61     32.39
 30.22     30.22     31.45     31.46     27.90

Merck 1st Coord:            1.3914
114.25    110.38     98.50    161.75    160.75    212.00    192.37
173.62    173.25    167.25    160.00    157.00
117.20    108.65    103.61    150.46    172.71    201.94    175.20
165.41    167.62    175.83    177.36    159.47

Intel 1st Coord:            1.8956
 22.00     22.50     25.75     36.00     40.27     54.28     39.56
 33.00     42.00     51.00     45.75     36.37
 24.99     23.61     22.77     33.27     40.24     48.14     42.80
 40.46     41.29     43.35     44.01     39.66

BethStl 1st Coord:          3.9414
  5.00      9.12     16.25      7.00     14.62     18.00     24.88
 21.87     21.25     20.25     21.00     16.25
  5.46      9.39     14.90      7.08     13.35     16.72     27.38
 23.13     21.47     21.00     20.31     16.17
```

10

Real Social Distance

There is a field of sociology in which even the name of the field is embattled. Whatever name you choose, the name itself is a shibboleth identifying your position on numerous issues of hot contention. So I will define the field operationally: I am talking about people's careers as they move (or do not move) from job to job. The moves may be long term, from their parents' place in society to their own, or the moves may be short term, year to year, during the course of a career. Defining the field in terms of data, Table 10.1 is a "mobility table"; that's what I'm talking about. These particular data are a classic of the field, describing occupational mobility, father to son, in Britain circa 1947. The "50" at the upper-right-hand corner of the table indicates that 50 of these men were "Professionals" and were sons of "Professionals," while 16 of these "Professionals" were sons of "Managers."

What's so controversial? Well, start from the key fact of mobility, particularly in the broader context of *social* mobility: The key fact is that not everyone is mobile. Not every new-born babe has equal chance at every job, at every income, at every skill, at every level of prestige and reward. Among these British men, no one made it from the bottom, column 1, to the top, row 1. This *im*mobility is no surprise, but — why not? Why is it unlikely that the son of an unskilled worker will make it to the top?

There are answers, but they are in conflict. If you answer, "Because some people are smart and some aren't," then you are suggesting that success is determined by ability and ability is inherited. Cream rises to the top. If you're at the top then you must be the cream. And if you're at the bottom, well . . . , there's probably a reason. We achieve unequal rewards because individuals have unequal merit. That's one view and it's controversial.

		|	|	FATHERS				
		P	M	I	I	S	S	U
	Professional & Higher Administrative	50	16	12	11	14	0	0
	Managerial &Executive	19	40	35	20	36	6	3
S O N S	Inspectional, Supervisory, &Other Non-Manual-Higher Grade	26	34	65	58	114	19	14
	Inspectional, Supervisory, &Other Non-Manual	8	18	66	110	185	40	32
	Skilled Manual &Routine Non-Manual	18	31	123	223	714	179	141
	Semi-Skilled Manual	6	8	23	64	258	143	91
	Unskilled Manual	2	3	21	32	189	71	106

From D. V. Glass and J. R. Hall, Social Mobility in Britain, in *Social Mobility in Britain*, David Glass, ed., Routledge & Kegan Paul Ltd., London, 1954, p. 183.

Table 10.1
Father-to-Son Occupational Changes in Britain, circa 1947

In sharp dissent, you might say "No. We are unequal because society discriminates against blacks, women, Catholics, and Southerners (in the U.S.), while it recruits white, male Eastern Protestants." This argument suggests that external attributes are the key to success, more so than ability. It suggests that we achieve unequal rewards because the world distributes rewards and imposes punishment according to "who you are," not by what you can accomplish. Society distributes rewards unequally by ascription, not by ability.

Now we've got an argument and that's not the end of it. You can argue from another direction and say, "Success is determined by your relation to capital," implying that society is divided into classes according to control of the means of production and that society prescribes different rules of the game and unequal rewards to different classes. Or, you might argue that "immobility is the result of unequal access to education," suggesting that society is ordered in ranks, but not necessarily divided into classes. The unequal-education argument suggests that inequalities in society are subject to control. Or, you might argue that inequality is inevitable — "If two people ride the same horse, then one rides in front and the other behind. Inequality is inevitable." With that kind of rhetoric you imply that life is tough: We have a status system, it is rank ordered and it is necessary. Your argument suggests that inequality is not subject to control.

Perhaps one of these alternatives "explains" immobility. Perhaps it explains why some people move "up" or stay up and others do not. Perhaps it explains why children from different backgrounds have unequal access to the goodies of society. You can see why the field is embattled: Short of religion, politics or personal slanders, it's hard to imagine a set of issues more likely to provoke intellectual trench warfare. The facts of mobility affect everyone from the individuals who do or do not "make it" to the social theorists, politicians, and ideologues who need to explain why some "made it" and others didn't. So, what are we studying when we study people's careers? Are we studying careers, achievement, occupational attainment, occupational mobility, class, or stratification? Are we measuring the efficacy of education? Are we testing the openness of a market economy? Are we examining the circulation of elites? Are we asking whether society is fair or unjust, getting better or getting worse? Are we seeking remedies? Do we want policy intervention on behalf of the good society? Are we attempting to stabilize the foundations of democracy? That's what's controversial about these data. We will begin to talk about methods that approach these questions later. For now, you have been warned: "Here there be dragons!"[1]

Now, to work. You know the procedure: As always, I want to analyze the variables, not the correlations but the variables, minimizing *a priori* assumptions about their nature. The variables are in this case "occupation," occupation of father and occupation of son. As always, I observe that the data imply that some categories of the variable are "closer" than others. Professionals are closer to Managers than to

---

1. The May 1992 American Journal of Sociology, Volume 97, Number 6, includes a symposium demonstrating both intrinsic measurement, on the part of Steve Rytina of McGill, and the intensity of debate on these issues. In that symposium, see Rytina's "Scaling the Intergenerational Continuity of Occupation: Is Occupational Inheritance Ascriptive after All?" p. 1658, and "Response to Hauser, and Logan and Grusky and Van Rompaey," p. 1729, as well as Robert Hauser and John Logan's "How Not to Measure Intergenerational Persistence," p. 1689, and David Grusky and Stephen Van Rompaey's "The Vertical Scaling of Occupations: Some Cautionary Comment and Reflections."

Unskilled Manual Labor. Next I wonder, rhetorically, whether the categories of the variable might not be organized according to some unknown interval scale. Following up, I specify a negative exponential "law" of distance and solve for the scale. And, as always, I test the scale and the negative exponential against the data. If the fit is good, then I infer support for the negative exponential law of distance and for the scale of categories.

Here, with these data, I propose that the movement is governed by a negative exponential of both social distance and distance squared and, sure enough, the fit to these data is good, in fact, excellent, as shown in Table 10.2. And from that I infer support for the hypothesis that mobility is a lawful function of distance and for the interval scale inferred from the British data. I move through the procedure rapidly because you know it and because there is a limit to the number of times I can repeat the same argument in great detail in each new context.

But with the usual data analysis completed so early in the discussion, let me push the examination further. I want to talk about nothing less than reality, and specifically about the reality of social distance. What is the proper stance toward this thing we are analyzing? Is there a real social distance, something more than the conventions of my numerical technique and more than a metaphor? Does the data analysis create a statistical summary of a complex world, data go in to the computer, summaries come out? Or is it a tool reading through the data to touch a reality? Most of us believe in physical reality: There is something "out there" perfectly capable of stubbing my toe when I walk into it in the middle of the night — regardless of my theories, regardless of my power of positive thinking, regardless of any social construction of reality that I might use to will such unpleasantries out of existence. There is a physical reality.

But is there a social reality? Even social scientists are a lot less sure about social reality. Mostly we don't talk about such questions: This "nature of reality" stuff is a little bit soft and it's risky for a hard-core quantitative social scientist to be seen in the company of such a discussion. But the issue is there. You see it in different attitudes toward the equations we write: There is a difference in attitude between those who claim the title "statistician" or "positivist" and those who

Table of Observed and Expected Values

	Profess	Manager	Inspec	Inspec	Skilled	Semi-sk	Unskill		Inferred Scale
Professio	50 47.2	16 18.7	12 15.0	11 9.3	14 12.1	0 1.8	0 1.0	1.06	Professional
Manageria	19 27.7	40 33.2	35 32.3	20 23.4	36 34.9	6 6.1	3 3.8	.62	Managerial
Inspec Hi	26 20.9	34 30.3	65 76.2	58 63.2	114 106.3	19 21.2	14 14.2	.23	Inspectional Higher
Inspec Lo	8 12.5	18 21.1	66 60.6	110 103.3	185 190.9	40 42.2	32 30.1	-.08	Inspectional Lower
Skilled	18 18.0	31 34.9	123 112.9	223 211.5	714 739.3	179 179.0	141 134.9	-.35	Skilled
Semi-skil	6 4.0	8 8.9	23 32.7	64 67.7	258 259.1	143 124.7	91 99.9	-.65	Semi-skilled
Unskilled	2 1.9	3 4.8	21 19.0	32 41.9	189 169.6	71 86.7	106 104.4	-.83	Unskilled

Chi-square = 33.8337

The "All" multiplier is 102.499. The row multipliers, in order from Professionals to Unskilled Labor, are .556, .568, .833, .961, 2.677, 1.323, and 1.127. The column multipliers, in the same order, are .829, .571, .891, 1.060, 2.694, .920, and .903. The coefficient of distance is standardized to 1 and the coefficient of distance squared is .558. The Chi-square is 33.8337.

Table 10.2
Father-to-Son Occupational Changes with Inferred Scale and Expected Values

identify themselves as "modelers." Roughly, very roughly, and with exceptions, the statisticians are agnostic about this reality stuff. Theirs is a blind-men-and-the-elephant approach. They learn that the elephant is big *and* like a tree trunk *and* like a fan *and* like a rope, and that the attributes are negatively correlated. The next research article will verify that the elephant is also like a truck, when it sits on you, and like a porcupine when you sit on it. Whether or not the elephant exists aside from the increasing collection of data is an issue of no practical significance. For the foreseeable future of their work it suffices to separate the big correlations from the small ones, to mark off the effects that some theory, some day, will have to account for. By contrast, and with exceptions, modelers adopt a different stance. When a modeler specifies a model of social distance and a law relating movement to distance, the hypothesis is that the model describes what's "really" going on out there.

Those of us with quantitative training assume both attitudes, depending on data, subject matter, whim, and a host of imponderables. Personally, I find myself in one camp or the other at different times and I assume that that is a common experience. Sometimes the equations are just simplifying data by organizing it, an accountant's summary. Sometimes the equations model real objects. When I analyze political attitudes or stock market prices I'm taking the first approach, simplifying, looking for regularities. When I'm analyzing the "friends and relations" data or mobility I'm talking about real social distance — not just an accounting system that helps me organize data, but a real social distance: It's not physically visible and I can't lay a ruler down beside it and measure it, but then we're not doing physical science. I use the data analysis to detect it and the equations to specify its form, indirectly from its pattern within the data. That's the handicap of the social sciences.

How do I convince you that there is a social reality? It matters: If you believe that research is data analysis, facts upon facts, correlations piled on correlations, knowledge measured by the height of the pile, then you revel in complexity. Complexity exists because the world is infinitely variable and simplicity is the illusion. More data yield more averages, more correlations, and more research publications without end.

By contrast, if you believe there is a hard-core reality to the way things work, then when the world looks complex you don't believe it, not entirely. If research pursues truth, then part of that complexity is an illusion, a puzzle that looks complex because you haven't figured it out. If you believe in that reality, then your research is a contest with nature; the challenge is to figure it out. If you believe that social research is data analysis then research is a contest with your peers; there is no "it" to be figured.

With the first attitude, the discipline that controls your research is style, the consensus of your competitors. If there is no "it" to be discovered then there is no firmer base from which to judge one analysis versus another. With the second attitude, the discipline that shapes your research is reality, at least in principle. That's my subject, to convince you that social reality, and social distance in particular, are real. It's important because, as scientists, our attitude toward reality makes a tremendous difference in the likelihood that we can achieve a social science.

So, is there a social reality? Broadly stated the only possible answer is "Yes." As a scientist I have to believe there is. I have to search for simplicity or give up on science. But when it gets to specifics, specifically, "Is there a social distance?" then the question gets interesting. I say "Probably, yes." But this is one of those things you can't prove. The best I can do is show you arguments that say to me: There *is* something out there and it is a lot more real than a statistical abstraction. I want to persuade you that there is a social reality and that, by extension, there are answers to the "great" questions surrounding the data on social mobility.

Social Reality, Argument 1: Parsimony
(The Aesthetic of Crystallized Carbon)

If you are thinking in "statistical" mode, mobility data are a great opportunity. Want facts? I can tell you the probability that the son of a "Professional" can sustain the status of his father. Referring to Table 10.1, there were $50 + 19 + 26 + ... + 2 = 129$ such sons of professionals among whom 50 were themselves professionals. So the probability that the son of a "Professional" can sustain the status of his father is $50/129 = .38$. More facts? I can tell you the probability that the son of an "Unskilled" worker, at the other end of the social scale, will inherit his father's status. For him the probability is $106/387 = .27$. More? I can compare the two, comparing Professionals to Unskilled workers with the ratio of these ratios, .38/.27 = 1.41. That tells you that the higher-status group is more likely to "inherit" its parents' positions. More? I can compute this measure of inheritance for each of the seven British occupations and compare each of them to an average for the whole. More, . . . ? I can compare sons of professionals to sons of managers, comparing them with respect to their access to professional jobs. I can effect the same comparison between sons of professionals and sons of supervisors. I can compare sons of professionals to sons of manual laborers, and so forth. More, . . .? Once you get the hang of it, there is no end to the facets worthy of display, and to the comparative descriptions of the people they represent.

There was one paper in the literature whose title captured the essence of this approach. The title was "How to ransack social mobility tables and other kinds of cross-classifications."[2] Goodman started with something simple, a nine number form of these same British data, Table 10.3, reduced to three rows and three columns ("Low," "Middle," and "Upper"). But working these nine numbers, the machinery began to grind, comparing and contrasting, and comparing the comparisons — using various sums and ratios of sums. Eventually the nine numbers combine and contrast to form twenty indices of British mobility. The machinery starts with something simple and revels in its ability to become complex, twenty numbers to describe nine data points. Some of the numbers bear suggestive names like "status inheritance," and "intrinsic status inheritance," Table 10.3. It's intimidating when you think how many numbers it would have taken to describe the original table, seven indices of status inheritance plus seven indices of intrinsic status inheritance, plus . . .

I have to admit that my mind is repelled, aesthetically, by this kind of detail. I like a few parsimonious principles that explain a lot of detail, by implication. I'm repelled when a little bit of data explodes into a plethora of principles. If that were what science demanded of us, well then too bad for my sense of aesthetics. If that were what was necessary, then there would be no choice but to get on with it. But it isn't.

---

2. Leo A. Goodman, "How to ransack social mobility tables and other kinds of cross-classifications," *American Journal of Sociology*, 1969, 75, 1-40.

Interaction Effect	Measured on:	
	British Data	Simulated British Data
U or M fathers and U or M subjects	1.11	1.22
U or M fathers and M or L subjects	.44	.19
U or M fathers and U or L subjects	1.56	1.41
M or L fathers and U or M subjects	.32	.19
M or L fathers and M or L subjects	.72	.82
M or L fathers and U or L subjects	1.03	1.01
U or L fathers and U or M subjects	1.43	1.41
U or L fathers and M or L subjects	1.16	1.02
U or L fathers and U or L subjects	2.59	2.42
Status inheritance of U status (interaction (U,U))	1.67	1.62
Status inheritance of M status (interaction (M,M))	.27	.41
Status inheritance of L status (interaction (L,L))	1.38	1.32
Difference between interaction (U,U) and (M,M)	1.40	1.20
Difference between interaction (M,M) and (L,L)	-1.11	-.91
Difference between interaction (U,U) and (L,L)	.29	.30
Intrinsic status inheritance of U status (with blank (M,M) and (L,L))	1.50	1.41
Intrinsic status inheritance of M status (with blank (U,U) and (L,L))	-.39	-.19
Intrinsic status inheritance of L status (with blank (U,U) and (M,M))	1.10	1.01
Intrinsic net status inheritance of all statuses	2.21	2.52
Fathers and subjects with different statuses (with blank diagonal cells)	.13	.00

U refers to Upper, M to Middle, L to Lower of the categories of Goodman's three-by-three simplification of the full table. Values shown for British data are from Goodman's 1969 article in *AJS*, cited in the text. Values shown for simulated data are from Levine's "Interaction in Father-Son Status Mobility," *Behavioral Science*, Volume 17, 1972, p. 463.

Table 10.3

Ransacking of Glass' British Mobility Data Compared to Ransacking of "Simulated Britain," Using Expected Values for the Full Seven-by-Seven Table Generated by the Distance Model.

You've already seen the opposite approach to these data, modeling, moving from the complex to the simple. The distance equation reduces forty-nine numbers of the full table to twenty, going down.[3] These twenty, *plus* the model, can reproduce the original forty-nine. To get technical for a moment, it reproduces the data with a chi-square of 33.83 using 29 degrees of freedom, a fit that is almost too close: If you went out and drew another sample, repeating the British study entirely, your new sample would probably not be this close to the original.[4] By implication, that's it. That's all we need. It's another case of there being less here than meets the eye: If the distance equation can reconstruct the data, then it can reconstruct or closely reconstruct the nine-number compression of the data, or the twenty-number description of the nine numbers, or the however-many-number description that "ransacking" might require for the full data. If social distance can reproduce the data, then it can nearly reproduce any of the ratios, or ratios of ratios, or logs of ratios of ratios that derive from the data.

One colleague suggests an analogy: Ransacking, he suggests, is conspicuous display, comparable to the way we would treat an exquisite diamond. You can display the diamond against a backdrop of black velvet, flooding it with light that brings out the reflections and diffractions within the diamond. Want to see more? Turn the diamond, change the light, change the backdrop. Want to see more? Turn it again. There is always another variation to be admired, without end. That's one approach. By contrast, a mineralogist would offer us a dissertation on the crystalline structure of carbon. The first approach, the diamond, is capable of infinite variation. The second approach is ascetic and disciplined. It builds a model. It attempts to give you the kernel from which the infinite variations derive.

Why prefer the aesthetic of carbon to the aesthetic of the diamond? I like the beauty of the diamond. I feel good when I see its reflections change in the light. But data are different. When data explode, when they are arranged and re-arranged in dazzling complexity, I get uneasy.

---

3. Six for the interval scale, thirteen independent numbers for the row and column effects, and one for the coefficient of distance-squared.

4. The original work showed chi-square = 29.74 with twenty-nine degrees of freedom, using a continuity correction. See Levine, 1972, cited in Table 10.3.

When I start with nine data points and am asked to think about twenty numbers in order to understand them, that's not beauty, that's confusion. The aesthetic of the diamond appreciates infinite variation. The aesthetic of the carbon appreciates parsimony, conciseness within which there exists the power to comprehend the infinite variation.

When you are working with data, reveling in complexity is wrong. We don't usually use that word in social science. We're usually more laissez-faire: *chacun à son goût*, to each his own method, and so forth. But no, reveling in unnecessary complexity is wrong because it gives the wrong message. The message is "This is complex," and that's wrong. Note, for example, the facet of "intrinsic status inheritance" in Table 10.3: The top and bottom workers experienced "intrinsic status inheritance" with a positive sign, 1.50 and 1.10, while the "middle class" had the opposite experience, −.39, or "intrinsic status *dis*inheritance." This "facet" of the diamond suggests that there's something weird about the British middle class as compared to other classes. That's wrong and you can demonstrate it by simulating Britain and observing what happens — using the equation that matches the British data. In this simulated Britain, using the equation, we know exactly what's going on because I wrote the equation and the equation gave no special attention to the British middle class, no "negative" treatment for them as compared to the top and bottom. Yet, sure enough, the peculiar facet, this negative inheritance, is reproduced by the simulated Britain. I have to conclude that the "facet" is not a property of Britain but a peculiarity of the exact placement of the velvet and the lights — a creation of the ratios and the logs. What needs to be explained here is not the British middle class, but the index that claims they act strangely.[5] That kind of parsimony, reducing the phenomenon to something simple, while retaining the

---

5. When you dig in to the equation you find an interesting choice: All three indices of intrinsic status inheritance use dichotomies featuring one class in comparison to two others. The contrast is categorical, *one* versus *other*. But the reality is ordered. The *one* versus *other* distinction ignores the fact that sometimes the "one" is in the middle and sometimes the "one" is at an end. Now your choice is whether you want to call that a finding or an error, a feature or a bug: Is the middle class different because they are in the middle or is the index an error because it ignores the order?

ability to reproduce what seemed complex — that's power. That kind of parsimony suggests we are closer to a reality, to a crystal of carbon.[6]

Social Reality, Argument 2:
Bumps in the Night

Data analysts expect smooth data: Complexity tends to create that sort of thing. One odd fact gets balanced by another and by another, so that when you look at data for thousands of people you expect a certain amount of homogenizing to have occurred, blurring strong signals. When we get smoothness, we can explain it: Ahah! The smooth phenomenon "must be" some kind of average, with a large number of contributing factors. It's the opposite of smoothness — it's the rough data that demand attention. We attend to data that are sharp where they should be smooth, that have distributions that are pointy where they should be round. Such evidence suggests we're in the presence of something fundamental, not an aggregate.

That's the principle of my second piece of evidence regarding the "reality" of the phenomenon in these mobility data. The data don't behave like an aggregate. To begin, let's look at those upper-class sons. There were 129 sons of Professional & Higher Administrative fathers. Among these sons the most frequent event, the modal event, was to find themselves in top positions. As a human being who lives in this world, I'm not surprised. But as a scientist I submit that that's very strange. We expect that sons of the top fathers will have the best chance of making it to the top, but this is too much. The distribution of sons, how many stayed on top, how many went down a notch, and so forth, has an unusual shape.

Consider: What should the shape be? And let me simulate Britain using several loaded dice. My first loaded die is named "John." John is a professional and John is the father of Junior. When the time comes for

---

6. The aesthetic also guides questions. I don't "believe" the negative coefficient of the distance-squared term. I know: It's there. And it improves the fit. But it feels wrong. My conjecture is that a simpler model is correct, a model without the distance-squared term. My guess is that the negative value of the distance-squared term is covering up the presence of more dimensions in this stratification system, more than one, or of heterogeneity in the definition of the seven categories.

Junior to get a job, we throw the die and whatever comes up determines Junior's fate. Since men like John tend to have sons who go to the top, let's simulate Britain with loaded dice, creating odds in the relation 7 to 6 to 5 to 4 to 3 to 2 to 1, favoring a top-status result for Junior. With these odds, Junior's chances are not bell shaped. His chances are biased and they tend to put him at the top, Figure 10.1a.

Now, my second loaded die is Mary. Mary is John's spouse and if Mary is a little *déclassé*, compared to John, she's going to hurt Junior's chances. But let's give Junior the best he can get, and represent Mary with another die, equally loaded on behalf of her son. Now, when the time comes for Junior to get a job, we throw both dice and the average inheritance determines Junior's fate.

So what happens to Junior? Strangely enough, even in this best case, it hurts. Even though both dice were loaded in his favor, on the average, men like Junior move down. His chance for the top will be better than anyone else's but, on the average, he moves down, Figure 10.1b.

This re-shaping of the distribution is the action of what's known as The Central Limit Theorem. Multiple causes averaged together tend toward bell-shaped, "normal" curves, regardless of the distribution of the separate contributions. This is the homogenizing induced by multiple causes: Even when the odds are all stacked in your favor, multiple causes work against you, inducing a degree of homogeneity. It's counter-intuitive but you can work it out for yourself: There is only one way for John Junior to get an average score of 7: Both dice must come up 7. (Pardon me for using seven-sided dice.) But there are two ways to get an average of 6.5: One comes up 7 while the other comes up 6, or vice versa. And there are three ways to get an average of 6. As a result, both of these lower status outcomes are more likely than staying put with an average score of 7. With multiple causes the modal son moves down.

And Junior has more than Mom and Dad working on his behalf. He goes to the "best" school. And this too works not for him but against him. If there are at least three factors, Mom, Dad, and school, working "on his behalf," then the modal result moves down again, Figure 10.1c.

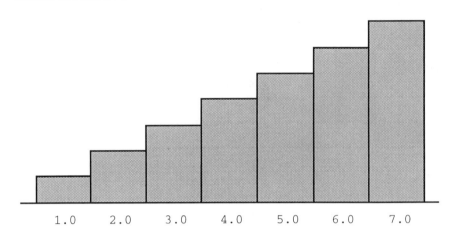

Figure 10.1a: One Loaded Die
Chances of "Making It" to the Top Using One Loaded
Die (with Seven Sides), Loaded in the Ratios 7 to 6 to 5 to 4 to 3 to 2 to 1

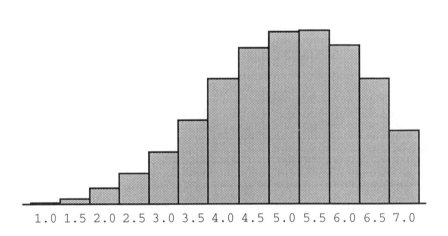

Figure 10.1b: Two Loaded Dice
Chances of "Making It" to the Top Using Two Loaded
Dice (with Seven Sides), Loaded in the Ratios 7 to 6 to 5 to 4 to 3 to 2 to 1

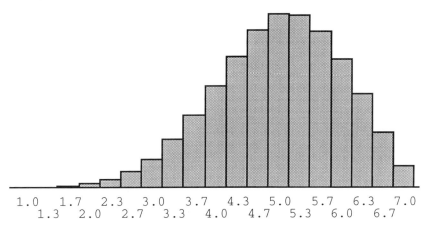

1.0   1.7   2.3   3.0   3.7   4.3   5.0   5.7   6.3   7.0
  1.3   2.0   2.7   3.3   4.0   4.7   5.3   6.0   6.7

Figure 10.1c: Three Loaded Dice
Chances of "Making It" to the Top Using Three Loaded
Dice (with Seven Sides), Loaded in the Ratios 7 to 6 to 5 to 4 to 3 to 2 to 1.

You see my point: With complex situations, with multiple contributing "causes," you tend to get bell-shaped results. By this kind of reasoning (and from our experience with data), sociologists expect bland bell-shaped results. But now look at the data: In fact, 50 out of 129 sons go to the top. By far, going to the top is the modal event.

You can, of course, argue with my argument for John. If I load the dice more strongly, then two or even three dice can be forced to produce "success" as the modal event for sons like John. But the tendency toward the bell shape should persist if we are dealing with a complicated event. Remember that these three dice, John, Mary, and the school, do not exhaust the "causes" of a son's career and even multiple causal models in the literature tend to explain less than half of the variance in mobility.[7] Each new hurdle for Junior is going to tend to smooth the curve.[8] And

---

7. See Blau and Duncan's original *American Occupational Structure,* New York, Wiley, 1967.

8. The situation is actually worse than it looks. The numbers in the British data are also heavily influenced by the numbers of jobs. Suppose we consider the number of sons making it to each status divided by the number who would make it if the only consideration were the number of jobs available. Of the 3,497 jobs, in total, 3.7% of the fathers' jobs were professional and 2.9% of the sons' were professional, so we would expect

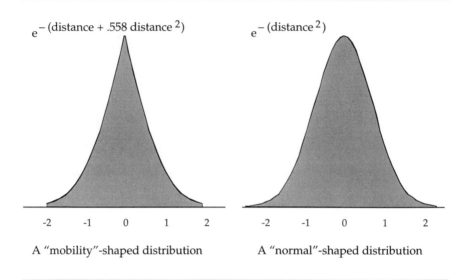

$$e^{-(\text{distance} + .558 \text{ distance}^2)} \qquad\qquad e^{-(\text{distance}^2)}$$

A "mobility"-shaped distribution   A "normal"-shaped distribution

Figure 10.2
Shape of the Distribution That "Fits" the Data, Left, Shown in Contrast to the
Shape of the Theoretical Gaussian, or "Normal," Distribution, Right

smooth curves are not the ones that fit these data. A smooth, "normal,"
distribution, the end result of shaping by the central limit theorem, is
shown on the right of Figure 10.2 where, by contrast, the "sharp"
negative exponential that fits the data, $e^{-(\text{distance} + .558 \text{ distance}^2)}$, is shown
on the left.

3.7% of 2.9% which is 3.80 of the sons (approximately 4) to have
professional status fathers and professional status jobs. The actual
number is 50, for a ratio of 50/3.80 = 13.16. For all 49 combinations, here
are the ratios (in the same order as for Table 1):

13.16	3.62	1.18	.72	.31	.00	.00
3.24	5.86	2.23	.85	.52	.29	.17
2.14	2.40	2.00	1.19	.80	.44	.38
.47	.91	1.46	1.62	.93	.67	.63
.34	.51	.87	1.05	1.16	.96	.89
.27	.31	.39	.73	1.01	.18	1.39
.13	.16	.50	.51	1.03	1.28	2.26

These ratios show that the numbers for the top-status men's sons are
even more unusual than they appeared. And now look at the lowest-
status men's sons: Too many of them stay on the bottom.

There is a subtle visual difference. One is sharp where the other is round. One has a single bend (on each side) where the other has a double bend, first concave and then convex. And, visually, the combined distance/distance-squared distribution on the left "looks like" a simple distance curve. Can we detect such subtle differences and use them? It appears that we can: If I limit the distance model to distance squared, corresponding to the shape on the right, I estimate a chi-squared error equal to 80.38. If I use simple distance, I estimate a chi-squared error equal to 50.82. And using the full model, using both, as shown on the left, I get a chi-squared error equal to 33.83.[9] The "pointy" curve matches the data with roughly half the error of the smooth "normal" curve: There is a recalcitrant bump in these data that refuses to be smoothed over, something that multiple regression or multiple-cause models are not likely to explain. And, by contrast, assuming the presence of social distance, the distance model is able to reproduce the data.

Social Reality, Argument 3:
Generality (Time Series)

I've argued the plausibility of social distance based on the parsimony it offers — it explains or "explains away" some otherwise complex results. I've argued the plausibility of social distance based on the irregularities that would not be created by a simple statistical averaging of complicated causes but which are predicted by the model. My third argument is another parsimony argument, observing what happens when I generalize the distance model to a broader problem. The broader problem is time series: People not only change jobs, they change jobs again and again. How do we describe mobility as a series of movements?

The most sophisticated modeling attempt to answer that question more or less exhausted itself, perhaps twenty years ago. At that time the thinking was that a series of moves *had to be* governed by something called a Markov process. But, empirically, it was hard to demonstrate a success with the method: Simple versions of the model failed to fit the

---

9. The degrees of freedom in each case are approximately the same, at 28, 28, and 29 degrees of freedom, respectively.

	Prf	Prf	Prp	MP	Clr	Sal	Sal	Crf	Crf	Crf	Op	Op	Srv	Lb	Lb	Fm	Fm
Professionals, Self-E	37	6	0	4	0	0	0	0	0	0	0	0	0	0	0	0	0
Professionals, Salaried	1	244	0	31	8	1	0	5	1	5	2	1	1	1	1	1	0
Proprietors–Commerce	0	0	64	14	1	6	3	0	1	1	0	3	3	0	0	4	2
M, O, P – Other	2	18	10	291	17	9	20	8	10	15	5	11	2	2	1	1	0
Clerical	0	12	0	10	150	1	3	2	0	7	10	4	1	3	4	1	0
Sales – Retail	0	0	3	6	1	40	1	1	0	1	0	1	1	0	0	1	0
Sales – Other	0	1	0	13	2	4	68	0	1	0	4	1	1	0	0	0	0
Craft – Manufacturing	0	9	1	10	5	0	1	229	8	11	28	6	8	3	1	0	0
Craft – Construction	1	3	1	5	3	0	1	6	165	11	2	5	3	1	8	4	1
Craft – Other	0	4	1	14	9	1	2	13	9	233	3	11	4	3	11	0	1
Operatives – Manuf.	0	2	1	4	6	1	1	34	3	3	328	11	9	18	9	2	1
Operatives – Other	0	5	2	9	6	2	2	1	9	20	13	240	6	3	24	0	4
Service	0	2	1	9	8	3	0	5	0	11	11	5	257	3	10	0	1
Labor – Manufacturing	0	1	0	1	3	0	0	4	0	4	24	1	8	57	5	0	0
Labor – Other	0	0	1	4	3	0	0	2	13	16	7	28	16	10	157	1	1
Farmers	0	2	2	1	1	1	1	4	3	2	1	4	4	2	5	230	10
Farm Labor	0	0	0	0	1	0	0	3	2	1	0	5	2	2	11	2	86

The label for Row 4 is Managers, Operators, and Proprietors, in industry "Other," that is not-retail, not commerce, not manufacturing or construction

Table 10.4

U.S. Male Occupational Mobility, 1967-1969, Parnes data, *op. cit.*, using categories modified by Levine and Spadaro, *op. cit.*

data, while complex versions of the model were too complex to be tested — you couldn't find a data set large enough for an application of the model. At that point the research more or less died.[10]

Now, let's re-open the problem: Let's take a look at a series of mobility tables. Leaving the father-to-son British data, let's look at U.S. data from the late 1960's and early 1970's. Table 10.4 shows one of three tables for *one* set of men: This table tabulates their mobility between 1967 and 1969 and the remaining data for these men extends to their mobility between 1967 and 1971, and their mobility between 1967 and 1973 (using the National Longitudinal Survey, Parnes 1975 re-analyzed by Levine and Spadaro, 1988).[11] If you "believe" in an underlying distance, and if mobility rates were roughly constant during this period, then what *should* a comparison of these three tables disclose?[12] Generally it should disclose that people moved more in four years than they did in two years, more in six years than they did in four. Empirically there will be more mobility and analytically, because of the increased mobility, the distances will appear to have shrunk.

That's what should happen according to the distance model and, approximately, that is what happens: We can analyze three tables, the two-year table, the four-year table, and the six-year table, parsimoniously with only one set of distances, shrinking the distances uniformly to account for the increased mobility in the long-term tables. The two-year map is converted, approximately, into the four-year map by multiplying all coordinates by .90 (estimated from the data), and the two-year map is converted to the six-year map by multiplying all coordinates by .81. Appendix 10.1 shows the observed and expected values using the one

---

10. See David McFarland's article "Intragenerational Social Mobility as a Markov Process," *American Sociological Review* 35, 1970, pages 463-476.

11. Referring to Herbert S. Parnes, *et al.*, *National Longitudinal Survey: 1966-73*, Ohio State University, Center for Human Resource Research, Columbus, 1975 and to Joel H. Levine and John Spadaro, "Occupational mobility: a structural model," in *Social Structures*, edited by Barry Wellman and S. D. Berkowitz, Cambridge University Press, Cambridge, 1988.

12. In fact, the U.S. economy was in a decline during the early 1970's.

map for all three time intervals.[13] [14] If that seems obvious to you: "Yes, of course. If you have more mobility it will look like the distances are shorter," then that's good — you are beginning to accept the distance model. It *is* obvious, but suffice it to say that other "obvious" solutions have not worked.[15]

So, I'm arguing that we're on the track of real social distance: It is parsimonious, in so far as it can explain away complicated phenomena like "intrinsic status inheritance." It accounts for data that are not "normal," presenting distributions that suggest a basic phenomenon, not the average of other processes. And it generalizes to a time series of mobility tables by a simple proportional change in the scale of effective distances.

Building a Model of Occupational Mobility: An Invitation

Does this give us the "compleat model of mobility"? Not likely. It opens a battery of questions that it will take an army of students to dispatch: Divide these men by age and the effects will certainly change. Divide these men by race — the effects will certainly change. Compare these men to women — the careers will be different. Add unemployment to the model. That will demand a new conceptual apparatus. For policy: What is the effect of creating one kind of job while closing others?

---

13. Technically, if these are interval scales, then these are all the same scale: The thing that defines an interval scale is the relative magnitudes of the intervals, not their absolute sizes. The fact that we are talking about magnitudes implies that we're edging toward something stronger than an interval scale.

14. These maps are the best two-dimensional maps, choosing to show *two* dimensions because two are easy to draw on a flat piece of paper. The best map appears to require four dimensions. In four dimensions, the map "fits" and one map, plus a scale factor that shrinks it, can be used to describe all three tables simultaneously (Levine and Spadaro, *op. cit.*).

15. The other "obvious" model is the Markov chain model, discussed briefly in Appendix 10.2.

All of these questions are open, but among all questions, one takes precedence and I invite you to help solve it. It's difficult to solve but accessible to anyone with a small computer. Once again, I direct your attention to the variable and ask: "What is an occupation?"

Consider my own occupation. I suspect that I, personally, have a unique occupation, at least in detail. As Mr. Rogers assures me, I am special, as is every other person in the world. Nowhere in the world is there a job that matches my particular teaching responsibilities, my particular profession, and the particulars of my administrative, scientific, and professional responsibilities. But there are times when uniqueness is too much of a burden: As a scientist studying such things I'm in big trouble if every last person in the world is unique, with a unique and special "occupation." That being said, I'm willing to concede that there are a few jobs in the world that are very much like mine and that are, "for all practical purposes," the same.

That's an occupation: It is a set of jobs that are, "for all practical purposes," the same. An occupation is an equivalence class. But which jobs are they? Which details are irrelevant and which ones are important? I am a sociologist. I work for an educational institution. I am salaried. Which is more important? Which characteristic exercises the greatest constraint on my present and my future? Is it the kind of work I do (sociology), is it my industry (education), or is it my relation to the means of production (I do not own the university)? In the process of defining "occupation" you have to figure out how the world works, you have to figure out what's important and what's not.

That is the fundamental problem in mobility research, fundamental because I can't even set up the data for other questions until I have figured out the categories that constitute the right way of dividing up occupations. For example, one of the classics of the field defined similarity by industry. Two people were in the same category if they worked in the same industry. Thus, if two people were both employed in "Service, Amusement, and Professions," they were treated as members of the same category. Never mind that one of them was the president of a bank (Service) while one of them was cleaning up slop in a circus (Amusement): Once the categories were defined, all such people were treated as equal. The data I refer to were used in Blumen, Kogen, and McCarthy's *Social Mobility as a Probability Process*, and there was very good reason for this nonsense, at least on the part of the analysts: That's the way the data came. Data were from the predecessor of the U.S. Social Security System, and that is the way workers were classified, by industry. Given the choice between using these categories and doing nothing at all, I too would have accepted the categories. But it is certain that Blumen, Kogen, and McCarthy's analysis suffered under an extreme handicap once they accepted these categories.

Here, in these three tables for U.S. mobility, I've defined equivalence by a combination of occupation, industry and whether or not the worker is self-employed.[16] But we should be able to do better. Here, for example, "Sales" includes:[17]

    380 ADVERTISING AGENTS AND SALESMEN
    381 AUCTIONEERS
    382 DEMONSTRATORS
    383 HUCKSTERS AND PEDDLERS
    385 INSURANCE AGENTS, BROKERS, AND UNDERWRITERS
    390 NEWSBOYS
    393 REAL ESTATE AGENTS AND BROKERS
    394 SALESMEN AND SALES CLERKS NOT ELSEWHERE
         CLASSIFIED
    395 STOCK AND BOND SALESMEN

And here is where we get back to "the big issues." For example, should I distinguish between sales workers who are salaried and those who are self-employed? Does their relation to the means of production significantly affect their careers (assuming that the self-employed own their means of production)? You answer that big question by experimenting with the categories, changing the criteria of categorical equivalence. If two categories differ only on the criterion "Salaried" versus "Self-Employed," and if the difference is important, then the two categories will be distant on the map. More generally, consider: If there are distances "out there," unknown to us but ready to be discovered, then what happens if I make a mistake in the categories? What happens

---

16. Following the standard procedure, while introducing a few changes in the specific combinations that build these categories — again following Blau and Duncan, *op. cit.*, and Levine and Spadaro, *op. cit.*

17. The three digits shown on each line are U.S. Census codes for these occupations.

if I draw the wrong categorical boundaries? Using the distance model two things *should* happen at once: First, the error in the categories should show up as error in fit. (A bad category has no location because it combines dissimilar things.) Second, the error in the categories should cause the distances to shrink. (The "wrong" classification reduces the detectable differences among categories.) These are the tools we have to work with, experimenting with the categories: Good categories will be marked by small errors and large distances.

So I invite you to help find good categories. The National Longitudinal Survey provides ample raw material. Occupation is described in great detail, with a three-digit code. Industry is described in similar detail. And we also have "class" defined, roughly, as salaried versus self-employed versus government. Altogether, with the data for 1967 to 1969 we can distinguish approximately 2,000 different jobs, combining distinctions by occupation, by industry, and by class. So does it matter whether or not a person is self-employed? Playing with the categories, you can check. Sometimes it matters and sometimes it doesn't. For example, it is conventional to distinguish whether trade workers are salaried or self-employed.[18] But, playing with the categories, it appears that people in trade cross this barrier, from self-employed to salaried and back, with comparative ease. The more important barrier is between wholesale trade and retail trade.[19]

That's one of thousands of distinctions that can be checked in the process of defining good categories, improving the fit. And it is an active area of current research, precisely because the mathematics now lets us get to the substance of the problem.[20] Do we need to keep track of race, sex, education, and family background? What attributes mark off whether people are the same or different, sociologically? Which divisions count, which ones don't? These are the questions you tackle

---

18. Blau and Duncan, *op. cit.*

19. Levine and Spadaro, *op. cit.*

20. See Ronald Breiger's "The Social Class Structure of Occupational Mobility," *American Journal of Sociology*, Volume 87, 1981, pages 578 through 611 and the articles and introduction in *Social Mobility and Social Structure*, edited by Ronald L. Breiger, Cambridge University Press, 1990.

when you choose the categories that define the rows and columns for your mobility table.

And there will be answers. The results should be interesting and they should be controversial because they will support some claims and deny others. No matter what personal background, ideological predilections, or random guesses you bring to the process of making these decisions, reality will get the last word. What is the American occupational structure? Some answers will be right, others will be wrong, some good, some bad. The answers are an "exercise for the reader," and for me.

Appendix 10.1
Three U.S. Mobility Tables, in Time Series, for One Set of Men

The three tables are for mobility between 1967 to 1969, between 1967 to 1971, and between 1967 to 1973. Numbers show the data, the expected values generated from the distance model, and the parameters used by the model

	Prof	Prof	Prop	MOP	Clr	Sal	Sal	Craf	Craf	Craf	Oper	Opr	Srv	Lab	Lab	Frm	Frm
Prof SelfEmp	37/36	6/4	0/1	4/2	0/1	0/1	0/1	0/1	0/2	0/1	0/1	0/1	0/1	0/0	0/1	0/1	0/0
Prof Salaried	1/2	244/250	0/1	31/21	8/9	1/2	0/4	5/5	1/2	5/4	2/3	1/3	1/2	1/1	1/1	1/1	0/1
Proprietors Commerce	0/0	0/2	64/65	14/13	1/3	6/7	3/3	0/1	1/3	1/3	0/1	3/2	3/3	0/1	0/3	4/1	2/1
Managers,Op Prop.Other	2/1	18/22	10/8	291/310	17/12	9/7	20/15	8/8	10/7	15/16	5/5	11/8	2/5	2/2	1/3	1/1	0/1
Clerical	0/0	12/9	0/1	10/11	150/154	1/2	3/2	2/5	0/3	7/7	10/6	4/6	1/5	3/2	4/2	1/1	0/1
Sales Retail	0/0	0/1	3/3	6/4	1/1	40/41	1/1	1/1	0/1	1/1	0/1	1/1	1/1	0/0	0/0	0/0	0/0
Sales Other	0/0	1/4	0/2	13/14	2/3	4/2	68/70	0/1	1/1	0/2	4/1	1/1	1/1	0/0	0/1	1/0	0/0
Craft Manu-facturing	0/0	9/5	1/1	10/8	5/6	0/1	1/1	229/238	8/5	11/11	28/29	6/7	8/6	3/4	1/3	0/1	0/1

	1	2	3	4	5	6	7	8	9	10	11	12	13	14	15	16	17
Craft Construction	1/1	3/2	1/2	5/7	3/3	0/1	1/1	6/4	165/162	11/14	2/2	5/8	3/3	1/1	8/8	4/3	1/2
Craft Other	0/0	4/4	4/2	14/15	9/7	1/1	2/2	13/10	9/13	233/237	3/4	11/13	4/7	3/2	11/9	0/1	1/1
Operatives Manufctrng	0/0	2/3	1/1	4/5	6/7	1/1	1/1	34/28	3/3	3/4	328/332	11/11	9/9	18/19	9/7	2/2	1/2
Operatives Other	0/0	5/3	2/2	9/10	6/8	2/1	2/1	1/8	9/10	20/18	13/14	240/239	6/8	3/4	24/20	0/3	4/3
Service	0/0	2/2	1/2	9/6	8/6	3/3	0/2	5/6	0/3	11/8	11/11	5/7	257/253	3/7	10/11	0/2	1/2
Labor Manufacturing	0/0	1/1	0/0	1/2	3/2	0/0	0/1	4/4	0/1	4/3	24/21	1/3	8/7	57/59	5/6	0/1	0/1
Labor Other	0/0	0/2	1/2	4/4	3/4	0/1	0/1	2/4	13/10	16/13	7/9	28/22	16/13	10/7	157/168	1/4	1/4
Farmers	0/1	2/2	2/2	1/2	1/2	1/1	1/1	4/2	3/6	2/2	1/4	4/5	4/4	2/1	5/6	230/229	10/7
Farm Labor	0/0	0/1	0/1	0/2	1/1	0/1	0/1	3/1	2/3	1/2	0/3	5/4	2/3	2/2	11/6	2/6	86/87

Time Series Mobility: 1967-1969, Frequencies and Expected Values

	Prof	Prof	Prop	MO	Cler	Sale	Sale	Craf	Craf	Craf	Craf	Oper	Oper	Serv	Labo	Labo	Farm	Farm
Prof SelfEmp	33 / 34.	7 / 4.	0 / 1.	3 / 3.	0 / 1.	1 / 0.	0 / 1.	0 / 1.	0 / 2.	1 / 1.	0 / 1.	0 / 1.	0 / 1.	0 / 0.	0 / 1.	0 / 1.	0 / 1.	0 / 0.
Prof Salaried	3 / 2.	208 / 218.	2 / 2.	28 / 25.	8 / 9.	1 / 2.	1 / 4.	5 / 5.	0 / 2.	7 / 5.	3 / 2.	2 / 3.	3 / 2.	1 / 1.	1 / 1.	3 / 1.	3 / 1.	0 / 1.
Proprietors Commerce	0 / 1.	1 / 3.	62 / 59.	19 / 15.	0 / 3.	7 / 6.	2 / 3.	0 / 1.	2 / 4.	1 / 4.	1 / 1.	1 / 2.	2 / 4.	1 / 0.	0 / 3.	2 / 1.	2 / 1.	2 / 1.
Managers, Op Prop. Other	1 / 1.	20 / 23.	8 / 9.	280 / 298.	13 / 12.	10 / 6.	20 / 15.	9 / 9.	11 / 7.	20 / 17.	4 / 4.	8 / 9.	7 / 6.	1 / 1.	3 / 3.	0 / 1.	2 / 1.	1 / 1.
Clerical	0 / 1.	13 / 10.	1 / 2.	14 / 14.	130 / 135.	1 / 2.	3 / 3.	7 / 6.	1 / 3.	6 / 8.	8 / 6.	5 / 7.	1 / 7.	1 / 2.	8 / 3.	0 / 1.	0 / 1.	0 / 1.
Sales Retail	1 / 0.	0 / 2.	2 / 4.	5 / 7.	0 / 2.	34 / 38.	2 / 2.	0 / 1.	0 / 1.	0 / 1.	0 / 1.	4 / 1.	2 / 2.	1 / 0.	0 / 1.	0 / 0.	0 / 0.	0 / 0.
Sales Other	1 / 0.	2 / 5.	2 / 2.	15 / 17.	2 / 3.	2 / 2.	65 / 62.	1 / 1.	1 / 1.	1 / 2.	3 / 1.	1 / 1.	0 / 2.	0 / 0.	0 / 1.	0 / 0.	1 / 0.	0 / 0.
Craft Manufacturing	0 / 0.	7 / 7.	1 / 1.	14 / 12.	4 / 7.	1 / 1.	0 / 2.	231 / 228.	8 / 6.	12 / 14.	29 / 29.	7 / 10.	9 / 8.	3 / 4.	4 / 4.	3 / 4.	0 / 1.	0 / 1.

Table values shown as observed frequency (top) and expected value (bottom).

Occupation	1	2	3	4	5	6	7	8	9	10	11	12	13	14	15	16	17
Craft Construction	0 / 1.	2 / 2.	1 / 3.	16 / 9.	1 / 4.	0 / 1.	1 / 1.	4 / 5.	140 / 146.	16 / 17.	1 / 3.	5 / 11.	4 / 4.	0 / 1.	12 / 10.	6 / 3.	2 / 2.
Craft Other	0 / 1.	5 / 5.	5 / 3.	20 / 20.	7 / 8.	2 / 1.	0 / 2.	10 / 11.	17 / 15.	221 / 224.	2 / 4.	18 / 17.	7 / 9.	1 / 2.	11 / 11.	0 / 1.	1 / 1.
Operatives Manufctrng	0 / 1.	3 / 4.	1 / 1.	8 / 8.	8 / 10.	0 / 1.	0 / 2.	38 / 37.	3 / 3.	22 / 6.	313 / 314.	19 / 18.	12 / 15.	20 / 20.	9 / 11.	2 / 3.	4 / 3.
Operatives Other	0 / 1.	4 / 4.	3 / 2.	12 / 12.	13 / 9.	1 / 1.	1 / 2.	3 / 9.	6 / 11.	23 / 20.	11 / 13.	243 / 238.	9 / 10.	1 / 3.	21 / 24.	2 / 3.	4 / 4.
Service	0 / 0.	7 / 2.	1 / 3.	12 / 7.	8 / 7.	2 / 3.	0 / 2.	5 / 7.	3 / 3.	7 / 10.	8 / 10.	9 / 9.	244 / 246.	2 / 6.	12 / 13.	0 / 3.	1 / 3.
Labor Manufacturing	0 / 0.	1 / 1.	0 / 1.	2 / 3.	4 / 3.	0 / 0.	0 / 1.	7 / 5.	0 / 1.	2 / 4.	25 / 22.	2 / 5.	8 / 10.	46 / 49.	10 / 8.	2 / 1.	0 / 2.
Labor Other	0 / 0.	3 / 2.	2 / 3.	3 / 5.	5 / 4.	0 / 1.	1 / 1.	1 / 4.	17 / 11.	12 / 15.	8 / 9.	28 / 27.	23 / 16.	7 / 6.	157 / 166.	1 / 5.	5 / 6.
Farmers	0 / 1.	1 / 2.	2 / 2.	2 / 3.	4 / 2.	1 / 1.	0 / 1.	3 / 2.	5 / 7.	1 / 3.	1 / 4.	9 / 7.	8 / 6.	4 / 1.	5 / 8.	215 / 218.	10 / 10.
Farm Labor	0 / 0.	0 / 1.	0 / 2.	0 / 2.	3 / 1.	0 / 1.	0 / 1.	0 / 1.	1 / 3.	0 / 2.	3 / 3.	2 / 6.	3 / 4.	2 / 2.	12 / 8.	5 / 7.	93 / 91.

Time Series Mobility: 1967-1971, Frequencies and Expected Values

	Prof	Prof	Prop	MO	Cler	Sale	Sale	Craf	Craf	Craf	Oper	Oper	Serv	Labo	Labo	Farm	Farm
Prof SelfEmp	28	10	0	2	0	1	0	1	0	0	0	0	0	0	0	0	0
	31.	5.	1.	3.	1.	1.	1.	1.	2.	1.	1.	1.	1.	0.	1.	1.	0.
Prof Salaried	4	210	2	30	11	0	2	6	0	3	0	2	2	1	1	4	0
	3.	209.	2.	29.	13.	3.	6.	6.	2.	5.	3.	4.	3.	1.	1.	1.	1.
Proprietors Commerce	0	1	57	11	0	6	2	2	3	3	0	2	3	1	0	3	2
	1.	3.	51.	14.	3.	6.	4.	1.	4.	3.	1.	3.	4.	0.	3.	1.	1.
Managers,Op Prop.Other	4	26	11	251	14	11	25	8	12	21	3	12	11	1	3	1	1
	1.	26.	12.	269.	16.	8.	20.	10.	9.	18.	6.	12.	8.	2.	4.	1.	1.
Clerical	0	10	1	15	127	1	2	5	0	8	9	6	1	3	4	0	0
	1.	10.	2.	14.	121.	2.	4.	6.	4.	7.	7.	8.	8.	2.	4.	1.	1.
Sales Retail	0	0	1	7	2	32	3	0	0	0	1	2	3	0	0	0	0
	0.	2.	4.	6.	2.	33.	2.	1.	1.	1.	1.	1.	3.	0.	1.	0.	0.
Sales Other	0	1	3	14	2	4	61	0	2	2	3	1	0	0	0	0	0
	0.	5.	3.	16.	3.	3.	58.	1.	1.	2.	1.	2.	2.	0.	1.	0.	0.
Craft Manu-facturing	0	5	1	14	6	1	1	207	7	10	31	4	12	3	6	0	0
	0.	7.	1.	13.	9.	1.	2.	196.	6.	14.	32.	12.	10.	4.	5.	1.	1.

Craft Construction	0 / 1.	1 / 2.	2 / 3.	20 / 10.	1 / 5.	0 / 1.	2 / 2.	4 / 6.	129 / 131.	8 / 16.	3 / 3.	11 / 12.	5 / 5.	1 / 1.	9 / 11.	5 / 4.	1 / 3.
Craft Other	0 / 1.	5 / 6.	5 / 4.	18 / 22.	6 / 10.	3 / 2.	3 / 3.	8 / 14.	19 / 18.	188 / 186.	5 / 5.	28 / 21.	9 / 13.	0 / 3.	15 / 14.	1 / 2.	1 / 2.
Operatives Manufctrng	0 / 0.	3 / 4.	1 / 2.	10 / 8.	11 / 12.	1 / 2.	1 / 3.	38 / 36.	4 / 4.	9 / 5.	273 / 277.	20 / 20.	16 / 18.	19 / 20.	12 / 12.	2 / 3.	5 / 4.
Operatives Other	0 / 1.	1 / 4.	2 / 2.	13 / 13.	12 / 10.	1 / 2.	1 / 2.	4 / 10.	8 / 12.	21 / 18.	17 / 15.	213 / 1208.	14 / 13.	1 / 4.	26 / 25.	3 / 4.	3 / 5.
Service	0 / 0.	4 / 2.	1 / 3.	12 / 7.	11 / 8.	2 / 3.	0 / 2.	2 / 7.	3 / 4.	6 / 9.	10 / 11.	9 / 10.	227 / 223.	6 / 6.	8 / 14.	0 / 3.	2 / 3.
Labor Manufacturing	0 / 0.	1 / 1.	0 / 1.	1 / 3.	3 / 3.	1 / 1.	0 / 1.	8 / 5.	1 / 1.	0 / 3.	22 / 21.	2 / 5.	13 / 11.	38 / 39.	8 / 8.	1 / 1.	0 / 2.
Labor Other	0 / 0.	2 / 2.	2 / 3.	2 / 5.	5 / 5.	0 / 1.	1 / 2.	0 / 4.	12 / 12.	13 / 13.	9 / 10.	27 / 27.	17 / 19.	8 / 6.	143 / 138.	2 / 5.	8 / 6.
Farmers	0 / 1.	1 / 2.	4 / 3.	2 / 3.	3 / 3.	0 / 1.	2 / 1.	1 / 2.	11 / 8.	2 / 3.	4 / 5.	8 / 8.	8 / 7.	2 / 2.	5 / 10.	197 / 200.	12 / 11.
Farm Labor	0 / 0.	0 / 1.	0 / 2.	0 / 2.	2 / 2.	0 / 1.	0 / 1.	1 / 1.	3 / 4.	0 / 2.	6 / 4.	1 / 6.	3 / 5.	3 / 2.	10 / 8.	6 / 7.	79 / 77.

Time Series Mobility: 1967-1973, Frequencies and Expected Values

Time Series Model: Coordinates (in four dimensions), row multipliers, column multipliers, polynomial, scale factors and chi-square

Prof.SE	2.450	3.003	-1.221	.944	8.672	7.145	7.101	4.138	4.698	4.318
Prof.Sal	2.212	-1.445	-1.221	.994	14.366	12.780	13.786	17.407	17.053	15.152
Prop C	1.715	.746	.962	-.083	9.367	8.302	7.055	6.888	7.110	7.204
MOPOther	1.649	-.667	-.643	-.090	16.472	14.350	15.047	18.833	20.776	17.846
Clerical	.252	-.965	.026	1.122	11.021	10.476	9.510	13.962	12.902	12.766
Sales Retl	1.993	-.397	2.209	.194	4.655	5.344	4.297	8.850	7.164	7.569
Sales Other	3.580	-0.629	0.034	-0.066	7.470	7.031	6.277	9.323	8.794	9.308
Craft Mfg.	-.546	-2.458	-.963	-.228	14.666	15.124	14.517	16.255	15.099	13.477
Craft Con.	-.154	1.847	-.643	-.236	11.737	11.597	11.032	13.835	12.562	11.833
Craft Other	.080	.003	-1.059	-.878	13.758	13.336	14.135	17.239	16.786	13.147
Oper.Mfg.	-1.788	-2.301	.034	.013	17.076	19.994	18.305	19.441	15.690	15.157
Oper.Other	-1.462	.091	-.689	.383	16.019	14.808	13.964	14.940	16.049	14.904
Service	-1.019	-.794	1.309	-.699	16.068	14.671	12.767	15.773	16.739	17.428
Labor Mfg.	-2.312	-1.521	.068	-.817	7.560	8.221	7.014	7.782	5.904	5.505
Labor Other	-1.462	.814	.019	-.748	13.975	13.306	11.790	12.012	12.479	11.667
Farmers	-1.880	3.393	.962	.103	20.359	20.780	19.289	11.228	10.493	10.348
Farm Labor	-3.307	1.278	.814	.041	11.929	11.159	9.704	7.263	8.127	7.959

Coefficients of the polynomial function of distance

    power 1   1.0000
    power 2   -0.0483

Scale Factors

    1: 1.   2: .902938   3: .812644

Chi-Square = 732.226

Appendix 10.2
Note on The Markov Model

The contrast between the distance model and a second obvious model, obvious except for the fact that the second model does not work (or has not yet been made to work), increases the confidence that these distances are real.

The other "obvious" model is the Markov chain model. For example, suppose I state that the probability of a British professional's son becoming a professional is .38. There's not much you can do with that statement in a single table: It is or it isn't. But if you take these things very seriously there is a great deal that you can question in the number .38. Consider: As I showed earlier, there are numbers you can compute when you're reporting a table of data. If among all of these numbers that I could have computed I choose to report a probability, then I'm saying, implicitly, that probabilities are more apt descriptions of mobility than other numbers I could have reported. The implication is that once you know that a father is a professional, then the mechanism of British society applies the probabilities and generates the careers of the sons.

With a single table and only two points in time, there is not much I can do to test that implication. The probabilities are whatever they are. But with two tables or three I can check the implication. I ask: How would a man get from "A" in 1967 to "B" in 1971? He could do it by

staying in A for two years, and then moving to B

He could do it by

moving to B, and then staying in B

Or by

moving to C, and then moving to B

Or by

moving to D, and then moving to B

and so forth.

There are seventeen ways to get from A to B in two steps and the first table in Table 10.1 gives us the basic probabilities from which to compute the probability of each of these seventeen combinations. If that's it, if these probabilities are the "dice" that determine a person's career, then we should be able to reconstruct the second table by simply multiplying and adding up the probabilities estimated from the first. But it doesn't work: The probabilities fail to reconstruct the second table or the third, and that's why the contrast between these two "obvious" models is interesting. Probability thinking, investing "reality" in the probabilities, leads to the wrong answers: It systematically under-estimates the number of people who change.

This effect, under-estimating the number of people who change (using the Markov model), is known in the literature as the Mover/Stayer effect. But the name, "Mover/Stayer," is not so much a name for the phenomenon as it is a name for one proposed solution. The proposed solution, by Blumen, Kogen, and McCarthy, was to analyze the mobility process into two processes, one of which was Markovian, the other of which was not — salvaging the Markov model by applying it to a hypothetical "Markovian" subset of the men.[*] This alternative has been difficult to implement because the more complicated the process, the more data that are needed to test it. And in this case the demands for data grew impractically large. Here, by contrast, vesting reality in the distances instead of the probabilities, we get a usable solution.

---

[*] Blumen, Kogen, and McCarthy, *op. cit.*

Epilogue

11

Theory

Ad Astra per Aspera

The subject is theory. I want to discuss theory in the context of scientific sociology. And lest you suspect that sociology has changed since you last looked, becoming theoretical and "scientific" in the sense popularly ascribed to physics, no. To talk about theory in our era and to use the word "scientific" is to debate what real sociology should be doing — defining the future.

The basic problem, "What should we be doing in the science of sociology?" plagues every serious sociologist every day. It plagues us because, privately, we are well aware of the modesty of our achievements. But these days the problem is out in the open in debates centering around Stanley Lieberson's book *Making it Count*.[1] Lieberson asks how you build a science, specifically sociology, without experiments. In experimental science the units of analysis are randomly assigned to different experimental conditions. But in sociology, with few exceptions, you can't do that. You can't assign human beings, much less families or corporations or whole societies, to experimental "treatment" groups with the randomness, independence, and comparability we would aspire to in a laboratory science. In sociology true experiments are usually difficult, unethical, or unthinkable. We're aware of that, but for generations we've acted otherwise. So Lieberson's question throws into doubt a large part of the practice, as distinct from the intentions, of contemporary sociology. Quoting Lieberson:

---

1. Stanley Lieberson, *Making It Count: The Improvement of Social Research and Theory*, University of California Press, 1985.

I have argued that several of the most widely accepted procedures in contemporary social research are often based on models and assumptions that are patently inappropriate and that, in such circumstances, their application is counter-productive. ... Assuming there is agreement, then at the very least we must recognize that "business as usual" — even if the alternative does not appear clear — is often nothing more than "ritualism as usual." ... there is no point in continuing to do something that sooner or later must be rejected and replaced.[2]

That's serious business: " ... The most widely accepted procedures ... are ... counter-productive." A sociologist is trained to question theories and hypotheses, the soft stuff, the words. But methodology and procedure were supposed to be exempt. When sociology was self-consciously pulling itself out of the mud and proclaiming itself a *science* it was politically useful to associate ourselves with "method" and the attendant illusion of mathematical purity. Where we had problems we hoped for a statistical fix, statistical controls in place of laboratory controls. Where we had problems with causal explanations we tried to use "variance explained" as a stand-in for "cause." For a generation, as sociology defined itself, serious skepticism was turned back on the skeptic, branding the skeptic as an outsider, probably hostile, probably a "theoretician" who had never proven his or her mettle by studying statistics. For a generation, skepticism about method was set aside.

No longer. Now Lieberson has called an end to the game. Today we have to question multiple regression, "percent of variance explained" and, implicitly, even tests of statistical probability. While we were busy defending ourselves we treated such things as truths on the order of 2 + 2 = 4. Who could question such things? But now we get statements like this from David Freedman, the author of one of our most widely used textbooks on method. Quoting Freedman on the practical use of regression:

A crude four-point scale may be useful. Regression is a method which —

---

2. Lieberson, *op. cit.*, p. 171.

1) usually works, although it is imperfect and may sometimes go wrong — like anything else;

2) sometimes works in the hands of skillful practitioners, but isn't suitable for routine use;

3) might work, but hasn't yet;

4) can't work.

Textbooks, courtroom testimony, and newspaper interviews often seem to put regression into category 1. *Although I have not had much luck in finding good examples, my own confidence interval is bracketed by 2) and 3); option 4) seems too pessimistic.*[3]

Perhaps we can negate the weakness in our statistical fix, saving the day by increased statistical sophistication. Perhaps there are niches in which statistical care and special circumstances can make "the Lieberson problem" inoperable, niches that we can broaden and generalize to the rest of sociology. Perhaps, but I doubt it. If we are comparing two children, one of whom went to a segregated school in a slum and one of whom went to an integrated school in an affluent suburb, we can think about a random experiment: We can imagine a case in which a flip of the coin consigned one child to one environment and one to the other. But rarely if ever can we perform such an experiment. And if we try to create a statistical substitute by "controlling" for differences in the parents' incomes, educations, occupations, aspirations for their children, time spent with children, and general family intervention in the lives of their children, then we're in big trouble: The number of children who match on all characteristics except the one, the number of children who are absolutely identical except that one grows up and goes to school in a slum and one grows up amid wealth — that number is close to zero.

Perhaps we can measure "cause," using precise measurement, timing, and observation of exceptions. Perhaps, but I doubt that too and

3. From David A. Freedman, "Statistical Models and Shoe Leather," Technical Report No. 217, Statistics Department, University of California, Berkeley, September 1989, p. 1, italics added. Revised for Sociological Methodology, 1991, Vol 27, *American Sociological Association*, 1991.

here, as in Chapter 2, I base my doubt on the modern interpretation of David Hume's *Enquiry Concerning Human Understanding* written in 1746. In brief: Cause is unobservable. Even in an experiment you don't *see* the cause.

Repeating the argument: Watch me as I take hold of the pencil in front of me on the table and slide the pencil across the table. We all know that I pushed the pencil. It did not pull my hand and it was not a coincidence that the two moved in the same direction. But the evidence of this cause-and-effect relation does not lie in the observable facts. We can quantify this experiment in utmost detail and repeat it a thousand times, but no image of "cause" will reflect light and project itself across your retina. The evidence lies in experience, in "theory" about my capacities and those of the pencil, and generally in a whole lot of reasoning that you added to what you observed: You have to think. Cause is unobservable, and no fair substituting diffuse phrases like "X explains ninety-nine and forty-four one-hundredths percent of the variance of Y" — even fractions of causes are unobservable.

If science requires true experiments, if our science requires a statistical measure of "cause," then we can fold the tent and be done with it. The Lieberson problem is insoluble. But the science does not require such things: The methods in question are means, not ends, and we are not obliged to rescue the methods. Contemporary waning of faith in one specific style of quantitative method does not prevent us, in principle, from pursuing the more general goal of "doing" social science, including quantitative social science. It does require that we re-think the matter, and for my taste that makes sociology a lot less mechanical and "method" a lot more intellectually interesting.

The key to re-thinking the matter is to ask what we were after: What scientific end were we pursuing when we entered this method-ological *cul de sac*? We were in hot pursuit of understanding, trying to understand what goes on "out there" in social relations. We were looking for underlying simplicity. We were looking for the similarities that unite superficially different phenomena. We were looking for theory.

The Continuum of Description:
Fact, Order, and Theory

What is theory? The one line answer is: "Theory is 'nothing but' a special kind of description." Theory lies at one end of a continuum of types of description that range in generality from specific facts at one end of the continuum to general theories at the other. There is surely a difference between fact and theory, between one side of a continuum and the other. It is certainly true that differences of degree gradually become differences of kind. But the continuum of increasing thought, falsifiability, and power that leads science to theory is a continuum of ever richer and more generalized description. You find theory by increasing descriptive sophistication, while attending to absolutely necessary classical virtues like precision, falsifiability, parsimony, generalization, goodness of fit, and elegance.

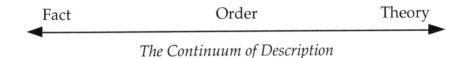

Fact   Order   Theory

The Continuum of Description

Let me give an example of three points on the continuum of description, beginning with a description of facts about a human group, continuing with a description of order in the pattern of group behavior, and continuing with increasingly theoretical descriptions of behavior. My human group for this discussion is, once again, the work group known as "the bank wiring room." For the bank wiring room we have data recording positive and negative ties, friends and enemies, and other interpersonal relations. Note: We do not have data on income, education, and family background — nothing to correlate and little on which the conventional statistical apparatus can grind out its results.[4] The bank wiring room data are mainline data for another brand of

---

4. The "Bank Wiring Room" data are generally accessed through data and description in chapters of George Homans' *The Human Group*, Harcourt, Brace & World, 1950. Refer also to Roethlisberger and Dixon, *Management and the Worker*, Harvard University Press, 1939.

quantitative sociology known variously as structural or network analysis. The data describe relations among fourteen men, day by day, as they threaded wires through a piece of plastic forming a "bank," and then connected the wires and soldered the connections in place. While the workers wired their banks, observers recorded their relations. With this background, let me describe the bank wiring room using three different degrees of description:

Facts

The "Friendships" and "Antagonisms" among these men are reported in Tables 11.1 and 11.2.[5] For example, Allen and Taylor were friends, as indicated by the *F* in row 1 column 8 of Table 11.1. Among other facts:

The average number of *friends* per person is 1.86; the standard deviation is 1.56; the range is from 0 friends to 4.

The distribution of the number of *friends* is skewed and bi-modal (five men had no friends, four men had three friends).

The average number of *antagonists* per person is 2.57; the standard deviation is 2.35; the range is from 0 antagonists to 8.

The distribution of *antagonists* per person is skewed.

The *correlation* between number of friends and number of antagonists is $r = -.58$ The correlation between the square root transformations of these variables is $-.59$.

Order

Those are facts: Data and summary statistics. Now let me describe order in the bank wiring room:

Friendship and Antagonism among these people was consistent with a partition of the wiring room into two sub-sets: An in-group and a non-group. The in-group of five men like each other. The non-group men had few friendships and many antagonisms. Re-

---

5. Homans, *op. cit.*, provides diagrams for Friendship, Antagonism, Games, Arguments About Windows, Help, and Trading of Jobs.

	Al I1	Ce S4	Do W4	Gr W9	Ha W7	Ob W8	St S1	Ta W3	Wi W1
Allen (I1)	-	.	.	.	.	.	.	F	.
Cermak (S4)	.	-	.	F	.	F	.	.	.
Donovan (W4)	.	.	-	.	.	.	F	F	F
Green (W9)	.	F	.	-	F	F	.	.	.
Hasulak (W7)	.	.	.	F	-	F	F	.	.
Oberleitner (W8)	.	F	.	F	F	-	.	.	.
Steinhardt (S1)	.	.	F	.	F	.	-	F	F
Taylor (W3)	F	.	F	.	.	.	F	-	F
Windowski (W1)	.	.	F	.	.	.	F	F	-

From the bank wiring room data presented in Homans, *The Human Group*, Harcourt Brace, 1950. Also see Roethlisberger and Dixon, *Management and the Worker,* 1939. The table shows the friendships for nine of the original fourteen men. (The remaining five men had no friends.) "W1" refers to Wireman 1. "S1" refers to Solderman 1. "I1" refers to Inspector 1.

Table 11.1
Friends

	Al I1	Ca W5	Ce S4	Do W4	Gr W9	Ha W7	Kr W6	Ma S2	Ma I3	Mu W2	Ob W8	St S1
Allen (I1)	-	.	.	.	.	.	.	.	A	A	.	.
Capek (W5)	.	-	.	A	A	A	A	A	A	.	A	A
Cermak (S4)	.	.	-	.	.	.	.	.	A	.	.	.
Donovan (W4)	.	A	.	-	.	.	.	.	.	.	.	.
Green (W9)	.	A	.	.	-	.	.	.	A	A	.	.
Hasulak (W7)	.	A	.	.	.	-	A	.	A	A	.	.
Krupa (W6)	.	A	.	.	.	A	-	.	A	.	.	.
Matchek (S2)	.	A	.	.	.	.	.	-	.	.	.	.
Mazmania (I3)	A	A	A	.	A	A	A	.	-	.	A	.
Mueller (W2)	A	.	.	.	A	A	.	.	.	-	A	.
Oberleit (W8)	.	A	.	.	.	.	.	.	A	A	-	.
Steinhar (S1)	.	A	.	.	.	.	.	.	.	.	.	-

From Homans, *op. cit.*, as for Table 11.1. The table shows the antagonisms among twelve of the original fourteen men. (The remaining two men had no antagonists.) "W1" refers to Wireman 1. "S1" refers to Solderman 1. "I1" refers to Inspector 1.

Table 11.2
Antagonists

arrangement of the data reveals the partition — marked by the dotted lines in Table 11.3.[6]

This description of order invokes structure, a reality behind the facts. Compared to simple facts, this requires thinking: It is not obvious that groups partition into sub-sets, exclusive sub-sets with boundaries — you're in or you're out. It is not obvious that a collection of people who do not like each other, the non-group, should be treated as an entity: They are not a clique that pals around together. In the first set seven out of ten possible friendships exist. That's a clique. But in the second set only five out of thirty-six exist. In the literature the members of these sets, members of the in group and the non-group, are known as "structurally equivalent" with respect to other members of their set.

Perhaps the strongest demonstration that statements about human order require thought, beyond the obvious facts, is presented by showing you some of the missing background of Table 11.3. When I spoke quickly and directed your attention to the re-arrangement of "*F*'s" and "*A*'s" in Table 11.3, I diverted you from a critical question: How did I find the re-arrangement I displayed in Table 11.3? The original data in Tables 11.1 and 11.2 and the re-arranged data in Table 11.3 are exactly the same. They only look different, but that "look" is critical to the imputation of order. Finding order, this kind of order among the facts, required a technical invention by Harrison White, Scott Boorman, and Ronald Breiger and a host of colleagues in hot pursuit of a simple question:[7] If there is an appropriate "partition" for these data,

---

6. The partition is the CONCOR solution for these data, referring to Harrison White, Scott Boorman, and Ronald Breiger's "Social Structure from Multiple Networks, I: Blockmodels of Roles and Positions," *American Journal of Sociology* 81, 1976, pages 730-780. CONCOR requires some assertion about every cell, including the diagonal. For Friendship, I assumed Friendship with one's self, on the diagonal. For Antagonism, I assumed non-antagonism with one's self. Also see Phipps Arabie, Scott Boorman, and Ronald Breiger, "An Algorithm for Clustering Relational Data with Applications to Social Network Analysis and Comparison with Multidimensional Scaling," *Journal of Mathematical Psychology*, Volume 12, pages 328-383.

7. *Op. cit.*

		IWSWW 14131	WSWWWSIWW 549762328			IWSWW 14131	WSWWWSIWW 549762328
All	(I1)	F F		All	(I1)		AA
Don	(W4)	FFFF		Don	(W4)		A
Ste	(S1)	FFFF	F	Ste	(S1)		A
Tay	(W3)	FFFFF		Tay	(W3)		
Win	(W1)	FFFF		Win	(W1)		
Cap	(W5)		F	Cap	(W5)	AA	AAAAA A
Cer	(S4)		FF F	Cer	(S4)		A
Gre	(W9)		FFF F	Gre	(W9)	A	AA
Has	(W7)	F	FF F	Has	(W7)	A	A AA
Kru	(W6)		F	Kru	(W6)	A	A A
Mat	(S2)		F	Mat	(S2)	A	A
Max	(I3)		F	Max	(I3)	A	AAAAA A
Mue	(W2)		F	Mue	(W2)	A	AA A
Obe	(W8)		FFF F	Obe	(W8)		A AA

Table 11.3

Sub-sets of the Bank Wiring Room, Partitioned by CONCOR, Showing the Five Person "In-Group" and the Nine Person "Non-Group"

how do you find it?[8]   You can't just keep re-arranging the data, swapping rows and columns until something pretty turns up: There are too many possibilities. White and friends came up with a technical invention, CONCOR, from the words "CONcatenated CORrelation." Let me show you some of the detail of CONCOR in order to make my point that it takes some thinking before these data can be described as orderly.

CONCOR, as a procedure, compares every person to every other person, treating all relations as real numbers — 1 if a relation is present, 0 if it's not. It acts as if "friendship" and "antagonism" had means, standard deviations and correlations, and it computes these numbers. For example, Allen's two friendships and three antagonisms (including presumed friendship with himself) are treated as five 1's within his complete list of 28 numbers. Donovan receives similar treatment:

8. Levine and Mullins, "Structuralist Analysis of Data in Sociology," Connections I, 1978, show the choices against a background of alternative roads not taken by White and his colleagues.

Allen:
```
10000000000010 00000000110000
```
Mean: .143 Standard Deviation: .350

Donovan:
```
00010000000111 01000000000000
```
Mean: .179 Standard Deviation: .383

Correlation:
r = .0761

CONCOR computes all the correlations, yielding the full table of correlations in Table 11.4. Now, don't ask me why CONCOR does this — CONCOR is what it is. Ask whether it's useful.

CONCOR continues. At stage two, it treats these correlations just as it treated data: Allen is treated as if he were the 14 numbers in Allen's column of correlations, 1.00, –.06, .13, . . . ; Donovan is treated as if he were the 14 numbers in Donovan's column. Once again the CONCOR procedure computes correlations, Table 11.5. Once again we get numbers. And then once again CONCOR gets correlations — and again, and again.

. . . Eventually the repetitions (the concatenated correlations) converge to numbers that are constant, either plus-one or minus-one, Table 11.6. And if you look at the locations of the plus-ones in Table 11.6, you will see how I identified the two sets, using CONCOR.

A simplified version of the computer program is in Appendix 11.1. It was a landmark in the structuralist literature. But the simple point is that the orderly description of the bank wiring room is a decidedly non-trivial enterprise. The description is objective. It is consistent with the facts. In this case it is partly computerized. But it is more than fact, and it is reaching toward the theoretical.

	All	Cap	Cer	Don	Gre	Has	Kru	Mat	Max	Mue	Obe	Ste	Tay	Win
All (I1)	1.00	-.06	.13	.08	.24	.19	.13	-.11	-.26	-.19	.24	.04	.34	.13
Cap (W5)	-.06	1.00	-.06	-.32	-.22	-.10	.16	-.19	.24	.28	-.22	-.36	-.32	-.28
Cer (S4)	.13	-.06	1.00	-.19	.71	.42	.13	-.11	-.26	-.19	.71	-.21	-.19	-.17
Don (W4)	.08	-.32	-.19	1.00	-.05	.12	.08	.23	-.09	-.22	-.05	.89	.76	.88
Gre (W9)	.24	-.22	.71	-.05	1.00	.73	.24	.16	-.18	-.27	.73	.10	-.27	-.24
Has (W7)	.19	-.10	.42	.12	.73	1.00	.19	.13	-.05	-.29	.73	.25	-.09	-.03
Kru (W6)	.13	.16	.13	.08	.24	.19	1.00	.28	.19	.08	.24	.04	-.19	-.17
Mat (S2)	-.11	-.19	-.11	.23	.16	.13	.28	1.00	.13	-.13	.16	.19	-.13	-.11
Max (I3)	-.26	.24	-.26	-.09	-.18	-.05	.19	.13	1.00	.53	-.18	-.14	-.29	-.26
Mue (W2)	-.19	.28	-.19	-.22	-.27	-.29	.08	-.13	.53	1.00	-.27	-.24	-.22	-.19
Obe (W8)	.24	-.22	.71	-.05	.73	.73	.24	.16	-.18	-.27	1.00	.10	-.27	-.24
Ste (S1)	.04	-.36	-.21	.89	.10	.25	.04	.19	-.14	-.24	.10	1.00	.67	.78
Tay (W3)	.34	-.32	-.19	.76	-.27	-.09	-.19	-.13	-.29	-.22	-.27	.67	1.00	.88
Win (W1)	.13	-.28	-.17	.88	-.24	-.03	-.17	-.11	-.26	-.19	-.24	.78	.88	1.00

Table 11.4

First Iteration of Correlations for Each Pair of People, for Both Relations Simultaneously.

		All	Cap	Cer	Don	Gre	Has	Kru	Mat	Max	Mue	Obe	Ste	Tay	Win
All	(I1)	1.00	-.32	.28	.10	.30	.29	-.08	-.28	-.65	-.54	.30	.12	.32	.18
Cap	(W5)	-.32	1.00	-.13	-.67	-.31	-.36	.26	-.30	.58	.65	-.31	-.73	-.57	-.57
Cer	(S4)	.28	-.13	1.00	-.48	.91	.76	.22	-.09	-.42	-.40	.91	-.37	-.47	-.48
Don	(W4)	.10	-.67	-.48	1.00	-.35	-.16	-.41	.12	-.43	-.47	-.35	.98	.92	.96
Gre	(W9)	.30	-.31	.91	-.35	1.00	.93	.30	-.18	-.40	-.52	.93	-.19	-.44	-.44
Has	(W7)	.29	-.36	.76	-.16	.93	1.00	.22	.19	-.42	-.62	.93	.01	-.29	-.44
Kru	(W6)	-.08	.26	.22	-.41	.30	.22	1.00	.40	.27	.10	.30	-.39	-.57	-.56
Mat	(S2)	-.28	-.30	-.09	.12	-.18	.19	.40	1.00	.12	.21	.18	-.15	-.18	-.14
Max	(I3)	-.65	.58	-.42	-.43	-.40	-.42	.27	.12	1.00	.83	-.40	-.48	-.51	-.47
Mue	(W2)	-.54	.65	-.40	-.47	-.52	-.62	.10	.21	.83	1.00	-.52	-.55	-.41	-.40
Obe	(W8)	.30	-.31	.91	-.35	.93	.93	.30	.18	-.40	-.52	1.00	-.19	-.44	-.44
Ste	(S1)	.12	-.73	-.37	.98	-.19	.01	-.39	-.15	-.48	-.55	-.19	1.00	.87	.92
Tay	(W3)	.32	-.57	-.47	.92	-.44	-.29	-.57	-.18	-.51	-.41	-.44	.87	1.00	.98
Win	(W1)	.18	-.57	-.48	.96	-.44	-.44	-.56	-.14	-.47	-.40	-.44	.92	.98	1.00

Table 11.5

Second Iteration of Correlations for Each Pair of People, Applied to Correlations in Table 11.4.

	All	Cap	Cer	Don	Gre	Has	Kru	Mat	Max	Mue	Obe	Ste	Tay	Win
All (I1)	1.0	-1.0	-1.0	1.0	-1.0	-1.0	-1.0	-1.0	-1.0	-1.0	-1.0	1.0	1.0	1.0
Cap (W5)	-1.0	1.0	1.0	-1.0	1.0	1.0	1.0	1.0	1.0	1.0	1.0	-1.0	-1.0	-1.0
Cer (S4)	-1.0	1.0	1.0	-1.0	1.0	1.0	1.0	1.0	1.0	1.0	1.0	-1.0	-1.0	-1.0
Don (W4)	1.0	-1.0	-1.0	1.0	-1.0	-1.0	-1.0	-1.0	-1.0	-1.0	-1.0	1.0	1.0	1.0
Gre (W9)	-1.0	1.0	1.0	-1.0	1.0	1.0	1.0	1.0	1.0	1.0	1.0	-1.0	-1.0	-1.0
Has (W7)	-1.0	1.0	1.0	-1.0	1.0	1.0	1.0	1.0	1.0	1.0	1.0	-1.0	-1.0	-1.0
Kru (W6)	-1.0	1.0	1.0	-1.0	1.0	1.0	1.0	1.0	1.0	1.0	1.0	-1.0	-1.0	-1.0
Mat (S2)	-1.0	1.0	1.0	-1.0	1.0	1.0	1.0	1.0	1.0	1.0	1.0	-1.0	-1.0	-1.0
Max (I3)	-1.0	1.0	1.0	-1.0	1.0	1.0	1.0	1.0	1.0	1.0	1.0	-1.0	-1.0	-1.0
Mue (W2)	-1.0	1.0	1.0	-1.0	1.0	1.0	1.0	1.0	1.0	1.0	1.0	-1.0	-1.0	-1.0
Obe (W8)	-1.0	1.0	1.0	-1.0	1.0	1.0	1.0	1.0	1.0	1.0	1.0	-1.0	-1.0	-1.0
Ste (S1)	1.0	-1.0	-1.0	1.0	-1.0	-1.0	-1.0	-1.0	-1.0	-1.0	-1.0	1.0	1.0	1.0
Tay (W3)	1.0	-1.0	-1.0	1.0	-1.0	-1.0	-1.0	-1.0	-1.0	-1.0	-1.0	1.0	1.0	1.0
Win (W1)	1.0	-1.0	-1.0	1.0	-1.0	-1.0	-1.0	-1.0	-1.0	-1.0	-1.0	1.0	1.0	1.0

Table 11.6

Convergence of Correlations after Twenty Concatenations of Correlation Applied to Correlations.

Theory (in the Making)

Now let me continue up the scale of description, from fact to order to something stronger. Stating the theory before I defend it:

> Strong relations, both friendship and antagonism, are experienced with people who are close. Friendship is simple: Friends are close and friendship attenuates with social distance. Antagonism is more complicated: Antagonists are not as close as friends. Initially, Antagonism increases with social distance. It peaks at short distances, and then attenuates.

I claim that this description becomes theory if it becomes sufficiently precise, sufficiently parsimonious, sufficiently general, and sufficiently elegant. It must also be falsifiable, that's essential, and it certainly helps if it is not demonstrably false. In Chapter 8 I introduced precision to this statement by expressing it as an equation and "fitting it" to the friendship and antagonism data in Tables 11.1 and 11.2.

Such precision is not enough by itself. It's useful because the precision of the equation says something that can be tested: It is falsifiable. And for these data the equation is not demonstrably false.

Is this description a theory? I'd say: "Not yet — too simple, not sufficiently general." But already its falsifiability adds something special — beyond the imputation of order. Consider the difference between this description and the previous imputation of order using CONCOR: If you don't like CONCOR then you and I can argue about your taste in such matters. I can challenge your taste with a pile of literature that likes CONCOR (hiding articles that don't). But "proof" by authority is not one of the favored tools of science and, if I can't persuade you, then with respect to CONCOR and its results, we will just continue in separate ways. Not so with the equation. If you don't like it, then too bad: Your likes or dislikes are not very important compared to an equation that fits. That's what's been added. You can, of course, disagree with my *interpretation* of the equation. Or, you can disagree by producing an alternative, one that fits better or does the same job more simply. If you can, then too bad for my equation. That's how you build a theory. That's how you have a disciplined discussion that moves forward.

"Description" is a lukewarm word in the present language of sociology. It doesn't have the punch of "reject the null hypothesis" or "partition the variance." But it may do the job. Perhaps the best thing to do with traditional methods — the stuff we now teach in classes labeled "Methods" — is to quietly walk away from them, not because they are bad but because they are embedded in arguments that make it difficult to clear our heads. I just sat through a discussion at another university where a very loud and self-certain fellow proclaimed that he was one of only two statisticians on his campus and that the role of sociological method is to teach students "CMS," a computer operating system, and "SPSS," a computer program.

Clearly the man who teaches CMS and SPSS knows better. He knows that statistics is not sociology, that being a statistician, if that's what he is, does not give him standing as a sociologist. He knows that statistics is one means to an end and that computer programs are only a means to that means to the end. Why does he say what he does? Because he is fighting people like a professor who tormented me when I was a student: "Mathematical sociology?" he said. "Yes, we love mathematical sociologists. We give them lots of money. They work real hard. They burn out quickly and we're rid of them." Against fools like that sociology fought back with computers, statistics, federal grants, and, when necessary, loud voices and other means of intimidation — including self-certain statements about the one true way to do sociology. I understand the argument. But those battles were won. And, in any case, the critics of thirty years ago are not our present students nor are they our colleagues. We need not prosecute old arguments with new students. We need not defend the canon of method for fear that the enterprise will crumble.

And if we don't put the questions that move our science forward, then others will. I would not like to stand before a traditional "methods" class and defend myself when a student fights through the numbers and technique for regressing weight on height, fights through all the means, variances, standardized variables, and covariances, fights through the confidence intervals and significance tests, and then, at the end of the battle, discovers the payoff: As I noted earlier, without all this good stuff a simple dumb prediction of a person's weight would make an error of

23 pounds (using the mean). And, with the technology? With the technology the error remains at 21 pounds. In the vernacular, "Big deal!"

I am not closing with a wishy-washy plea for theoreticians to learn more method and for methodologists to learn more theory. No, the point is that they are already woven together and that, when we pretend that theory and method are separate, the most interesting parts of the work go unexamined while all sorts of "theories" creep in through the "methods," disguised as *a priori* assumptions.

If you assume that political identity is a polarity, strong Republican versus strong Democrat, and then attend to the correlates of this form of political identity, you are building your results on an untested foundation. If you assume that real-world friendship and antagonism are comparable to mathematical relations, an untested model is adopted. When you try to mark off the time of human events by the pace of an astronomical clock you adopt a model from another science whose applicability to our own is an open question. When you set up equations to predict individual social mobility as a linear function of prior causal events — the more events, the less the variance — you assume a contestable theory of social reality.

Can a social scientist "do" theory? Obviously the question accepts only one answer: "Yes." But the word "theory" is corrupt in current social science. To some social scientists the word "theory" has no meaning, only a connotation of high status. For them, whatever they are doing — that's theory. By contrast, to some, "theory" connotes low status. For them "theory" connotes verbal speculation by ponderous thinkers who know nothing of science. To others, "theory" is a term in contrast to "reality." For them, the further the research can be removed from data the better — I don't do windows. I don't do data. I'm a theoretician. To others, "theory" means "not proven" as in: "Why should I believe you? That's only a theory." Let's not fight over the definition. We are trying to describe the social world. We are trying for description that has generality, precision, parsimony, falsifiability, and matches the data.

Appendix 11.1

```
!Program:  CONCOR


DIM x(1,1),junk(10),r_mat(1,1),current(1,1),lab$(1),idx(1)

PRINT "Name of data file?"?
!INPUT fn$
LET  fn$="?WrgFrAn"?OPEN  #2:  name  "ConCorOut",  create
"newold"?ERASE #2
OPEN #1: name fn$
INPUT #1:n
INPUT #1:v
PRINT   n;"?ows   and   ";v;"   columns"?MAT   redim
X(n,v),r_mat(v,v),lab$(v)
FOR i=1 to n
    MAT INPUT #1:junk(v)
    FOR j=1 to v
        LET x(i,j)=junk(j)
    NEXT j
NEXT i
FOR i=1 to v
    LINE INPUT #1:lab$(i)
NEXT i
MAT current=x
CALL cor_mat(n,v,current, r_mat(,))
!MAT PRINT using "--.##"?r_mat
FOR i=1 to 20
    MAT current=r_mat
    CALL cor_mat(v,v,current, r_mat)
    PRINT i
    !MAT PRINT using "--.##"?r_mat
NEXT i
!MAT PRINT x;
!MAT PRINT using "--.##"?r_mat
!MAT PRINT lab$;
!Sort
MAT redim idx(v)
FOR i=1 to v
    LET idx(i)=i
NEXT i
FOR i=2 to v
    LET j=i
    DO until j=1 or r_mat(1,idx(j))<0 and r_mat(1,idx(j-1))>0
        LET s=idx(j)
        LET idx(j)=idx(j-1)
        LET idx(j-1)=s
        LET j=j-1
    LOOP
NEXT i
FOR i=1 to v
    IF i>1 then
```

```
              IF  r_mat(1,idx(i))<0  and  r_mat(1,idx(i-1))>0  then  LET
begin2=i
    END IF
NEXT i
!Sort alphabetically within two subsets
FOR i=2 to begin2-1
    LET j=i
    DO until j=1 or lab$(idx(j))>lab$(idx(j-1))
       LET s=idx(j)
       LET idx(j)=idx(j-1)
       LET idx(j-1)=s
       LET j=j-1
    LOOP
NEXT i
FOR i=begin2+1 to v
    LET j=i
    DO until j=begin2 or lab$(idx(j))>lab$(idx(j-1))
       LET s=idx(j)
       LET idx(j)=idx(j-1)
       LET idx(j-1)=s
       LET j=j-1
    LOOP
NEXT i

!Print
PRINT #2
FOR letter=1 to 8
    FOR table = 1 to 2
        PRINT #2:"              ";
        FOR i=1 to v
            IF i=begin2 then PRINT #2:"  ";
            PRINT #2:lab$(idx(i))[letter:letter]&" ";
        NEXT i
    NEXT table
    PRINT #2
NEXT letter
FOR row=1 to v
    IF row=begin2 then PRINT #2:"          --------------------
--------          ---------------------------"?
    FOR table = 1 to 2
        PRINT #2, using " <####### " :lab$(idx(row));
        FOR col=1 to v
            IF col=begin2 then PRINT #2:"? ";
            IF x((table-1)*v+idx(row),idx(col))=1 then
                IF table = 1 then PRINT #2:"? "; else PRINT #2:"?
";
            ELSE
                PRINT #2:"   ";
            END IF
        NEXT col
    NEXT table
    PRINT #2
```

```
NEXT row


END
SUB cor_mat(nrow,ncol,m(,), r(,))
    DIM mean(1),sd(1)
    MAT redim mean(ncol),sd(ncol)
    FOR v=1 to ncol
        LET sum=0
        FOR i=1 to nrow
            LET sum=sum+m(i,v)
        NEXT i
        LET mean(v)=sum/nrow
        LET ss=0
        FOR i=1 to nrow
            LET ss=ss+(m(i,v)-mean(v))^2
        NEXT i
        LET sd(v)=sqr(ss/nrow)
    NEXT v
    FOR V1=1 to ncol                   !Pairs of variables
        FOR V2=v1 to ncol
            CALL
get_corr(nrow,v1,v2,m(,),mean(v1),mean(v2),sd(v1),sd(v2),r(v1,v2
))
            LET r(v2,v1)=r(v1,v2)
        NEXT v2
    NEXT v1
END SUB
SUB get_corr(nrow,v1,v2,m(,),m1,m2,sd1,sd2,r)
    LET r=0
    FOR i=1 to nrow
        LET r=r+((m(i,v1)-m1)/sd1)*((m(i,v2)-m2)/sd2)
    NEXT i
    LET r=r/nrow
END SUB



Sample Data File (Data for Friendship and Antagonism):

28
14
1,0,1,1,0,0,0,0,0,1,0,0,0,0
0,1,0,0,0,0,0,0,0,0,0,0,0,0
1,0,1,1,0,0,0,0,0,1,0,0,1,0
1,0,1,1,0,0,0,0,0,1,0,0,0,0
0,0,0,0,1,0,0,0,0,0,0,0,0,0
0,0,0,0,0,1,0,0,0,0,0,0,0,0
0,0,0,0,0,0,1,1,1,1,0,0,0,0
0,0,0,0,0,0,1,1,1,0,0,1,0,0
0,0,0,0,0,0,1,1,1,0,0,1,0,0
1,0,1,1,0,0,1,0,0,1,0,0,0,0
```

```
0,0,0,0,0,0,0,0,0,0,1,0,0,0
0,0,0,0,0,0,0,1,1,0,0,1,0,0
0,0,1,0,0,0,0,0,0,0,0,0,1,0
0,0,0,0,0,0,0,0,0,0,0,0,0,1
0,0,0,0,0,0,0,0,0,0,0,0,0,0
0,0,0,0,0,0,1,1,1,0,0,0,1,0
0,0,0,0,0,0,0,0,0,0,0,0,0,0
0,0,0,0,1,0,0,0,0,0,0,0,0,0
0,0,0,1,0,1,1,1,1,1,1,0,0,1
0,0,0,0,1,0,1,0,0,0,0,0,0,1
0,1,0,0,1,1,0,0,0,0,0,0,0,1
0,1,0,0,1,0,0,0,0,0,0,0,0,1
0,1,0,0,1,0,0,0,0,0,0,0,0,1
0,0,0,0,1,0,0,0,0,0,0,0,0,0
0,0,0,0,1,0,0,0,0,0,0,0,0,0
0,0,0,0,0,0,0,0,0,0,0,0,0,1
0,1,0,0,0,0,0,0,0,0,0,0,0,1
0,0,0,0,1,1,1,1,1,0,0,1,1,0
Win (W1)
Mue (W2)
Tay (W3)
Don (W4)
Cap (W5)
Kru (W6)
Has (W7)
Obe (W8)
Gre (W9)
Ste (S1)
Mat (S2)
Cer (S4)
All (I1)
Max (I3)
```

About the Book
and Author

How do you use numbers and equations to describe things like religion and politics? Quantitative social science is made easier as we follow master workman Joel Levine into his toolshed, where he discusses the use of various quantitative methods, sharpens some, and suggests alternatives to others. His wide-ranging discussions lead through data analysis, statistics, philosophy, and close analysis of well-known examples to a clearer understanding of social science.

Levine shows why quantitative social science must develop by its own rules, distinct from those that govern the disciplines of mathematics and statistics. Throughout, he emphasizes the use, misuse, and meaning of common techniques and the extension of basic tools to new problems.

For students, the book shows the practical consequences of sometimes-hidden links between theory and method. It explains how to let measurements emerge during the analysis of data in ways that minimize *a priori* assumptions while maximizing the information extracted. For scholars, the book joins the debate between methodologists and theoreticians about the future of social science. It presents a unified analysis of diverse empirical problems in economic time series, political identity, small-group sociometry, and occupational stratification.

Joel H. Levine is professor of mathematical social sciences at Dartmouth College.

Index